WORLD MILITARY HELICOPTERS

Elfan ap Rees

JANE'S

First published in the United Kingdom in 1986 by
Jane's Publishing Company Limited
238 City Road, London EC1V 2PU

Distributed in the Philippines and the
USA and its dependencies by
Jane's Publishing Inc
115 Fifth Avenue
New York, NY 10003

ISBN 0 7106 0374 6

Computer typesetting by Method Limited, Epping, Essex
Printed and bound in the United Kingdom by
Biddles Ltd, Guildford and King's Lynn

PREFACE

Like any military procurement programme, the development of new military helicopters is always subject to budget cuts, specification changes and other hazards before metal can be cut. For that reason current projects such as the US Army plans for a new light scout/attack helicopter (LHX), the Franco-German attack and escort helicopter (PAH-2/HAC/HAP) and the European tactical transport/ASW helicopter (NH-90) are not included in this review. Similarly, pure experimental helicopters such as the Bell and Sikorsky ACAP (all composite airframe programme), funded by the military for possible application to new generation aircraft, are also excluded. The line has been drawn at manned military helicopters actually in service, flying as prototypes or under construction.

CONTENTS

INTRODUCTION

THE HELICOPTER TODAY is a valued weapon in any nation's armoury. It has not always been so. Indeed 40 years ago, when the helicopter first began to be listed in military inventories, there were many who regarded it with downright suspicion. While its hovering capability was accepted as being unique, its practical application was very much open to question, for poor performance and lack of power often meant a struggle to get airborne, even with just the pilot and his trusting crewman on board.

If anything in particular was responsible for converting at least some of the sceptics to helicopter enthusiasts, it was the series of post-Second World War conflicts that spilled over from the end of the 1940s into the early 1950s, to whit those in Indo-China, Malaya, and Korea. In Indo-China the French Army (ALAT) developed casevac and observation techniques with the Hiller 360, and troop and cargo carrying with the Westland-Sikorsky WS-51 Dragonfly and WS-55 Whirlwind, while in Malaya the Royal Air Force and Royal Navy did much the same thing with just the WS-51 and S-55, learning the hard way the difficulties of operating helicopters in tropical climates. Meanwhile, the drawn-out Korean War between 1950 and 1953 saw the further refinement of the casevac and observation roles by the US Army with the Bell H-13 Sioux, while the US and Royal Navies formalised the use of helicopters for carrier-based plane guard and SAR operations.

By the mid-1950s acceptance of the helicopter by the military planners had reached a point where the British relied on 16 Whirlwinds and six Bristol Sycamores to launch the first helicopter commando assault at Suez in 1956, operating from two carriers offshore and moving over 400 troops with their ammunition and equipment in one and a half hours. Meanwhile the ALAT was further developing the helicopter role in the rugged terrain of Algeria by arming their new turbine-engined Alouettes and larger helicopters with machine-guns and rockets for ground attack work. By the end of the decade France had upwards of 500 military helicopters in service, many of them operational in Algeria.

Incredibly some of these early helicopters from the 1950s are still in service today but, in December 1961, an event occurred which was to mark the beginning of a significant step forward in military helicopter development. On the 11th of that month a US Navy carrier unloaded in Saigon harbour 32 US Army helicopters, which on the Christmas Eve carried out the first airmobile combat action in Vietnam. By the end of the Vietnam War ten years later, the piston-engined helicopter was history, the attack helicopter was a reality, and heavylift work, combat-rescue and casevac, troop assaults, minesweeping, anti-submarine patrols, vertical replenishment (VERTREP) and similar operations were well established and practised.

Since 1970 three further conflicts have been notable for their contribution to military helicopter design and strategic use. The long-running war in Afghanistan has undoubtedly provided the Soviet Union with valuable data on Hip, Hind and Halo operations in the field as well as contributing to the development of the new Havoc attack helicopter which is now being evaluated in that theatre. Meanwhile the clash between Israeli and Syrian forces in Lebanon provided a further insight into the use of helicopters as anti-armour weapon platforms in a Middle East environment.

More recently the unfortunate clash between Argentina and the United Kingdom in the Falkland Isles demonstrated most dramatically the strategic value of the modern military helicopter, as well as exposing some of its vulnerabilities and weak points. For the British forces in particular the reality of war provided lessons that no amount of exercising could accomplish, lessons that are already being incorporated in existing service helicopters as well as being embodied in the next generation.

As to the next generation, there can be little doubt that the use of new avionics, including computerised health monitoring, advanced weapons control, more navigation aids and battlefield warning systems etc will lighten the currently high crew workload, while new materials and rotor systems will improve nap-of-the-earth performance and survivability. By the year 2000 the military helicopter will probably be three to four times as potent a weapon as the helicopter today, and an even more essential ingredient in any nation's armed forces.

Elfan ap Rees
May 1986

Acknowledgements

A book such as this can never be the work of one person, and thanks are therefore due to the many friends and colleagues in the helicopter industry who over the years, and sometimes unwittingly, have contributed to the contents.

It is quite impossible to name them all but I would like to thank the following for their especial help: Marty Reisch and Dick Tipton (Bell Helicopter), Jean Louis-Espes (Aérospatiale), Christina Gotzheim (MBB), Rob Mack and Hal Klopper (McDonnell Douglas Helicopters), Bianca Corbella (Agusta), Bruce Jay and Bob Torgeson (Boeing Vertol), Bob Stangarone and Jim Ventrilio (Sikorsky), Ian Woodward and Peter Batten (Westland).

In addition I owe thanks to those who helped in the production of this book, particularly Joan Probert who typed the entire manuscript, John Phillips for his research and preparation of the Military Fleet appendix, and my daughter Claire who selected the 200 plus photographs from the thousands in the *HELICOPTER International* library, Brendan Gallagher and Alex Vanags-Baginskis of Jane's for their help and patience, and John W R Taylor, the redoubtable Editor of Jane's *All the World's Aircraft*, who put me up to writing the book in the first place.

Last but not least, a very big thanks to a special person, my wife Linda, whose consistent support and encouragement over the past 25 years has made it all possible.

SE 313B/SA 318C Alouette II

The British Army Air Corps has been a long-time operator of the Alouette 2, and still has examples on strength in support of UN operations in Cyprus.

Originally designated the SE 3130, the Alouette II was developed by one of the predecessor companies to Aérospatiale, Sud-Est Aviation, which had been engaged in experimental helicopter development since the mid-1940s.

By 1949 Sud-Est was test-flying the piston-engined SE 3120 Alouette I, but the arrival of the first turboshaft powerplants from Turboméca in the early 1950s and the obvious power-to-weight advantages offered, led to a redesign of the aircraft. The result was the five-seat Alouette II (F-WHHE), which made its initial flight on 12 March 1955.

A second prototype flew soon afterwards and, just three months later, on 3 June, the aircraft proved its potential by setting up a new class altitude record of 8,209 m (26,932 ft). The layout of the Alouette II followed classic light helicopter design of the period, with a bubble-style cabin and open-framework centre fuselage and tail boom. The 360 shp Turboméca Artouste engine was positioned horizontally atop the centre fuselage with a direct drive into the main gearbox and thence to the articulated three-blade main rotor and two-blade tail rotor. A standard skid undercarriage could be replaced by a quadricycle wheeled undercarriage for shipboard operations.

The size of the Alouette II made it ideal for a number of emerging military helicopter roles, especially liaison, observation, and ambulance work which needed to be carried out away from sophisticated maintenance facilities. Initial orders were quickly placed by all three French Services, and the first delivery was made to the Armée de l'Air on 11 May 1956. The first Alouette II for the Aviation Lègére de l'Armée de Terre (ALAT) followed a month later. Both aircraft were still operational in 1986.

In 1957 the type was redesignated the SE 313B and over the next seven years some 924 were built before production switched to the SA 318C. First flown on 31 January 1961, this introduced an improved and more modern Turboméca powerplant the Astazou IIA, which produced the same power as the original Artouste but gave a better fuel consumption and was more reliable.

Early military customers for the SE 313B, apart from the home market, had included the Austrian Air Force, Belgian Army, Swiss Army, the British Army Air Corps and the German armed forces. The latter was a major export customer, taking delivery of some 247 SE 313Bs and 53 of the later SA 318C. By 1975 382 SA 318Cs had been added to the production total, by which time the design had been largely superseded by the SA 341 Gazelle. Production of the basic Alouette II was therefore terminated.

Although now out of production for some ten years, large numbers of SE 313B and SA 318C variants still remain in military operation where they continue to provide useful service. The original role profile has expanded to include anti-tank and anti-submarine missions, using SS.11 wire-guided missiles or torpedoes, as well as search and rescue and pilot training.

Meanwhile in 1968 development began of an uprated variant, the SA 315B Llama, which married the basic SE 313B airframe to the dynamics system of the SA 316B Alouette III, including the 870 shp Turbomeca Artouste IIIB engine derated to 550 shp. This provided exceptional hot/high and sling load performance, increasing the normal gross weight to 1,950 kg (4,300 lb) and allowing the Lama to carry up to 1,135 kg (2,500 lb) on the hook.

Technical specifications

Helicopter SE 3130 Alouette II
Type General purpose
Year 1955
Engine 530 shp Turboméca Artouste IIC
Rotor diameter 10.20 m (33 ft 5 in)
Fuselage length 9.70 m (31 ft 10 in)
Height 2.75 m (9 ft)
Empty weight 890 kg (1,962 lb)
Gross weight 1,500 kg (3,307 lb)
Maximum speed 175 km/h (108 mph)
Hovering ceiling IGE 2,000 m (6,560 ft)
Service ceiling 3,200 m (10,498 ft)
Range 600 km (373 miles)
Capacity Pilot + 4 passengers

Military sales of the SA 315B by Aérospatiale have been limited to a handful of customers such as Chile, although this variant remains in small scale production at the Marignane factory. In addition the aircraft has been in production since 1972 by Hindustan Aeronautics in India as the Chetak. To date over 150 have been produced by this source, with many entering service with the Indian Air Force.

The SA 315B Llama variant of the Alouette is operated in some numbers by military air arms in the various mountainous areas of the world. H-10 is a Chilean Air Force example. (S. N. Simms).

SE 316B/SA 319 Alouette III

The Alouette III was a natural growth development of the SE 3130 Alouette II by Sud-Est Aviation, which originally designated the new helicopter, the SE 3160.

The dynamic layout followed that established by the earlier aircraft, but introduced the more powerful 550 shp Turboméca Artouste III turboshaft, with an extended diameter main rotor and three-bladed tail rotor to take advantage of the enhanced performance. A widened front fuselage provided space for seven occupants while the centre section and tail boom were faired over and a tricycle undercarriage installed.

The prototype Alouette III (F-ZWVQ) made its initial flight on 28 February 1959 and, in June 1960, the new aircraft reached a height of 4,810 m (15,780 ft) on Mont Blanc, carrying seven passengers. Later that year, it flew to 6,004 m (19,698 ft) on the Himalayan mountain of Deo Tibaa with two pilots and 250 kg (550 lb) of freight.

Meanwhile, military trials were carried out with various forms of weapons fit, including wire-guided air-ground missiles and pivot-mounted gun installations. These were particularly aimed at supporting French military operations in the Algerian conflict, although this ended before the Alouette III entered service.

In fact initial deliveries of the Alouette III were mainly made to overseas customers, commencing with three aircraft for the Burmese Air Force in July-October 1961 and followed by examples for the South African Air Force and Rhodesian Air Force. The French ALAT and Aéronavale took five and six aircraft respectively from the initial production batch, and other early military customers included Peru and the Danish Navy.

Like its smaller predecessor, the Alouette 3 has been sold world-wide to a number of air arms, including Abu Dhabi which purchased the SA 316B for the utility role.

With the French ALAT, the Alouette 3 served in the anti-tank role prior to being superseded by the SA 342 Gazelle. Nevertheless the Alouette still remains in service with all three French air arms.

In 1965 an Alouette III began flying with an Astazou XII turboshaft, which offered a 25 percent reduction in fuel consumption for a 30 shp increase in available power. This variant, designated the SA 319B, subsequently went into production alongside the SA 316.

By 1978 French production of the Alouette III had topped 1,400 aircraft, and the type was in widespread military service in over 60 countries. In addition, the type had been selected for licence production in India and Romania. India, where the aircraft has been named the Chetak by the local manufacturer, Hindustan Aircraft, has built nearly 300 for home military and government use to date, as well as exporting a small number to other countries including the Soviet Union.

In Romania, the SA 316B version is produced by CNAR and over 200 examples have been built to date, including a number exported via Aérospatiale to Pakistan, Algeria and Angola etc. Production continues at both licence sources, but ended in France in 1983.

Technical specifications

Helicopter SE 3160 Alouette III
Type General purpose
Year 1959
Engine 870 shp Turboméca Artouste IIIB
Rotor diameter 11.00 m (36 ft 1 in)
Fuselage length 10.03 m (32 ft 11 in)
Height 3.09 m (10 ft 2 in)
Empty weight 1,090 kg (2,403 lb)
Gross weight 2,100 kg (4,630 lb)
Maximum speed 210 km/h (130 mph)
Hovering ceiling IGE 2,000 m (6,560 ft)
Service ceiling 4,250 m (13,943 ft)
Range 500 km (310 miles)
Capacity Pilot + 6 passengers

SA 321 Super Frelon

Design of the Super Frelon, the largest helicopter yet produced by the French helicopter industry, was originally initiated in the late 1950s to meet a specification for a troop transport.

The resultant SE 3200 Frelon, which first flew on 10 June 1959, was an innovative design which used three 750 shp Turboméca Turmo IIIB engines mounted atop the fuselage and feeding into a common main gearbox. This drove a four blade main rotor and five blade tail rotor. All fuel was contained in podded tanks on either side of the main fuselage, which was thus kept clear for the carriage of passengers or freight.

The SE 3200 was not successful and development was suspended in favour of a larger design which took advantage of Sikorsky experience with the experimental S-60 and smaller S-61. Designated the SA 3210 Super Frelon, the new prototype first flew on 7 December 1962. While the tri-engine layout was retained, the power was much increased by introducing 1,320 shp Turmo IIIC engines driving a larger diameter six blade main rotor system. The fuselage was similarly enlarged, with a rear ramp entry, inboard fuel tankage and an amphibious hull.

The first prototype, (F-ZWWE), configured for the original troop transport requirement, was followed by a second example configured for the anti-submarine role. This version introduced folding main rotor blades, sponsons, and a hinged tailboom for shipboard operations, and was the result of growing interest by the French Navy in acquiring a suitably sized ASW helicopter for its aircraft carriers.

After the two prototypes Sud Aviation built four pre-production SA 321 Super Frelons, progressively introducing further refinements and role equipment modifications such as search radar and sonar. Meanwhile the French Aéronavale placed a firm order for 17 SA 321Gs while, in July 1963, the first prototype was stripped down and modified to set new world speed records over 3 km (1.86 miles) - 341.23 km/h (212 mph), 15/25 km (9/15 miles) - 350.47 km/h (218 mph), and 100 km (62 miles) -334.28 km/h (208 mph).

The first production SA 321G flew on 30 November 1965, standardising on the uprated 1,550 shp Turmo IIIC engine and equipped with two Sylphe radars, all-weather navigation and auto-stabilisation systems, and mine-laying and mine sweeping gear. Standard armament was four torpedoes but subsequently two Exocet anti-ship missiles were also included. In total 25 SA 321Gs were eventually delivered for land-based and shipboard operation by Flotille 32F from bases on the French Atlantic and Mediterranean coasts. The majority of these are still in service but are scheduled for replacement in the late 1990s.

Although the French Air Force and Army showed little interest in ordering Super Frelons for its original trooping role, several overseas governments were more open to suggestion, and the fourth production aircraft was completed as the first of 12 SA 321Ks for the Israeli Air Force. This version deleted the outboard sponsons and other naval modifications, reverting to a simple tricycle undercarriage layout and an unimpeded

Below: Overseas customers for the SA 321 have included Libya, which operates several examples on long range SAR and transport duties. (G. Mangion).

This Super Frelon is one of 14 in service with the South African Air Force in the assault role. Note the simplified landing gear of the de-navalised SA 321.

7 m long cabin with full width ramp loading. More recently, the Israeli Air Force has sought to upgrade the fleet by replacing the original Turmo engines with two 3,925 shp General Electric T64 powerplants, but it is not known if this plan has proceeded beyond a feasibility study.

The trooping version of the Super Frelon was also ordered by South Africa, which took delivery of 16 SA 321Ls between April 1967 and September 1969 and by Iraq, which has received at least 16 aircraft and modified some to carry the Exocet missile for operations in the Gulf area.

Meanwhile, two semi-maritime sales were made to China and Libya. The latter purchased the SA 321M Search and Rescue configured variant, and took delivery of the final production Super Frelon in 1981. China meanwhile received 13 SA 321Js for land-and ship-based utility and anti-submarine missions. In common with the French Aéronavale aircraft, three ASW configured machines are now being updated with a SFIM autopilot with an automatic coupler, a Crouzet Nadir navigation system, OMERA ORB-32 radar, HS-12 sonar and a Thomson-CSF Lamparo sonobuoy processor.

A grand total of 110 Super Frelons were eventually built. This included the six prototypes, several of which are still operated on trials work in France, a single VIP-configured aircraft handed over to the Zaire Air Force in November 1975, and four airframes which remained unsold and have been dismantled for spares.

On 12 December 1985 the first of two prototype Zhishengi Zhi-8 helicopters made its initial flight at the Changho manufacturing plant in Jiangshi Province in China. Described as a heavy lift helicopter, with a gross weight of 13 tonnes the aircraft bears a close resemblance to the SA 321G variant, re-engineered for local production. China plans to build ten Zhi-8s in the current 5-year plan.

Technical specifications

Helicopter SA 321G Super Frelon
Type Multipurpose
Year 1965
Engine 3 × 1,550 shp Turboméca Turmo IIIC
Rotor diameter 18.90 m (62 ft)
Fuselage length 19.40 m (63 ft 8 in)
Overall length 23.03 m (75 ft 7 in)
Height 6.66 m (21 ft 10 in)
Empty weight 6,863 kg (15,130 lb)
Gross weight 13,000 kg (28,660 lb)
Maximum speed 275 km/h (170 mph)
Hovering ceiling IGE 2,170 m (7,120 ft)
Service ceiling 3,150 m (10,335 ft)
Range 820 km (509 miles)
Capacity 3 crew + 27-30 troops (transport version)
Armament 4 torpedoes + 2 × Exocet anti-ship missiles

SA 330 Puma

Following a decision by the French Army and Air Force not to pursue a transport variant of the original SA 3200 Frelon, a new specification was issued in 1962 for a medium-weight tactical transport helicopter capable of all weather operation.

To meet this requirement Sud Aviation scaled down the tri-engined Frelon to produce a twin-engined aircraft of some 7,000 kg (15,432 lb) gross weight, able to carry up to 16 troops or 3,000 kg (6,614 lb) of externally slung cargo. Originally intended to be powered by two 1,300 shp Turbo-méca Bastan VII turbines, these were changed for two 1,300 shp Turmo IIIC4 engines by the time a mock-up appeared at the 1963 Paris Air Show as the Alouette IV. Immediately afterwards, the French government allocated FFr 20 million to fund the development of eight prototype and pre-production aircraft.

The first prototype, (F-ZWNN), designated the SA 330A, made its initial flight at the Marignane factory on 15 April 1965 and was followed at intervals by the second prototype and six pre-production machines. In 1967 the aircraft was selected as part of an Anglo-French helicopter agreement, under which development and pro-

The Puma has been in Royal Air Force service since 1971 and is due for replacement in the mid-1990s. This odd camouflage scheme was adopted by No 230 Sqdn on the occasion of an international 'Tiger Meet'.

A number of SA 330s found their way to various emerging countries as presidential/VIP aircraft. 5V-MAK carries Togo Air Force colours.

South Africa was a major customer for the Puma prior to the UN embargo, taking delivery of some 67 examples. It is now likely that the local aviation industry has sufficient experience to build its own hybrid variant.

duction of the SA 330, SA 341 and WG-13 would be shared by Sud Aviation and Westland, with all three types entering military service in both countries. In consequence, the eighth SA 330A (F-ZJUX/XW 241) was transferred soon after completion to the UK for Royal Air Force evaluation and trials, and the name Puma jointly adopted.

Production at the Sud Aviation Marignane factory began in 1968 and the first aircraft was rolled out, unpainted, on 12 September, although delivery was not to take place for several months. Apart from the French ALAT, early orders were placed by Portugal and South Africa, and these helicopters were slotted in between ALAT deliveries. All such early export aircraft were designated SA 330C. By the close of 1969, 16 military production Pumas had been delivered, six to the Portuguese Air Force and ten to ALAT, and the first for the South African Air Force followed soon afterwards. South Africa later became a major Puma customer, with 66 aircraft delivered before the UN embargo became effective in the late 1970s.

The Westland production line was started in 1969 and, under the terms of the joint agreement, assembled those Pumas ordered for the Royal Air Force, as well as supplying components to the French production line totalling some 45 percent of the completed aircraft. A similar agreement existed between Turboméca and Rolls-Royce to cover the Turmo powerplant. The RAF eventually purchased 48 SA 330E variants, the first of which was flown on 25 November 1970. Deliveries to the Operational Conversion Unit began in January 1971 and the first front-line squadron formed up in June.

A continuing improvement programme by Aérospatiale (which succeeded Sud Aviation in 1970) saw the introduction of uprated 1,575 shp Turmo IVC engines and fibreglass main rotor blades in the mid-1970s, and these were progressively adopted for all new production aircraft, as well as being retrospectively installed in earlier examples. The increased performance resulting from these modifications opened up the hot and high markets in the Middle East and elsewhere and, by 1980, total Puma production had topped 600 aircraft. In addition, a licence agreement was signed with Nurtanio to assemble 11 machines for local Indonesian use. The final three Pumas were delivered to the French Air Force in 1982, bringing total production to 679 aircraft.

However, Aérospatiale had previously reached an agreement with CNAR-Brasov in 1978 to set up production under licence in Romania, and at least 90 aircraft had been delivered from this new source by mid-1983. Initial production concentrated on satisfying Romanian domestic military needs but since 1979 aircraft have also been delivered to export customers, including the Kenyan Air Force and Sudan.

Meanwhile, despite the arrival on the home scene of the updated and improved AS 332 Super Puma, many Pumas will remain in service until at least the end of this century. Present ALAT plans see the aircraft being replaced by the European Consortium NATO NH-90 from the late 1990s onward, and this new design may find favour with other existing Puma operators.

Technical specifications

Helicopter SA 330H Puma
Type Medium transport
Year 1968
Engine 2 × 1,580 shp Turboméca Turmo IVC
Rotor diameter 15.08 m (49 ft 3 in)
Fuselage length 14.06 m (46 ft 2 in)
Overall length 18.15 m (55 ft 6 in)
Height 4.38 m (14 ft 4 in)
Empty weight 3,536 kg (7,795 lb)
Gross weight 7,000 kg (15,432 lb)
Maximum speed 273 km/h (170 mph)
Hovering ceiling IGE 2,230 m (7,316 ft)
Service ceiling 6,000 m (19,684 ft)
Range 570 km (354 miles)
Capacity 2 crew + 16 combat-equipped troops

AS 332B/M Super Puma

The Super Puma has sold well in the export market as a military transport. This example, carrying temporary French markings, is in Kuwait Air Force colours.

Following the loss of a number of helicopters during the Falklands crisis, Argentina placed an order for 24 Super Pumas to re-equip the Army. AE-525 was one of the first delivered.

The naval variant of the Super Puma, the AS 332F, is able to carry two Exocet anti-shipping missiles, mounted one on each side of the main cabin. Other modifications include the introduction of a chin-mounted search radar. This is the prototype AS 332F, F-WZJK.

Soon after production had begun of the SA 330 Puma, the Aérospatiale design team began looking at a growth version as a successor, using a more powerful powerplant and an improved rotor system to produce a stretched aircraft with a better payload.

Serious design work began in 1974 and in 1977 a Puma fuselage was taken from the production line and modified as the AS 331 prototype with an uprated transmission and two new 1,780 shp Turboméca Makila engines. First flown on 5 September 1977, this aircraft was followed a year later by a more definitive prototype designated the AS 332 Super Puma.

The AS 332 further introduced a new energy-absorbing landing gear, an increased fuel capacity, more efficient fibreglass main and tail rotors, a lengthened nose section, and revised fin and tail plane contours to improve handling. The first AS 332 (F-WZJA) made its initial flight at Marignane on 13 September 1978, and was followed by five pre-production aircraft, including one (F-WZJN) with a further cabin stretch of 0.76 m (2 ft 6 in) to provide room for four extra passengers.

With the Puma well established with the French Air Force and ALAT, and sales of the military export variants going well, Aérospatiale's initial thrust with the Super Puma was in the civil market, but the fifth aircraft was completed as the AS 332B military prototype. As such it carried out various development trials from 1981 onwards, including extensive icing trials to clear the type for flight in all icing conditions.

Military sales of the AS 332B variant began in March 1982 with the delivery of the first two of four aircraft to Ecuador and continued with VIP-configured machines for Chile and Oman and six for Abu Dhabi. The latter were later followed by two stretched cabin variants, the AS 332M, for VIP use.

While the AS 332M continues to sell in some numbers alongside its very successful AS 332L civil equivalent, the majority of military Super Puma customers continue to opt for the short-fuselage AS 332, now available in both the B transport version and the AS 332F naval variant. The latter has been developed as an anti-submarine/anti-shipping variant with two Exocet missiles or torpedoes, capable of land or ship-based operations. Although the carriage of the Exocet in the anti-shipping role is an option exercised by the AS 332B, specific development of the naval variant, with a folding tail rotor pylon, radar and sonar equipment and a deck landing device, is now being undertaken by PT Nurtanio in Indonesia, where the aircraft has been assembled under licence since 1984. The AS 332M is also being locally assembled in Singapore.

By the end of 1985 military Super Puma sales had exceeded the 100 mark.

Technical specifications

Helicopter AS 332M Super Puma
Type Medium transport
Year 1978
Engine 2 × 1,780 shp Turboméca Makila 1A
Rotor diameter 15.60 m (51 ft 2.25 in)
Fuselage length 16.25 m (53 ft 3.75 in)
Overall length 18.70 m (61 ft 4.25 ft)
Height 4.92 m (16 ft 1.75 in)
Empty weight 4,265 kg (9,402 lb)
Gross weight 8,350 kg (18,410 lb)
Maximum speed 296 km/h (184 mph)
Hovering ceiling IGE 2,700 m (8,850 ft)
Service ceiling n/a
Range 635 km (394 miles)
Capacity 2 pilots + 22 passengers

SA 341/342 Gazelle

The origins of the Aérospatiale Gazelle, currently still in production with over 1,200 built to date, go back to the early 1960s when the Sud Aviation design team began to consider a replacement for the highly successful SE 313B Alouette II. By 1963, with political encouragement, the team was working in collaboration with a Westland design group to produce a light observation helicopter which could be common to both the British and French Armies.

By using well-proven Alouette dynamic components and a 523 shp Turboméca Astazou II engine, the joint team came up with a streamlined four-seat helicopter, the WS-22, which offered some performance advantage over the Alouette II but insufficient improvement to warrant a go-ahead. While the British Army ordered the Bell 47G Sioux instead, the Sud team returned to the drawing board and began work on a new design, which incorporated a new fibreglass rigid-rotor system developed in association with Bölkow of Germany. Initially known as the X-300, this new project matured in 1966 as the SA 340, a four-seat aircraft with the Bölkow rigid rotor and the then revolutionary 'fenestron' – a multi-bladed small diameter fan mounted within the fin area, which replaced the tail rotor and was expected to allow all the engine power to be concentrated on driving the main rotor during cruise flight.

On 16 January 1967, the UK and France signed a Memorandum of Understanding to jointly develop and produce the SA 340, together with the SA 330 Puma and WG-13 Lynx, and this event was followed, in the February, by the roll-out of the SA 340 prototype. Initially this aircraft (F-WOFH) had neither the rigid rotor or the fenestron, as both were still in the early stages of development, and it was not until April 1968 that a more definitive second prototype (F-ZWRA) began flying. This aircraft quickly demonstrated that much work still needed to be done and, although the fenestron was eventually successful, in 1969 the decision was made to replace the rigid rotor system with a semi-articulated rotorhead matched to fibreglass blades.

In this form the aircraft was redesignated the SA 341, and in July 1969 was named the Gazelle. Four SA 341 prototypes were built, and the third of these (F-ZWRI/XW 276) was transferred to Westland in August 1969 to act as the British Army trials aircraft.

In July 1970, the French and UK Governments authorised production of an initial batch of 110 Gazelles to meet initial ALAT and British services requirements, and tooling up began at the Aérospatiale and Westland factories. The first production aircraft subsequently made its initial flight at Marignane on 6 August 1971, but new

Over 1,000 Gazelles have now been built by Aérospatiale, together with others produced under licence. Yugoslavia has assembled a large number of SA 341s for its own forces, which uses the type in the liaison, scout and anti-tank role.

The Middle East has been a major purchaser of the SA 342 Gazelle variant. This example, equipped for the anti-tank role with the Syrian Air Force, was captured in the Lebanon by the Israeli Defence Forces.

in-flight vibration and ground resonance problems now appeared and further production was slowed down until the difficulties were overcome. By May 1972 suitable modifications to the main rotor blades and gearbox mounting were in hand, and production resumed. Total orders had now reached the 300 mark.

The first military Gazelles to be produced were from the Westland production line, building the SA 341B, SA 341C and SA 341D for the British Army, Royal Navy and Royal Air Force respectively. Initial aircraft for these three services formed a joint trials unit in May 1973, before the type took up a training role with all three services. As deliveries of SA 341Bs increased, the Army Air Corps began to use them for front-line observation and liaison work, replacing the veteran Sioux.

In France, the first SA 341Fs for the ALAT were delivered in early 1973, although the fourth aircraft was immediately earmarked for armament trials with the HOT anti-tank missile. These tests demonstrated that the aircraft could carry four missiles with a minimal effect on range, but meanwhile the development by Turboméca of the uprated 870 shp Astazou XIVH engine offered the opportunity to increase the payload by two more missiles in a temperate climate, or improve the hot/high performance.

This new higher-powered anti-tank variant, the SA 342K, immediately attracted a number of orders from the Middle East, including Egypt and Iraq. In addition the ALAT chose to update 110 of its SA 341Fs to the HOT configuration and to order a number of new machines. These were redesignated the SA 342M.

First military SA 342 deliveries began in April 1975 with the 156th production Gazelle, one of 20 aircraft for Kuwait, and eventually all aircraft being built by Aérospatiale were to this standard. Westland, however, continued to assemble the SA 341 until UK production ended in January 1984 with delivery of the 281st aircraft. In addition, a licence agreement signed with Yugoslavia in 1974 saw 132 SA 341H aircraft assembled locally for military and government use, as well as the supply of some airframes to Aérospatiale for completion for other customers.

A further chapter in Gazelle production began in 1982 when Egypt, which had already taken delivery of 60 SA 342Ks, signed a licence production agreement to locally assemble a further 30 aircraft. This agreement included the progressive manufacture of components at the Helwan factory, and options to build additional Gazelles for other Middle East customers.

By 1985 total Gazelle production had comfortably passed the 1,000 mark and orders had reached 1,146. These figures included 298 aircraft for the ALAT, the last of which are just entering service. Also recently delivered has been an attrition batch for the Syrian Air Force, bringing total sales to this customer to 67 aircraft. In all, the Gazelle family is currently operational with some 19 military and para-military services, and will remain a major weapon for many armed forces into the next century.

Technical specifications

Helicopter SA 341F Gazelle
Type Multipurpose
Year 1971
Engine 590 shp Turboméca Astazou IIIA
Rotor diameter 10.50 m (34 ft 5 in)
Fuselage length 9.53 m (31 ft 3 in)
Overall length 11.97 m (39 ft 3 in)
Height 3.15 m (10 ft 4 in)
Empty weight 917 kg (2,022 lb)
Gross weight 1,800 kg (3,968 lb)
Maximum speed 264 km/h (164 mph)
Hovering ceiling IGE 2,850 m (9,350 ft)
Service ceiling 5,000 m (16,404 ft)
Range 670 km (416 miles)
Capacity Pilot + 4 troops
Armament 4 or 6 HOT anti-tank missiles or podded 2.75 in (69 mm) rockets, 7.62 mm machine guns, etc

AS 350B/L Ecureuil

Development of the AS 350 was originally initiated by Aérospatiale in the early 1970s as a civil 5/6 seat helicopter, using new materials and construction techniques, and designed to succeed the Alouette and challenge contemporary 'aesthetic' helicopters such as the Bell JetRanger.

Although some early design work was done in association with Westland Helicopters, the British manufacturer eventually chose not to continue the liaison and, in April 1973, Aérospatiale decided to go ahead with the project alone and build two prototypes. The first of these (F-WVKI) was powered by a 592 shp Avco-Lycoming LTS-101 engine, in order to improve acceptance in the powerful American civil market, but the second (F-WVKH) adopted the 641 shp Turboméca Arriel turboshaft for sales elsewhere in the world.

Central to the AS 350 was a new rotor system, using a Starflex glassfibre head with a single maintenance-free composite balljoint replacing the conventional blade hinges. This head was married to three glassfibre main blades. The two-blade tail rotor followed a similar pattern with a flexible glassfibre spar replacing the hinge system. Glassfibre was also extensively used in the manufacture of the fuselage and other components, resulting in a weight-saving structure which easily lent itself to economic production.

The AS 350 Ecureuil has found favour with several countries as a training and liaison aircraft. This example is one of 18 in service with the Royal Australian Air Force. Others operate with the RAN.

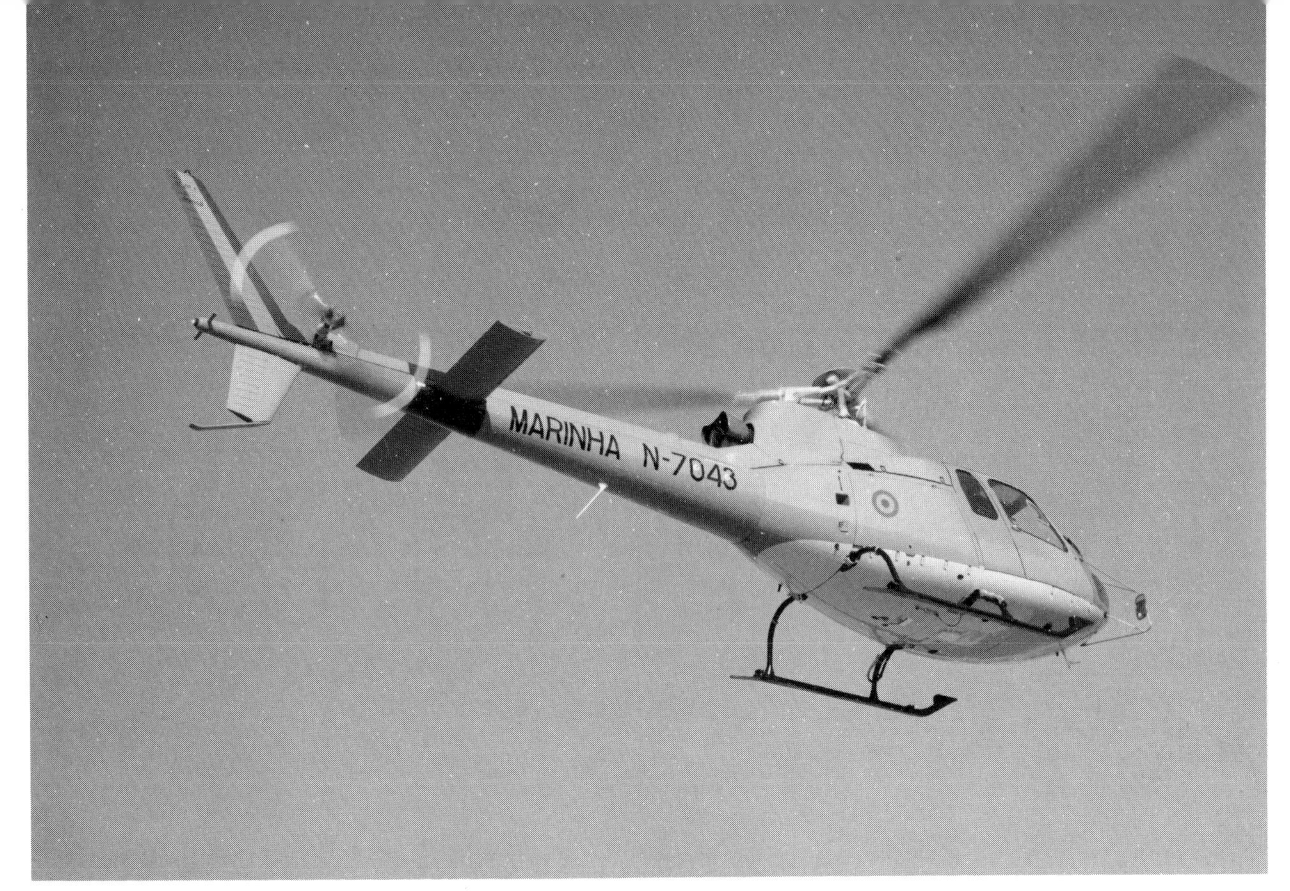

In Brazil the Ecureuil has been assembled locally by Helibras as the HB-350 Esquilo. N-7043 is operated by the Brazilian Navy.

The first AS 350 prototype made its initial flight on 27 June 1974, followed by the Arriel-powered variant on 14 February 1975. Development continued throughout 1976 and production began the following year in anticipation of certification. This was granted by the French DGAC in October 1977 and by the US FAA soon afterwards, with customer deliveries beginning in March 1978.

Initially sales of these variants, the AS 350B Ecureuil (Arriel engine) and AS 350C/AS 350D AStar (LTS101), concentrated on the civil market, although some marketing activity was carried out in the military trainer market. As a result of this the Brazilian Navy was first to place an order, for nine AS 350Bs to be assembled locally by a joint Franco-Brazilian enterprise entitled Helibras. These aircraft entered service in the training and liaison role. A further 15 were ordered in early 1985. Helibras also assembled seven for government use, while Aérospatiale likewise sold the occasional aircraft to other government customers for such and para-military duties.

The next major military sale came in 1982 when the Australian government selected the AS 350B to perform a training/liaison/search and rescue role with the Royal Australian Air Force. A total of 18 aircraft had been ordered by early 1984 and, in addition, nine AS 350Bs were ordered for similar duties with the Royal Australian Navy. Deliveries of these machines began in April 1984 and the type was fully operational by early 1985.

Meanwhile, Aérospatiale had been developing a specifically tailored military variant, the AS 350L, which appeared in 1984. This version offers the option of various weapons packs, mounted on stub pylons, but no major orders have yet been announced.

Technical specifications

Helicopter AS 350 Ecureuil I
Type Light transport
Year 1975
Engine 641 shp Turboméca Arriel
Rotor diameter 10.69 m (35 ft 1 in)
Fuselage length 10.91 m (35 ft 9 in)
Overall length 12.99 m (42 ft 7 in)
Height 3.08 m (10 ft 1 in)
Empty weight 1,027 kg (2,264 lb)
Gross weight 1,900 kg (4,188 lb)
Maximum speed 272 km/h (169 mph)
Hovering ceiling IGE 4.050 m (13,287 ft)
Service ceiling 5,800 m (19,028 ft)
Range 750 km (466 miles)
Capacity Pilot + 5 passengers

AS 355M Ecureuil 2

The AS 355F is now in service with the French Air Force, which has taken delivery of some eight aircraft out of an expected total order for 44.

The early acceptance of the AS 350 in the civil market prompted Aérospatiale in 1978 to begin development of a twin-engined model, particularly for offshore and urbanised areas where the safety advantages of a second engine were important.

Construction of the first of two prototypes, (F-WZLA), built around two 425 shp Allison 250-C20F engines, began in early 1979 and the aircraft first flew on 27 September. Essentially the airframe and most components, including the main rotor hub and mast, were identical to the single-engined AS 350, but the transmission was uprated to take advantage of the additional power. The upper fuselage structure was also changed to accept the twin engines.

Following certification in October 1980, deliveries of the initial production version, the AS 355E, began in early 1981. Meanwhile, Aérospatiale had developed the improved AS 355F, which introduced new design main rotor blades and other modifications to allow an increase in payload and gross take-off weight. This became available in mid-1981 and in late 1982 was further certificated for IFR operation. Subsequently, Aérospatiale introduced in January 1984 the AS 355FI, which featured improved tail rotor performance and a five percent decrease in torque limitation. This allowed more power to be transmitted to the main gearbox, and further increased payload and take-off weight.

Export sales of the military AS 355 have to date been relatively slow. Note the engine intake filters on this Djibouti aircraft.

Both the AS 355E and F variants of the Ecureuil 2 were aimed at the civil helicopter market and sales of the first 300 aircraft were almost exclusively in this sector, apart from the odd VIP/para-military example. However, in 1983, the French Air Force evinced an interest in acquiring 50 machines for strategic base surveillance and liaison/training duties. This version was to be armed with Matra Mistral air-to-air missiles for defensive purposes and prompted the development of a military version of the Ecureuil 2, designated the AS 355M. A demonstrator, fitted with a weapons pylon, was completed in May 1983.

Initial deliveries of the AS 355M to the French Air Force began in 1984, but only the first few aircraft are entering service with the Allison engine installation. Later machines will standardise on the 450 shp Turboméca TM319 powerplant, which offers an increase in power and a better specific fuel consumption. This new combination is expected to be available during 1986 and will improve the military options. Aérospatiale is currently promoting both a light anti-tank variant, with TOW or HOT missiles, and a naval anti-shipping version.

Meanwhile, small sales of the Allison-engined AS 355M have been made to other customers, notably in Africa.

Technical specifications

Helicopter AS 355M Ecureuil 2
Type Twin-turbine light surveillance
Year 1983
Engine 2 × 425 shp Allison 250-C20F turboshafts
Rotor diameter 10.69 m (35 ft 0.75 in)
Fuselage length 10.91 m (35 ft 9.5 in)
Overall length 12.99 m (42 ft 7.5 in)
Height 3.15 m (10 ft 4 in)
Empty weight 1,275 kg (2,811 lb)
Gross weight 2,300 kg (5,070 lb)
Maximum speed 215 km/h (133 mph)
Hovering ceiling IGE 2,050 m (6,725 ft)
Service ceiling 4,400 m (14,435 ft)
Range 740 km (460 miles)
Capacity Pilot + 5 passengers
Armament Provision for carrying Matra SATCP infra-red missiles or rockets and gun. TOW anti-tank missile available

SA 365/SA 366 Dauphin/Panther

Early versions of the Dauphin family were unsuccessful in gaining military orders, although several examples were used for trials. F-WZAK, the sole SA 361H variant, was employed extensively on night-vision trials and is seen here equipped with FLIR in a nose housing, a roof-mounted sight, and eight HOT anti-tank missiles.

Designed to replace the successful Alouette III, particularly in the growing civil market, development of the eight-seat Dauphin originally began as a single-engined configuration, designated the SA 360, and based on a scaled-up SA 341 layout with a fenestron tail.

The first of two such prototypes, (F-WSQL), powered by the 980 shp Turboméca Astazou XVI engine, made an initial flight on 1 June 1972 and after 18 months development the aircraft went into production as the SA 360C. In the event, the design proved to be underpowered and the market for a single-engined helicopter in this class too limited, and production ended with the 34th example.

Concurrent with marketing of the SA 360C in the civil market, Aérospatiale made strenuous efforts to win military orders, especially when it became apparent that a number of completed SA 360C airframes would have no buyers. Consequently, three aircraft were allocated for military trials. The first of these was the SA 360H, powered by the uprated 1,400 shp Astazou XX engine, and this was followed by the SA 361B, which further introduced a new Starflex composite hinge-less rotorhead based on that previously developed for the smaller AS 350. Both these prototypes were promoted as assault helicopters but failed to win any orders and subsequently reverted to trials use. The SA 360H in particular became the SA 361H and was used to test day/night vision systems and anti-tank weaponry against future French ALAT requirements. The third military SA 360 was the converted first production aircraft, which was used for limited French Navy trials at sea, in particular aboard the *Jeanne d'Arc* in 1978.

Some of the military trials conducted with the SA 360 and SA 361 were, however, connected with the successor to the single-engined Dauphin, the SA 365C Twin Dauphin. This new version introduced a number of improvements over the original design, notably the Starflex head and fibreglass rotor blades coupled with twin 650 shp Turboméca Arriel turboshafts. The prototype (F-WVKE) began test flying on 24 January 1975 and the type succeeded the SA 360C on the production line in 1977, with deliveries commencing the following year.

Above: Development of the naval SA 365F Dauphin has been carried out in conjunction with Saudi Arabia, which has taken delivery of a small number of SAR-configured aircraft, as shown here, and is now receiving . . .

. . . *Below:* a quantity of sophisticated ASV variants for operation from coastal patrol vessels in the surface attack and OTHT role.

One of the early SA 365N development aircraft, F-WZJV, has been converted as the prototype SA 365M Panther with uprated Turbomeca TM333 engines and provision for day/night vision and sighting systems with anti-armour or ground attack armament.

The SA 365C was a useful improvement over its predecessor but sales continued to be slow, and relatively few found their way into the military market. Those that did were used mainly in the transport role, although three were supplied to the Royal Hong Kong Auxiliary Air Force for search and rescue and policing duties.

SA 365C production ended with the 79th aircraft, by which time the type had already been superseded by the SA 365N Dauphin II. This new version resulted from a further redesign of the basic aircraft, begun in 1977, and culminated with the first flight of the prototype (F-WZJD) on 31 March 1979.

The SA 365N retained the basic dynamic system of the SA 365C, including the Starflex head, but introduced many refinements. These included a fully retractable tricycle undercarriage, improved rotor blades, uprated engines, increased fuel capacity and a better cabin layout for up to 14 occupants. In addition, the airframe incorporated new construction techniques, in particular the use of composites to improve the overall weight and production costs.

Although some aerodynamic changes and other modifications were found necessary, most of these had been recognised by the time a second SA 365N had joined the test programme in late 1979 and, in February 1980, this aircraft demonstrated the type's capability by setting up new record performances over the Paris-London-Paris route. At 3,800 kg (8,378 lb) gross weight, the SA 365M Panther. The prototype for this variant (F-WZJV) was converted from an early SA 365N demonstrator during 1983, and first flew at Marignane on 29 February 1984. In addition to the new tail unit and some local strengthening of the airframe, the SA 365M introduced two 838 shp Turboméca TM333 engines, offering substantial extra power but with better fuel efficiency than the Arriel. The new powerplant allows an increase in gross weight to 4,100 kg (9,040 lb), and an improved hot/high performance.

Concurrent with development of the SA 366G (Page 26), Aérospatiale began working on two specific military variants of the SA 365N, the SA 365F naval version and the SA 365M anti-tank and light assault transport. While the latter was primarily a private-venture exercise in association with the French avionics and weapons industry, the SA 365F development programme was underwritten by Saudi Arabia, which on 13 October 1980 ordered 24 aircraft for the Saudi Navy to perform an anti-surface vessel (ASV) and search and rescue (SAR) role.

Accordingly, the original SA 365N prototype was reworked in 1981 to flight test the equipment and weapons systems intended for the SA 365F, making its first flight in this form on 22 February 1982. It was followed five months later by the first of four Saudi SA 365s configured for the SAR role with Omera ORB 32 radar, rescue winch and deck harpoon. This aircraft carried out deck landing qualification trials at RAE Bedford and at sea during 1982-83 alongside the first production anti-ship version.

The ASV SA 365F introduced the Agrion 15 radar in a pivoting chin radome and stub pylons mounting four AS.15TT anti-ship missiles, as well as a MAD installation on the port side of the rear fuselage. This equipment allows the aircraft to track and scan simultaneously over long ranges and to provide over-the-horizon targeting for long range missiles launched from ship or shore. Compatibility and firing trials were finally completed in mid-1985, soon after deliveries to the Royal Saudi Navy.

Shortly afterwards, the delivery to the Irish Air Corps and Irish Naval Air Service of five SA 365Fs for fishery surveillance, SAR and coastal patrol work began. These aircraft are equipped with a Bendix RDR L500 search radar, SFIM L55 autopilot, CDV L55 four-axis flight coupler, Crouzet navigation system and EFIS instrumentation. An ASW version, with sonar equipment and homing torpedoes, is also being marketed.

Production SA 365Fs differ from the early trials examples by introducing 700 shp Turboméca Arriel 520M (navalised) engines and a larger carbon fibre 11-blade fenestron tail unit to improve hover performance, especially with the wind from three-quarters aft. The new tail weighs some 20 percent less than the original SA 365N metal unit, while the enlarged tail rotor provides 37 percent extra thrust.

This larger tail unit was originally developed for the SA 366G programme but has been adopted, not only for the SA 365F, but also for the SA 365M Panther. The prototype for this variant F-WZJV was converted from an early SA 365N demonstrator during 1983, and first flew at Marignane on 29 February 1984. In addition to the new tail unit and some local strengthening of the airframe, the SA 365M introduced two 838 shp Turboméca TM333 engines, offering substantial extra power but with better fuel efficiency than the Arriel. The new powerplant allows an increase in gross weight to 4,100 kg (9,040 lb), and an improved hot/high performance.

The earlier trials with the SA 360H and SA 361 prototypes have already confirmed the basic compatibility of the Dauphin airframe with various night vision and sighting systems and a variety of armament, including eight HOT anti-tank missiles, and these options are now available to SA 365M customers. The first of these is Angola, which ordered four aircraft during 1985 with options on a further 21.

Production of the SA 365F, SA 365M and SA 366G is currently intermingled on the basic SA 365N assembly line, and overall sales of the generic family had topped 350 aircraft by the end of 1985. This total included several SA 365Ns delivered for para-military use and 50 SA 365Ns sold to China for operation by both commercial and military elements of the Administration.

Technical specifications

Helicopter SA 365M Panther
Type Day/night attack/transport
Year 1984
Engine 2 × 838 shp Turboméca TM333
Rotor diameter 11.93 m (39 ft 1.75 in)
Fuselage length 12.07 m (39 ft 7 in)
Overall length 13.74 m (45 ft 1 in)
Height 4.00 m (13 ft 4 in)
Empty weight 2,300 kg (5,070 lb)
Gross weight 4,100 kg (9,040 lb)
Maximum speed 280 km/h (174 mph)
Hovering ceiling IGE 3,200 m (10,500 ft)
Service ceiling 6,000 m (19,680 ft)
Range 750 km (466 miles)
Capacity Pilot + 8 passengers
Armament 8 × HOT anti-tank missiles or podded rockets, machine guns, etc.

SA 366G Dolphin

Currently being delivered from the Aérospatiale facility in Grand Prairie, Texas, is the SA 366G variant for the US Coast Guard. Powered by Avco-Lycoming LTS-101 engines, and with extensive avionics and other changes, the SA 366G is also under consideration by several other countries.

The Aérospatiale SA 366G originated as an Americanised variant of the SA 365 Dauphin (page 22), with 680 shp Avco-Lycoming LTS-101 turboshafts replacing the Turboméca Arriel engines and US avionics and equipment.

The original SA 366 concept envisaged a version of the SA 365C Twin Dauphin and, in fact, one of the original prototypes was actually completed and flown in January 1975, with the LTS-101 installation and under the SA 366G designation, before being converted to SA 365C standard.

Subsequently, in parallel with the redesign of the SA 365C which led to the SA 365N, Aérospatiale began development of a new SA 366G, which was tailored to meet a US Coast Guard specification for a new Short Range Rescue (SRR) helicopter. Initially the company was in competition with the Bell 222 and Sikorsky S-76, but the latter was withdrawn in 1978 and eventually, in June 1979, the SA 366G was announced as the winner. The resultant $215 million fixed-price contract covered 90 aircraft, designated HH-65A Dolphin by the USCG, and basically comprising

Originally destined for the US Coast Guard, N60035 is one of two SA 366G Dolphins delivered to Israel in May 1985 to undergo extensive evaluation against a local SAR requirement.

an SA 365N airframe outfitted with US engines, avionics and other equipment.

The first SA 366G (F-WZJT/4101), sequentially the second production SA 365N fuselage, was completed in 1980 and first flown on 23 July before being delivered later that year to the Aérospatiale facility at Grand Prairie Texas, where all SA 366Gs were destined to be assembled and fitted out. Four aircraft were initially built and allocated to development trials, but a serious shortage of engines throughout 1981, followed by a need to increase the tail rotor thrust to meet a payload extension, much delayed progress.

The latter problem was overcome by a complete redesign of the fenestron tail unit, introducing an enlarged fin of all-composite construction and a new increased-diameter 11-blade tail rotor. The result was a weight saving of some 9 kg (20 lb) and an increase in thrust of some 37 percent, allowing the helicopter to hover in winds of plus 30 knots (34.5 mph/55 km/h), as well as permitting an extra 120 kg (265 lb) take-off weight.

Meanwhile, continuing trials uncovered further problems in August 1982, when high altitude engine stalls occurred, and in the October the contract was rewritten to allow all aircraft to be delivered to a new SA 366G-1 standard, which included the new tail unit, engine/intake modifications to overcome the stall problem, and a fully machined engine compressor to increase efficiency from 75 to 80 percent. Subsequently, further modifications were necessary to the engine intake system to overcome a surge condition caused by snow ingestion and deliveries to the USCG finally began in November 1984.

The delays in the SA 366G programme were not all attributable to development problems, as the USCG undertook a deliberate policy of updating the aircraft and its equipment between 1979 and 1984. As a result, production SA 366Gs now incorporate a Lucas electronic fuel control system and a freon environmental control unit is being added, as well as a Northrop FLIR system to aid night and bad weather rescue operations. Other equipment on the SA 366G-1 includes a full communications package, plus a data link for automatic transmission of the aircraft state and position to ship or shore base, a passive failure AFCS and an omnidirectional airspeed system.

Following the original order for 90 aircraft, the USCG ordered a further six SA 366G-1s in late 1984. As the HH-65A, the type will eventually be deployed at USCG shore bases around the US coastline and will also operate from the USCG cutter fleet. In the event of hostilities, the aircraft would come under US Navy control.

Aérospatiale is now marketing the SA 366G for similar SAR and coastal patrol missions in several other countries, and delivered two ex-USCG trials machines to Israel in May 1985 for service evaluation. If this is successful, sales of up to 25 more aircraft may follow.

Technical specifications

Helicopter SA 366G Dolphin
Type Short Range Recovery (SRR)
Year 1980
Engine 2 × 680 shp Avco Lycoming LTS-101-750A-1 turboshafts
Rotor diameter 11.93 m (39 ft 1.75 in)
Fuselage length 11.44 m (37 ft 6.5 in)
Overall length 13.46 m (44 ft 2 in)
Height 3.51 m (11 ft 6.25 in)
Empty weight 2,718 kg (5,992 lb)
Gross weight 4,050 kg (8,928 lb)
Maximum speed 257 km/h (160 mph)
Hovering ceiling IGE 2,290 m (7,510 ft)
Range 307 km (191 miles)
Capacity 3 crew
Equipment Communications/navigation and all-weather search equipment; nose-mounted Northrop See Hawk infra-red sensor

Agusta 109A/109K

Top: One overseas customer for the military A 109 has been Argentina, which is expected to build new aircraft for the Army under licence, following the loss or capture of several of its original machines in the Falklands in 1982.

Below: The Agusta A 109 is in service with the Italian Army in an interim anti-tank role, pending the introduction of the definitive A 129 attack helicopter.

Although Agusta designed several indigenous helicopters between 1956 and 1969, none were developed beyond prototype and pre-production aircraft until the arrival of the A 109 in 1971.

The new helicopter was originally designed to provide a high speed executive transport in the civil market, pitched in size between the popular JetRanger family and the larger twin-engined civil transports then available. The aircraft was of a very aesthetic appearance, with twin 420 shp Allison 250-C20 engines closely cowled atop the fuselage, a retractable undercarriage, and a narrow body with room for up to eight occupants.

The rotor system was based on a conventional four blade articulated main rotor with a two blade tail rotor.

The prototype A 109 (I-AGUO) was assembled in the spring of 1971 and, at the time of its first flight on 4 August, was well in advance of any competitors in its class. Unfortunately, a ground resonance accident to the first prototype delayed serious flight trials until a second prototype (I-AGUX) flew in 1972. This was subsequently joined by a third aircraft in military configuration (I-AGUL) in 1973 and a fourth prototype for civil use.

Certification of the A 109 took place in May 1975, by which date the company had already laid down an initial production batch, including five aircraft for evaluation by the Italian Army in the scout/anti-tank/liaison role. These were delivered

Re-engined with the more powerful Turbomeca TM333 powerplant and with a new fixed undercarriage and other refinements, the A 109K is aimed specifically at the military market. First orders have yet to be confirmed.

in 1977, with three fitted out with the Hughes M65 TOW missile system. Although no follow-on order for this variant was received, the TOW aircraft contributed useful data to the development of the later A 129 attack helicopter, while Argentina took delivery of nine multi-role combat A 109s in 1979.

Meanwhile Agusta developed several other specific military variants for potential customers including an ESM/ECM electronic warfare version, one with external launch pylons for two Meteor Mirach-100 remotely-piloted vehicles with on-board relay and retrieval capability, a command/control variant for target designation and direction of a helicopter attack force, and a naval version. The latter is aimed at anti-surface and anti-submarine missions, with the capability of attack with air-to-surface missiles or homing torpedoes. Detection equipment installed includes a long range search radar fitted under the nose, and a retractable MAD unit. The aircraft can also be used for stand-off guidance of ship-launched missiles.

By late 1985, some 275 A 109As had been produced, including 30 aircraft built on spec and subsequently allocated to the Italian Army for scout/anti-tank familiarisation prior to the introduction of the A 129. Other military deliveries have included six aircraft to the Venezuelan Army and two machines for the British Army to supplement a pair of captured Argentinian A 109s being used for special anti-terrorist duties. In addition, at least 20 A 109As have entered service with Italian para-military operators such as the Carabinieri.

In the early 1980s Agusta began development of an uprated A 109, for hot/high operation and aimed specifically at the military market in the Middle East and Africa. Designated the A 109K, this new version introduced two 700 shp Turboméca Arriel 1K engines in place of the Allison powerplants, a transmission uprated to 816 shp maximum continuous operation, and a new tail rotor of slightly reduced diameter but with a more efficient aerofoil section and protection against sand erosion. Other major changes included the adoption of a fixed undercarriage and a lengthened nose to provide more sensor and avionics space.

Flight tests of the new dynamics began in April 1983 and this was followed by the first flight of the definitive A 109K prototype (I-DACE) in March 1984. This aircraft has since been fitted with a new composite rotor head, with elastomeric bearings and new profile composite blades which will be standard on production aircraft.

Technical specifications

Helicopter Agusta A 109A
Type Light transport
Year 1975
Engine 2 × 420 shp Allison 250-C20B
Rotor diameter 11.00 m (36 ft 1 in)
Fuselage length 11.16 m (36 ft 7 in)
Overall length 13.08 m (42 ft 11 in)
Height 3.32 m (10 ft 11 in)
Empty weight 1,360 kg (3,000 lb)
Gross weight 2,450 kg (5,400 lb)
Maximum speed 310 km/h (193 mph)
Hovering ceiling IGE 3,050 m (10,000 ft)
Service ceiling 4,572 m (15,000 ft)
Range 570 km (354 miles)
Capacity 2 crew + 5/6 passengers
Armament 4 × TOW anti-tank missiles or podded 7.62 mm machine guns, rockets, etc

A129 Mangusta

The Agusta A 129 is a dedicated multi-role combat helicopter on order for the Italian Army for the anti-tank role. Noteworthy in this view is the nose-mounted sensor and sighting system and the crashworthy undercarriage.

Design of this dedicated day/night light attack helicopter was initiated by Agusta in 1978 as a derivative of the A 109A for the anti-tank/scout role with the Italian Army. As the concept matured, however, the original design was replaced by a totally new project which laid heavy emphasis on survivability and advanced avionics. Several further design changes followed before the format was frozen in 1980.

The construction of five prototypes, including a ground test vehicle, was 70 percent funded by the Italian government and the first aircraft (MM590) made its first flight in early September 1983, before being demonstrated to the media on 15th. This was followed by the completion of the ground test vehicle in early 1984 and the first flights of the second and third prototypes in February and June 1984. These early aircraft were primarily airframe and dynamics test machines but the fourth prototype, first flown in mid 1985, introduced the Harris digital integrated multiplex system, controlling communication/navigation/armament/engine/power distribution and utility sub-systems. The fifth prototype was representative of the production A 129, with the full TOW armament and sighting systems.

Development of the A 129 has allowed for future engine changes by designing a modular transmission, which permits specific units to be changed to match different powerplants. New A 129 variants could be powered by the RTM322, in a single engine layout.

During 1985 Agusta projected this transport variant of the A 129, using the dynamic components of the attack helicopter but with a new forward fuselage providing passenger accommodation.

The initial version of the A 129 uses a fully articulated four-blade main rotor with a two-blade semi-rigid tail rotor. The fibreglass blades are designed to have a ballistic tolerance against hits from 12.7 mm ammunition and considerable tolerance against 23 mm hits. The 70 percent composite airframe is also resistant to 12.7 mm ammunitition, including the transmission which has a 30 min run-dry capability. Power is provided by two 952 shp Rolls-Royce Gem 2 engines mounted on either side of the arrow cross-section fuselage. The pilot and weapons operator sit in stepped tandem cockpits, with the pilot night vision FLIR, sensor and sighting systems in the extreme nose. A mast-mounted sight is optional, as is provision of laser designation and tracking equipment.

Armament is carried on four weapons pylons below the stub wings, with typically eight TOW missiles in the outboard positions and podded rockets, guns, bombs or other stores inboard. Both passive and active protection systems are included, with radar and laser warning receivers, jammers and a chaff/flare dispenser installed.

A total of 60 A 129 Mk 1 are currently on order for the Italian Army, with deliveries due to commence in 1987. A second batch, probably with the mast-mounted sight, is expected to follow on in 1991. Some export sales are also anticipated, especially from South America, the Middle East and within Europe.

The UK, Spain and the Netherlands are currently discussing with Agusta the development of a more powerful A 129 Mk 2, with the Gem engines replaced by a single 2,100 shp Rolls-Royce/Turboméca RTM322 powerplant and other modifications, including the introduction of the third generation Trigat anti-tank missile and the Westland BERP advanced rotor. A joint feasibility study was launched in September 1985 which, if successful, will lead to joint production in the early 1990s.

Also on offer by Agusta is a proposed naval version of the Mk 1, optimised for the anti-shipping role and over-the-horizon-targetting, and the A 129LUH tactical transport. This utilises the A 129 dynamics married to a new 10-14 seat fuselage. Gross weight of this utility variant would be in the region of 4,500 kg (9,920 lb), with a maximum cruise speed of 175 mph (277 km/h).

Technical specifications

Helicopter Agusta A 129
Type Light scout/anti-armour helicopter
Year 1983
Engine 2 × 952 shp Rolls-Royce Gem 2 Mk 1004D
Rotor diameter 11.90 m (39 ft 0.5 in)
Fuselage length 12.275 m (40 ft 3.25 in)
Overall length 14.29 m (46 ft 10.5 in)
Height 3.35 m (11 ft)
Empty weight 2,529 kg (5,575 lb)
Gross weight 3,700 kg (8,157 lb)
Maximum speed 270 km/h (168 mph)
Hovering ceiling IGE 3,290 m (10,800 ft)
Service ceiling 2,390 m (7,850 ft)
Range 750 km (465 miles)
Capacity 2 crew
Armament 8 × HOT or TOW anti-tank missiles plus podded 7.62 mm or 12.7 mm machine guns or rockets, etc

Atlas Alpha XH1

The Atlas XH 1 has been developed in South Africa, using the dynamics system and rear fuselage components of the SA 316B Alouette III. No production decision has yet been made.

Developed as a result of the international arms embargo imposed on South Africa, the Alpha XH1 represents the first home-grown military helicopter to be produced by the Atlas Aircraft Corporation, although this company had gained much previous experience overhauling and rebuilding Alouette, Puma and Wasp helicopters for the South African armed forces.

Design of the XH1 was begun in March 1981, following a decision by the South African Air Force that its prime helicopter requirement was for a light attack helicopter to fill a gap in its inventory. In addition such a design was felt to be best suited to the level of technology currently available within the company, since it could be based upon the dynamics system of an existing in-service type. Accordingly Atlas took the locally manufactured rotor and transmission system of the Aérospatiale SA 316B Alouette III , together with a Turboméca powerplant (probably the 870 shp Artouste IIIB), and married these components to a new fuselage. The latter employs a tail boom closely based on that of the Alouette III, with a welded steel tube centre fuselage and a tandem-seat front section. The powerplant is partially cowled and general airframe construction is of metal semi-monoque with some composite components. A crashworthy main undercarriage with a tailwheel layout is designed to improve survivability, and a swept tailfin with additional tailplane endplate fins provides directional stability in the event of a tail rotor failure.

The cockpit area provides for a weapons operator seated in front of and below the pilot, with side entry doors and extensive glazing. In the extreme nose is provision for a radar and associated avionics, while below the front fuselage is a turret-mounted 20 mm GA.1 cannon, slaved to the weapons operator's helmet sight. Alternative weapons can be carried on stub pylons immediately forward of the main undercarriage.

A prototype Alpha XH1 made its first flight on 3 February 1985, under conditions of great secrecy, and its existence was not publicly revealed until 8 March 1986. During this period a number of modifications were made and further changes are likely before any decision on production is confirmed.

Technical specifications

Helicopter Atlas Alpha XH1
Type Light attack helicopter
Year 1985
Engine (est) 870 shp Turboméca Artouste IIIB
Rotor diameter 11.02 m (36 ft 1.25 in)
Fuselage length (est) 10.98 m (36 ft)
Height (est) 3.05 m (10 ft)
Empty weight (est) 1,200 kg (2,646 lb)
Gross weight 2,200 kg (4,851 lb)
Maximum speed (est) 200 km/h (125 mph)
Ceiling (est) 12,352 m (20,500 ft)
Range (est) 530 km (330 miles)
Capacity 2 crew
Armament 1 × 20 mm GA.1 cannon or four pylon-mounted 7.62 mm machine guns, unguided rockets, etc.

Bell Model 47

Despite its mid-1940 origins, the simplicity of the Bell 47, coupled with the vast numbers built has ensured that the type is still to be found in military service 40 years later.

Military variants of the Model 47 were largely based on the US Army H-13 Sioux, initially powered by the 200 hp Franklin engines but also using a 250 hp Lycoming powerplant with and without supercharging. The two-bladed teeter-rotor, with a stabilising bar, a bubble canopy enclosing a two/three-seat cockpit, skid under-carriage, and a simple skeletal fuselage and tailboom were common characteristics of most military variants, although some four-seat 47J aircraft with a covered fuselage and tail boom also found their way into service with the US Navy and other forces.

Licence agreements also saw the Bell 47 being built under licence by Kawasaki in Japan, Agusta in Italy, where over 1,100 AB-47G and J variants were assembled, and by Westland in the UK, where 100 47Gs were built for the Army Air Corps. Production finally ended in 1973 with the delivery of two Agusta-built aircraft to Zambia, by which time over 6,000 aircraft had been built.

In service the Bell 47 was primarily used in the observation, communication and training roles although, with stretcher pods fitted, it was also

The Bell 47 has been produced in a number of different variants since it was first introduced into service in 1946. This example is one of six assembled under licence in the UK by Westland for South Yemen.

Probably the most familiar helicopter yet built, the H-13 Sioux. This example, an H-13K 59-4972 for the US Army, was one of two built in 1960 to Model 47G-3 standard with the 225 hp Franklin 6VS-335 engine.

employed as an ambulance helicopter during its early military career. Only in the 1970s, with the arrival of more sophisticated types, did this military career begin to wane.

Surviving military Bell 47s are mostly all based on the G sub-variant, which introduced an increased fuel capacity in podded shoulder tanks and a controllable tail stabiliser. Initial 47Gs, produced from 1953, were powered by the 200 hp Franklin 0-335-3 piston engine and all 265 built were issued to the US Army as the OH-13G. The 47G-2 (OH-13H) introduced a 250 hp Lycoming 0-435-23 engine, with all-metal rotor blades and other improvements. Delivery of 453 aircraft to the US Army began in late 1965, while others were built for a number of overseas air arms. Finally, the 47G-3 standardised on an extended tailboom and the uprated 270 hp Lycoming engine, with a turbocharger in the 47G-3B-2 version, while the 47G-4 offered the 305 hp Lycoming 0-540 powerplant.

While the ready availability of spares makes continued operation of the Bell 47 feasible to the end of the century, increasing maintenance costs are likely to force the last military examples into retirement well before that date.

Technical specifications

Helicopter Bell 47G-3B
Type Observation/liaison
Year 1961
Engine 270 hp Lycoming TVO-435
Rotor diameter 11.35 m (37 ft 3 in)
Fuselage length 9.62 m (31 ft 7 in)
Height 2.83 m (9 ft 3 in)
Empty weight 814 kg (1,795 lb)
Gross weight 1,340 kg (2,954 lb)
Maximum speed 169 km/h (105 mph)
Hovering ceiling IGE 6,100 m (20,013 ft)
Service ceiling 5,330 m (17,487 ft)
Range 507 km (315 miles)
Capacity Pilot + 2 passengers

Bell Model 204

The Bell Model 204 was designed in 1954 to meet a US Army requirement for a utility helicopter to meet primarily a casualty evacuation role, plus troop-carrying and other missions, identified as a result of experience in the Korean War. Other key points of the specification were an 8,000 lb (3,629 kg) payload, and the ability to be air-transportable by C-124 or C-130.

By selecting a turbine powerplant mounted horizontally above the rear cabin, and marrying this to the two-blade teeter-rotor system, Bell was able to develop a classic design which, with some updating, is still in production 30 years later. The US Army initially ordered three prototypes of the new design and the first of these, the XH-40 55-4459, first flew at Fort Worth on 22 October 1956, powered by the new 825 shp Lycoming XT53 turboshaft. In August 1958 Bell delivered six prototype YH-40 aircraft to the US Army for evaluation. These machines introduced a 30 cm (11.8 in) stretch in the cabin, increased skid clearance, an enlarged cabin door and other changes, but retained the XT53 powerplant. Field trials with the YH-40 soon led to an order for nine pre-production aircraft, designated the HU-1 under contemporary US Army nomenclature. It was this designation that led to the popular name of 'Huey' being adopted for the type, after the Disney character who achieved fame as one of Donald Duck's mischievous nephews. The official name, however, was 'Iroquois', in line with US Army policy of naming its aircraft after Indian tribes.

The first HU-1, 57-6095, was handed over to the US Army in September 1958 and promptly despatched to Alaska for cold weather trials. The HU-1 introduced the 860 shp Lycoming T53-L-1A turboshaft, derated to 770 shp, and made provision for up to three crew and four passengers in a bulged cabin which allowed stowage for stretchers in the prime casevac role.

In March 1959, the US Army consolidated its faith in the Iroquois by placing a major order for 173 HU-1As, deliveries of which commenced in the following June. Similar to the HU-1, this new variant introduced a T53-L-1 powerplant further derated to 680 shp and a gross weight of 7,200 lbs (3,266 kg). 14 entered service as instrument

Early versions of the Bell UH-1, built under the company designation Model 204, still remain in service with a number of air arms. This is an Agusta-built AB204B operated by the Swedish Army.

trainers under the designation TH-1A, but most of the aircraft went to frontline units at home and abroad and, in 1962, some went into operation in Vietnam, armed with 7.62 mm machine guns and ground attack rockets.

In April 1960, the first HU-1B was flown, introducing an improved rotor system which featured a taller rotor mast and increased chord on the main blades, with aluminium honeycomb replacing the previous spar construction and repositioned blade weights. The new rotor system improved the CG range and, coupled with an uprated 960 shp T53-L-5 engine, allowed a 50 percent increase in cabin loading and a new gross weight of 8,500 lb (3,856 kg). Deliveries to the US Army of the HU-1B were to total 1,010 aircraft, with later aircraft standardising on the 1,100 shp T53-L-11 engine, and all HU-1s being retrospectively designated UH-1 under a revised nomenclature system in 1962. Many UH-1Bs were to see service in Vietnam, undertaking casevac missions and armed escort work with the larger troop-carrying piston-engined helicopters then in operation.

The equivalent Bell designation for the UH-1B was the Model 204B, first ordered by the Royal Australian Air Force in April 1961. Essentially identical to the UH-1B, the Australian aircraft also saw service in Vietnam with 16 being eventually delivered, and the last only recently having been retired. Other military 204Bs were delivered by Bell to New Zealand, Indonesia, Norway, and Colombia. The type was also built under licence by Fuji for local Japanese service.

Meanwhile Bell also signed a licence agreement with Agusta, which developed its own variant, the AB-204B, powered by the 1,050 shp Bristol-Siddeley Gnome turboshaft. This engine was a licence development of the General Electric T-58. The first AB-204B flew in Italy on 10 May 1961 and was initially followed by production aircraft for the Italian Army. Subsequent deliveries, variously powered by the Gnome, T-53 or T-58 engine, and with 44 ft and 48 ft (13.4 m and 14.6 m) diameter rotors, were made to Austria, Ethiopia, Spain, Sweden, Saudi Arabia, Turkey and Holland, as well as to the Italian Navy.

The latter took delivery of 30 AB-204AS, a specialised anti-submarine variant with an automatic stabilisation system, dunking sonar, Ekco search radar and provision for two Mk 44 torpedoes. Two AB204AS were also delivered to the Spanish Navy.

In the United States the adoption of further main rotor improvements, coupled with an increase chord tail pylon with anti-torque camber, led naturally to the UH-1C, 749 of which followed the previously delivered UH-1Bs into the US

The Bell UH-1H is standard equipment for many military services world-wide. This Royal Australian Air Force example is one of four which were detached to support the United Nations' emergency force in the Middle East.

The US Air Force version of the early Model 204 Iroquois UH-1B was the UH-1F, 120 of which were delivered for training and other roles powered by the 1,100 shp General Electric T58 engine. 63-13141 was the first such example.

Army. UH-1Cs re-engined with the 1,400 shp T53-L-13 engine were later redesignated UH-1Ms. Other Model 204 variants based on the UH-1B and UH-1C entered service with the US Navy, including the UH-1E, which was an armed UH-1B development for the Marine Corps, the HH-1K built for SAR operations with the 1,400 shp T53-L-13 turboshaft, the UH-1L general utility helicopter, and the TH-1L trainer.

Meanwhile the work done by Agusta in marrying the Gnome engine to the 204B airframe in 1961 proved of benefit two years later when the US Air Force selected the UH-1B, powered by the 1,290 shp General Electric T58 engine, to fulfil a utility support and base rescue role. In addition to the extra power, the T58 offered the advantage of commonality with the USAF Sikorsky HH-3 fleet. The first UH-1F flew on 20 February 1964 and 120 basic aircraft were eventually delivered, as well as 26 TH-1F instrument trainers. Subsequently 20 UH-1F were modified to UH-1P standard to carry out psychological warfare missions in Vietnam during the late 1960s.

With the introduction of newer variants of the UH-1 family, in particular the Model 205, surplus American military Model 204s found their way to various US friendly countries while some Agusta-built examples also remain in service.

Technical specifications

Helicopter Bell Model 204 (HU-1A)
Type Utility/transport
Year 1959
Engine 860 shp Lycoming T53-L-1A
Rotor diameter 13.40 m (44 ft)
Fuselage length 12.98 m (42 ft 7 in)
Overall length 13.59 m (44 ft 7 in)
Height 3.87 m (12 ft 8 in)
Empty weight 2,050 kg (4,520 lb)
Gross weight 3,856 kg (8,500 lb)
Maximum speed 238 km/h (148 mph)
Hovering ceiling IGE 3,230 m (10,600 ft)
Service ceiling 3,500 m (11,483 ft)
Range 615 km (382 miles)
Capacity 2 pilots + 8 troops
Armament 2 × 7.62 mm machine guns

Bell Model 205

The arrival in 1959 of the HU-1A Model 204 in the US Army rapidly led to a requirement to stretch the basic design and provide a tactical transport version. This was urgently needed to replace the piston-engined Sikorsky H-34 and Vertol H-21s then being used by the American forces in the Vietnam war theatre.

Bell therefore developed the Model 205, introducing a 3 ft 5 in (1.06 m) fuselage stretch matched to the 1,100 shp Lycoming T53-L-11 powerplant and a 48 ft (14.6 m) diameter wide-chord main rotor. Large sliding doors gave easy access to an enlarged cabin, able to accommodate up to 14 armed troops, or six stretchers and three passengers, up to a gross payload of 4,900 lb (2,222 kg). Maximum take-off weight was set at 9,500 lb (4,309 kg), a 1,000 lb (454 kg) increase over the earlier model.

The prototype Model 205, 60-6028, designated the YHU-1D, first flew on 16 August 1961 and was followed by six prototype/pre-production aircraft. In April 1962 one of these machines set up new time to height records of 6,000 m (19,685 ft) in 5 min 47.4 sec, and 3,000 m (9,843 ft) in 2 min 17.3 sec, breaking the times previously set by a UH-1A, as well as setting up a new 1,000 km (621 mile) closed circuit speed record of 134.9 mph (217.2 km/h).

Production UH-1D aircraft began rolling off the Bell line in May 1963. Eight initial machines were followed by orders for 22, 47 and 94 respectively before the US Army placed the first of several major contracts for the type. By late 1964 some 375 were in action in Vietnam, with 30 aircraft a month being delivered to the war zone by mid-1965. A total of 20,08 UH-1Ds were eventually received by the US Army, including a small number converted to HH-1D configuration for rescue work.

A major overseas order for the UH-1D came to Bell in April 1965, when the West German government placed a contract for 406 aircraft, for local assembly by Dornier. In the event, only 350 were actually delivered, including two US pattern aircraft, with the last being handed over in 1971. Most entered service with the Army and the Air Force, including a number allocated to the SAR role.

Other UH-1Ds were supplied to the Canadian, Australian, New Zealand and Brazilian Air Forces while, with the arrival of later variants and the eventual introduction of the Sikorsky

The West German Army is still a large scale 'Huey' operator, with over 180 UH-1Ds still in front line service and expected to remain operational until the end of the century.

Black Hawk in the US Army inventory, a good number of surplus American UH-1Ds were passed on to other countries as military aid.

In 1967 the UH-1D was phased out of production at the Bell plant in favour of the UH-1H, which introduced the uprated 1,114 shp Lycoming T53-L-13 engine. Some 5,500 UH-1Hs have been built by Bell to date and many UH-1Ds were also converted to the new standard during their military career. Three other variants, modified in relatively small numbers, were the HH-1H for base rescue, the EH-1H electronic warfare version, and the UH-1V rescue medevac conversion. The basic UH-1H was also built under

licence in Taiwan, Japan and Italy, with the two latter sources still in production in 1985 and about to be joined by a new production line established by the Turkish Army in Ankara.

In Italy, Agusta began producing the UH-1D version, designated the AB205, in 1963 and followed this with the AB205A (equivalent to the UH-1H). By 1986 several hundred aircraft had been produced, not only for the Italian armed forces but for a number of Middle East and African countries as well.

Like the earlier variants of the ubiquitous Huey, the UH-1H has been recently displaced in some numbers from the US Army inventory, although many aircraft will remain operational for several years yet. Others have moved on to other countries, and will likely be in front line service to at least the turn of the century.

Technical specifications

Helicopter Bell Model 205 (UH-1H)
Type General purpose
Year 1963
Engine 1,400 shp Lycoming T53-L-13
Rotor diameter 14.63 m (48 ft)
Fuselage length 12.77 m (41 ft 10 in)
Overall length 17.40 m (57 ft)
Height 4.42 m (14 ft 6 in)
Empty weight 2,177 kg (4,800 lb)
Gross weight 4,310 kg (9,500 lb)
Maximum speed 222 km/h (138 mph)
Hovering ceiling IGE 4,145 m (13,600 ft)
Service ceiling 6,700 m (21,980 ft)
Range 580 km (360 miles)
Capacity 2 pilots + 11-14 troops

Bell Model 206

The Model 206 was originally designed by Bell for the 1961 US Army Light Observation Helicopter (LOH) competition, in which it was matched against projects by Hiller and Hughes.

Prototypes of each competitor were ordered in spring 1961 and the first of eight Bell prototypes (N73999), designated the Model 206, flew on 8 December 1962. Five of these were funded by the US Army as the OH-4A and participated in the fly-off competition against the Hiller OH-5A and Hughes OH-6A in 1964. The Bell entry was powered by a 250 shp Allison T-63 engine driving a main rotor based on the Model 47 principle with a stabiliser bar. The four-seat cabin was extensively glazed, with a bubble nose section, and stressed to withstand 15g vertically.

In the event Bell lost the competition to the Hughes OH-6A, but the company decided to redesign the helicopter to a more commercial specification and this emerged in 1965 as the Model 206A JetRanger. The new design was based on the dynamic components of its military forerunner but featured a more aesthetic airframe design with a five-seat cabin, and introduced the more powerful 317 shp Allison 250-C18 civil version of the T63 engine.

The prototype Model 206A (N8560F) first flew on 10 January 1966 and was launched into commercial production later that year, with deliveries beginning in January 1967. The immediate success of the JetRanger soon led to a reawakening of US military interest and an order from the US Navy for 40 TH-57A SeaRangers, configured with dual controls and naval avionics but otherwise identical to the basic Model 206A. Deliveries of the TH-57A took place in 1968, by which time the US Army had re-opened its LOH competition and ordered 2,200 of a new JetRanger variant, designated the OH-58A Kiowa.

The prototype OH-58A, modified from a standard JetRanger airframe, was completed in August 1968 and was followed by the first

The newest variant of the Bell OH-58 Kiowa to enter service is the OH-58D Scout, the subject of a major updating programme which includes the introduction of a four-bladed main rotor, new avionics and a mast-mounted sight/sensor system. Now operational with the US Army, all OH-58Ds being built are conversions of early OH-58A and OH-58B airframes.

As the JetRanger the Model 206B found a large commercial market in the late 1960s, but additionally entered widespread military service as a liaison and training aircraft. The US Navy has been a major customer for the TH-57 variant, which it uses for basic and advanced instrument training.

production aircraft, 68-16687, in February 1969. Apart from internal layout changes and different avionics, the OH-58A also differed from the Model 206A by introducing an increased diameter main rotor and provision for light armament. By late 1969 OH-58As were operational in Vietnam and production continued until November 1973, when the final machine for the US Army was handed over.

The OH-58A variant was also delivered to the Canadian Armed Forces, which purchased 74 COH-58As (later re-designated CH-136) in 1971-72 for observation and pilot training duties. In addition 56 aircraft were supplied to the Australian military between 1971 and 1978, with the first 14 assembled by Bell and the remainder licence-built locally by the Commonwealth Aircraft Corporation.

The introduction of the more powerful 400 shp Allison 250-C20 engine led in 1972 to the availability of the OH-58B, 23 of which were supplied by Bell to Israel in 1974. This variant was also purchased by the Austrian Air Force, which took delivery of 12 aircraft in 1976, and by Spain and Turkey, which were provided with 12 and three examples respectively in the same period.

In 1976 the US Army adopted a Bell proposal to upgrade its OH-58A fleet, incorporating the further uprated 420 shp Allison 250-C20B (T63-A-720) engine, infra-red exhaust protection, a flat-plate cockpit canopy to reduce glint, a new NVG instrument panel and other modifications. Three OH-58As were initially converted to the new configuration as OH-58Cs and in March 1978 Bell began the conversion of 435 aircraft to production OH-58C standard. A further 150 were converted by Israel Aircraft Industries for US Army units in West Germany.

Meanwhile the original Model 206A JetRanger had been succeeded by the Model 206B JetRanger II, powered by 400 shp 250-C20, and subsequently by the 206B JetRanger III, using the 420 shp 250-C20B. Despite the commercial tag, all three JetRanger variants were produced for military customers to fulfill observation, training and communications roles. Exports by Bell included four Model 206As for the Chilean Navy and similarly small numbers of 206Bs for a variety of small military air arms. The largest Model 206B orders to date have been from Canada for 14 JetRanger IIIs in 1981 to replace CH-136s in the basic training role, and from the Brazilian Navy in 1985 for 16 aircraft for an IFR training role. In

In an attempt to broaden the military market for the 206L Long Ranger, Bell has developed the 206L Texas Ranger, fitted with a roof-mounted sight system for a TOW anti-tank missile system. The aircraft can also be operated in utility and similar military roles, but has not yet attracted any firm orders.

addition, the US Navy purchased 21 TH-57B JetRanger IIIs during 1984 for the primary training role, having previously placed a large order for 76 TH-57C variants. This latter version differed from earlier TH-57s by introducing a full IFR instrument panel, Sfena Ministab ASE, an environmental control unit, jettisonable doors, rotorbrake and provision for an external cargo hook, with a resultant increase in empty weight of 300 lb (136 kg).

As the result of a licence agreement with Agusta, the various Model 206 versions have also been produced in Italy since 1967, with a large number of military aircraft being sold into European and Middle East countries. Designated AB 206A-1, 39 of the initial version were purchased by the Italian Army, with others going to such customers as Abu Dhabi, Sweden, Turkey, Iran and Saudi Arabia. Some of these aircraft were fitted with a water injection system to boost performance in hot/high conditions, but with the advent of the AB 206B-1, powered by the 400 shp Allison 250-C20 engine, customers such as the Italian Army and Iran switched to the new version.

The success of the Model 206 JetRanger family in the military market led Bell to produce, in 1980, an armed variant of its commercial Model 206L LongRanger, a stretched version of the JetRanger powered by a 500 shp Allison 250-C28 engine and first flown on 11 September 1974. Known as the Model 206L TexasRanger, the military demonstrator prototype was closely based on the commercial airframe, but introduced a strengthened tailboom and a reinforced rear fuselage to offset blast pressure from missile launches. In addition, various quick-change design features were incorporated to facilitate rapid role changes from an eight passenger transport through to light anti-armour missions.

In the latter role, the TexasRanger can carry four TOW missiles in two launchers, plus four spare missiles in the cabin. A roof-mounted sight allows target sighting to be carried out from a covert position. Alternative weaponry which can be mounted on the lateral pylons includes two pods, each containing seven 2.75-in (70 mm) rockets or 7.62 mm machine guns, or a total of four anti-aircraft missiles.

To date only the demonstrator TexasRanger, N206L, has been built. The proposed production version would differ by introducing the uprated 650 shp 250-C30 powerplant with a larger 416 litre (91.5 gall) crash resistant fuel system.

Technical specifications

Helicopter Bell OH-58C Kiowa
Type Observation/light transport
Year 1976
Engine 420 shp Allison T63-A-720
Rotor diameter 10.77 m (35 ft 4 in)
Fuselage length 9.93 m (32 ft 6 in)
Overall length 12.49 m (41 ft)
Height 2.91 m (9 ft 6 in)
Empty weight 825 kg (1,818 lb)
Gross weight 1,451 kg (3,200 lb)
Maximum speed 222 km/h (138 mph)
Hovering ceiling IGE 4,025 m (13,200 ft)
Service ceiling 5,640 m (18,500 ft)
Range 480 km (298 miles)
Capacity 2 pilots + 3 passengers

Bell Model 209 (AH-1G/Q/S)

Only two years after the first flight of the prototype Model 204 Iroquois, Bell began to examine the market for an attack/reconnaissance helicopter, able to carry out armed escort and fighter missions in support of Army ground units and airborne forces.

This led, in 1962, to the D255 Iroquois Warrior project, which utilised Model 204 dynamics and other components married to a tandem two-seat cockpit and provision for heavy armament, including a turret faired into the nose. To further the project Bell built a concept demonstrator around the basics of a Model 47 Sioux. This machine, the Model 207 Sioux Scout, flew in July 1963 and toured a number of US Army bases over the next several months before undergoing evaluation by the 11th Air Assault Division in early 1964.

Later in 1964, the US Army selected Lockheed and Sikorsky to compete for the development of an Advanced Aerial Fire Support System (AAFS), effectively a long range and high performance helicopter gunship which was eventually cancelled at the end of the decade. Bell, eliminated from the competition, decided to go it alone and in March 1965 began construction of a revised prototype, designated Model 209.

By this time, intensification of the Vietnam War was forcing the US Army to consider an interim AAFS which could be quickly launched into production. This was urgently needed to supplement and replace the UH-1Bs and UH-1Cs then being increasingly used in a gunship role and as escorts for the newly arriving -and faster -UH-1D troop carriers. In August 1965 five types were put up for consideration, including armed versions of the Boeing Vertol CH-47, Kaman UH-2 and Sikorsky S-61 as well as the Bell Model 209.

The prototype Model 209, N209J, first flew on 7 September 1965, powered by the 1,100 shp Lycoming T53-L-11 engine and sharing the dynamics of the Model 205 UH-1D. New was a retractable skid undercarriage and a ventral fin, neither of which were adopted as permanent features. On 25 October N209J set up an official world speed record in its class of 200 mph (321.9 km/h) and, by the end of the year, the US Army had made its choice. On 4 April 1966 a contract was signed for two pre-production prototypes, followed nine days later by an order for 112 aircraft.

Initially allocated the designation UH-1H, the new helicopter was almost immediately redesignated the AH-1G and named the HueyCobra, a change in US Army tradition forced by a combination of the 'Huey' nickname for the UH-1 family and the Cobra title already given to UH-1 gunships in Vietnam.

The first production AH-1G, 66-15246, flew in September 1966, standardising on a taller tailfin and introducing an initial armament of a 7.62 mm multi-barrelled minigun in a TAT-102 chin turret, with four underwing hard points able to carry rocket launchers or additional guns in pods. Crew protection included armour-plated seats and stowable cockpit side panels. Initial crew conversion got underway in July 1967 and, on 29 August, the first six AH-1Gs allocated to the US Army in Vietnam departed the Bell factory for Bien Hoa. Six days later the first combat mission was flown.

Although almost all the 1,127 AH-1Gs built were destined for US Army service, 38 aircraft were diverted to the US Marine Corps in 1969, to support Marine activities in Vietnam. Experience in that war theatre also led to modifications during the AH-1G production run. The most obvious was the repositioning of the tail rotor from the left to right side of the fin to improve handling in quartering tail wind conditions. In addition, the turret armament was upgraded to mount either twin 7.62 mm miniguns or a grenade launcher. Some machines were also fitted with an upturned exhaust deflector to provide some infrared protection from SA-7 missiles. Others were modified as TH-1G trainers, with instructor flight controls and an instrument panel in the second cockpit.

Overseas sales of the AH-1G were confined to six aircraft for Israel and eight to the Spanish Navy. The latter were operated in the anti-shipping role, occasionally deploying aboard the aircraft carrier *Dedalo*, but have now been withdrawn from service.

With the revival of the AAFS programme in the early 1970s and a change in emphasis towards an attack helicopter with full anti-armour capability, Bell built two prototype King Cobras, grossing 14,000 lb (6,354 kg) apiece, and featuring uprated dynamic systems based on the Bell 214. Armament included a 30 mm turret gun, eight TOW anti-tank missiles and other stores, as well as provision for FLIR, HUD, laser rangefinder and

The current production verson of the single-engined Cobra is the AH-1S, armed with eight TOW anti-armour missiles. 1008 is one of 24 such aircraft delivered to Jordan in 1985.

other equipment in a revised nose section. In the event the AAFS requirement was abandoned in favour of a new Advanced Attack Helicopter (AAH) competition, which led to the McDonnell Douglas AH-64 (page 97), but the experience with the King Cobra was incorporated by Bell in a proposal to integrate the TOW system into the US Army AH-1G fleet.

In January 1974 the US Army accepted the proposal, with a contract to convert 101 AH-1Gs to TOW configuration as AH-1Qs. This programme included the installation of fixed fittings for eight wing-mounted missiles, and a nose-mounted sight linked to a Sperry helmet system. The initial order was followed by a second for 189 conversions at the end of 1974, and production deliveries began in June 1975, 93 AG-1Qs being converted by Bell before this mark was superseded by the Mod AH-1S.

The Mod AH-1S resulted from the need to equip the AH-1Q with a powerful engine to offset the weight increase imposed by the TOW installation. The new powerplant, an 1,800 shp Lycoming T53-L-703, gave an extra 400 shp and was matched to an uprated transmission and gearbox to allow operation at a new gross weight of 10,000 lb (4,540 kg). In addition the opportunity was taken to incorporate some structural strengthening to maximise manoeuvrability. A total of 20 AH-1Q were brought up to the new standard by Bell, while 63 were converted in Germany by Dornier using modification kits. In all, 407 original AH-1Gs have been brought up to Mod AH-1S configuration, including ten aircraft further converted as TH-1S by Northrop to provide night vision system training for future AH-64 pilots.

Meanwhile Bell had further developed the AH-1 design to improve survivability and effectiveness in an anti-tank environment, resulting in the definitive AH-1S. This new production variant standardised on the Mod AH-1S changes and further introduced a flat plate cockpit canopy, an improved nap-of-the-earth instrument layout, revised avionics, and a 20 mm gun in the nose turret with a laser rangefinder incorporated in the nose sight.

The first production AH-1S was handed over to the US Army in March 1977 and was followed by 65 similar aircraft, before a switch was made to composite main rotor blades designed for unlimited life and resistant to weapons of up to 23 mm calibre. A total of 100 AH-1S were completed by September 1978 and these were then followed by 98 Up-gun AH-1S, which further introduced a universal gun turret, able to mount 20 mm or 30 mm cannon, an improved weapons control system and a 10 kV alternator to handle the additional electrical power.

In October 1979 the Up-gun AH-1S was followed off the Bell production line by the first Modernised AH-1S. This Step 3 AH-1S variant featured all the earlier improvements but additionally incorpor-

ated a new fire control subsystem, low speed air data system, Doppler navigation, infra-red jammer and suppressor, and a new laser-augmented stabilised sight to improve gun and rocket accuracy.

By the beginning of 1985, a total of 338 AH-1S had been delivered to the US Army, of which 240 were to Modernised AH-1S standard. The latter included 27 for the National Guard, with another 23 due to follow. In addition Bell had delivered 20 to Israel, and had begun deliveries of 20 aircraft to Pakistan. Since that time, 24 Modernised AH-1S have been delivered to the Royal Jordanian Air Force, followed by a further 10 machines for Israel.

Since 1984 the Modernised AH-1S has also been in production in Japan, assembled under licence by Fuji for the Ground Self Defence Force. Local production was preceded by the delivery of two pattern aircraft from Bell for evaluation, and up to 54 machines are expected to be acquired over the next several years.

The Bell AH-1S is also now in production in Japan, where it is entering service with the Ground Self Defence Force. JG-3401 is one of two development aircraft delivered by Bell prior to local production.

Technical specifications

Helicopter Bell AH-1S
Type Anti-armour attack helicopter
Year 1977
Engine 1,800 shp Avco Lycoming T53-L-703
Rotor diameter 13.41 m (44 ft)
Fuselage length 13.59 m (44 ft 7 in)
Height 4.09 m (13 ft 5 in)
Empty weight 2,939 kg (6,479 lb)
Gross weight 4,535 kg (10,000 lb)
Maximum speed 227 km/h (141 mph)
Hovering ceiling IGE 3,720 m (12,200 ft)
Service ceiling 3,720 m (12,200 ft)
Range 507 km (315 miles)
Capacity 2 crew
Armament Various weapons and TOW missiles

Bell Model 209 (AH-1J/T/W)

By marrying the Pratt & Whitney Canada Twin-Pac powerplant developed for the Bell 212 to the Cobra airframe, Bell produced the AH-1J for the US Marine Corps. Seen here is a modified AH-1J of the Imperial Iranian Army.

Development by Bell of a twin-engined version of the UH-1 during the latter half of the 1960s (page 49) for the Canadian and US military, quickly led to interest by the US Marine Corps in acquiring a similar version of the AH-1G HueyCobra, 24 of which entered Corps service in 1969. Such interest was initially fuelled by USMC operations with the single-engined UH-1 in 1966-67, when 17 aircraft were lost due to engine problems, but had to be contained while priority was given to AH-1G production. However, Marine losses in 1968 accelerated a twin-engined AH-1 programme, destined to supersede a fiscal 1969 proposal to order 38 single-engined AH-1J HueyCobras featuring a rotorbrake, new avionics and a 20 mm cannon in the chin turret.

Thus, when the prototype AH-1J, 157757, was rolled out on 10 October 1969, it not only introduced the above modifications, but also featured the 1,800 shp Pratt & Whitney T400 TwinPac installation flown earlier that year on the Model 212 civil variant of the UH-1. The transmission was flat-rated at 1,100 shp with a 1,250 shp five minute emergency rating. Two further prototypes followed later that year before production deliveries of the AH-1J began in July 1970. Deployment to Vietnam for evaluation got underway in the following February, by which time 49 AH-1Js, now named the SeaCobra, were in USMC service. These were followed by 18 further examples in 1974-75. Two others were retained by Bell for modification to develop a TOW missile capability.

Meanwhile, support by the US government for the Shah of Iran had resulted in an order being placed for 202 AH-1J on behalf of the Imperial Iranian Air Force. The first of these aircraft, 3-4401, was completed in May 1974 and was followed by 140 similar machines before production switched to the anti-armour AH-1J (TOW) in April 1976. Development of the TOW anti-tank missile installation had already been carried out by Bell in 1974-75 for the US Army AH-1G programme, but this new Iranian variant went still further by upgrading the AH-1J dynamics. Changes began with the introduction of the more powerful 1,970 shp Pratt & Whitney T402 TwinPac, instead of the 1,800 shp T400, with a transmission uprated to 2,050 shp. In addition a larger 48 ft (14.6 m) diameter main rotor, a new 8 ft 8 in (2.6 m) tail rotor and other dynamic modifications, already introduced on the Iranian Model 214A utility transport, were also incorporated. A total of 62 AH-1J (TOW), commencing with 3-4541, were delivered to Iran between May 1976 and November 1977. In addition, eight similar aircraft were built for the Republic of Korea.

Development of the AH-1J (TOW) was also supported by the USMC, which sought to include

Further development of the AH-1J resulted in the US Marine Corps taking delivery of the AH-1T, armed with the TOW anti-tank missile system.

this capability on its own future AH-1J contracts, together with other improvements. In the event this led to a new variant, the AH-1T, the first two of which were completed in April 1976. These prototypes incorporated all the dynamic changes introduced on the AH-1J (TOW), but also underwent some fuselage stretching and the adoption of a ventral fin to improve CG and handling. Delivery of 55 production AH-1Ts began in December 1977 and was completed in October 1979.

The last of these aircraft, 161022, was however retained by Bell for further upgrading and in November 1979 was fitted with two 1,625 shp General Electric T700 engines for evaluation by company and Marine pilots. Flown in April 1980, the re-engined aircraft featured a new gross weight of 15,000 lb (6,806 kg), a 5,000 lb (2,268 kg) increase over the original AH-1J. After some budgetary delay, 161022 was re-engined in 1983 with the -401 marinised version of the T700, already in production for the US Navy SH-60B programme, and on 16 November 1983 made its first flight as the prototype AH-1T + SuperCobra.

This was followed in early 1984 by a USMC order for 44 AH-1T, subsequently designated the AH-1W, configured to carry either TOW or Hellfire anti-armour missiles, together with provision for two AIM-9L Sidewinder or Stinger air-to-air missiles or ground attack rockets and other underwing stores, and new defensive avionics.

Re-engining an AH-1T with a pair of General Electric T700 powerplants resulted in the AH-1T Plus Super Cobra prototype 161022, subsequently ordered for the US Marine Corps as the AH-1W. The first of 44 AH-1Ws was handed over in the spring of 1986.

Deliveries of the AH-1W began in March 1986 and are currently due to be completed in 1987. In addition standard AH-1Ts will be upgraded to AH-1W configuration.

Technical specifications

Helicopter Bell Model 209 (AH-1T)
Type Two-seat combat
Year 1980
Engine 1,970 shp Pratt & Whitney T400-WV-402
Rotor diameter 14.63 m (48 ft)
Fuselage length 14.68 m (48 ft 2 in)
Overall length 16.26 m (53 ft 4 in)
Height 4.15 m (13 ft 7 in)
Empty weight 3,635 kg (8,014 lb)
Gross weight 6,350 kg (14,000 lb)
Maximum speed 277 km/h (172 mph)
Hovering ceiling IGE 3,800 m (12,470 ft)
Service ceiling 3,795 m (12,450 ft)
Range 576 km (358 miles)
Capacity 2 crew
Armament Various weapons and TOW missiles

Bell Model 212/412

Interest in developing a twin-engined version of the Model 205 Iroquois originated within Bell during 1964, when deployment of early UH-1s in Vietnam demonstrated the need for more power and the improved safety factor conferred by two engines.

Research initially led to the one-off Model 208, a converted UH-1D powered by two 600 shp Continental T72 engines coupled to a common reduction gearbox and output shaft, first flown on 29 April 1965. In 1967 the research switched to Italy where Agusta, already building the Model 205 under licence, test flew in 1967 the AB 205BG powered by two Bristol Siddeley Gnome engines, and subsequently the AB 205TA with twin 700 shp Turboméca Astazous.

However, a Canadian interest in acquiring the UH-1 powered by a locally manufactured powerplant, led in 1968 to the development by Pratt & Whitney (Canada) of the PT6T-3 TwinPac, comprising two engines mounted side by side and producing a coupled output of 1,800 shp. Installed in a modified Model 205 airframe, redesignated as the Model 212 (N1402W), this combination first flew at the Bell plant in April 1969.

Initial development was carried out as a commercial enterprise, but an order for 50 military aircraft, designated CUH-1N, with options for 20 more was received from the Canadian government, concurrently with an initial order for 141 UH-1N from the US Air Force and Navy.

Deliveries began in September 1970 with the first (68-10778) of 79 UH-1Ns for the USAF, which deployed them worldwide including 22 HH-1N rescue machines and a number configured as VH-1N VIP transports. The US Navy and the Marine Corps eventually took delivery of 204 UH-1Ns, including six in the VH-1N configuration. Most of the Navy aircraft were deployed on base rescue while six Marine units were equipped with the type for the assault role from April 1971.

Canadian deliveries began in May 1971, with this variant being redesignated as the CH-135,

In US Navy service the Model 212 is designated the UH-1N and employed on training and utility duties. This machine was photographed with the ship's flight aboard the USS *Saipan*. (R. Walker).

A relatively recent customer for the Model 212 has been the Sri Lankan Air Force, which has purchased a number of examples since the Tamil uprising in 1984 and subsequent guerilla activity.

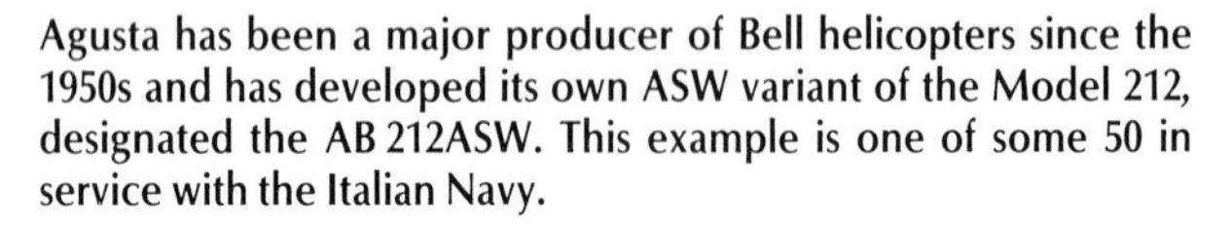
Agusta has been a major producer of Bell helicopters since the 1950s and has developed its own ASW variant of the Model 212, designated the AB 212ASW. This example is one of some 50 in service with the Italian Navy.

The Peruvian Navy also operates the AB 212ASW, with six aircraft armed with Sea Killer missiles performing an ASW/ASV role aboard the navy's frigates.

The Bell Model 412 is essentially a version of the 212 with a new technology four-bladed main rotor. This is one of two 412s operated by the Venezuelan Air Force.

The Model 412 is also operational with the Royal Thai Air Force in a VIP role alongside a large number of earlier UH-1 variants.

while a further major military order came from the Israeli Air Force, which took delivery of 62 aircraft under the Model 212 designation in 1975-76. Subsequently small numbers of 212s have entered service with many air arms in the military transport role.

Since 1981 the basic airframe has also been available with a new four-blade composite main rotor system as the Model 412, either as a new aircraft or as a retrofit installation. The new rotor offers some advantages in terms of payload and range but has not yet led to any major military orders.

Technical specifications

Helicopter Bell Model 212 (UH-1N)
Type Tactical transport
Year 1969
Engine 2 × 1,800 shp Pratt & Whitney Canada PT6T-3
Rotor diameter 14.69 m (48 ft 2 in)
Fuselage length 12.92 m (42 ft 5 in)
Height 4.39 m (14 ft 5 in)
Empty weight 2,517 kg (5,550 lb)
Gross weight 5,085 kg (11,210 lb)
Maximum speed 203 km/h (126 mph)
Hovering ceiling IGE 3,930 m (12,894 ft)
Service ceiling 5,304 m (17,405 ft)
Range 440 km (273 miles)
Capacity 2 pilots + 13 troops

Bell Model 214

The Model 214 programme arose from a requirement to considerably uprate the power available in the Model 205 to provide a 15-seat troop transport in the hot and high terrain of the Middle East, specifically in Iran.

Thus, in 1970, Bell built a single prototype Model 214 Huey Plus, a strengthened UH-1H airframe powered by a 1,900 shp Lycoming T53-L-702 turboshaft, and incorporating uprated dynamics including a new 48 ft (14.6 m) diameter main rotor with increased chord. Subsequently, this aircraft was re-engined with a more powerful 2,050 shp Lycoming T55-L-7C engine and the rotor system further refined to improve lift and reduce maintenance. Thus modified, the prototype was shipped in August 1972 to Iran and, at the end of that year, a $63 million contract was signed for 287 aircraft, to be powered by the still further uprated 2,930 shp LTC4B-8D engine.

The first of three definitive Model 214A prototypes was flown by Bell on 13 March 1974, and these were followed by the first production aircraft one year later. This machine, 6-4651, was delivered to Iran in April 1975 and, at the end of that month, set up a series of time-to-height records in its class, as well as maintaining level flight at an altitude of 29,760 ft (9,074.6 m). Deliveries of the 214A to the Imperial Iranian Army continued through 1976 and 1977, with six additional aircraft being ordered to follow on during 1978. Plans for the joint manufacture of a further 50 Model 214As, prior to the introduction of a production line in Iran, collapsed with the 1979 revolution.

The Iranian Air Force also took delivery of 39 Model 214s, ordered in February 1976 equipped for the SAR role and designated Model 214C. The first example, 4-9420, was flown in October 1976 and deliveries were completed in March 1978.

The Model 214B designation had meanwhile been allocated to a commercialised variant, introducing such changes as an engine fire extinguisher system and push-out escape windows. Most of the 70 aircraft built between 1976 and 1982 went to commercial operators but five were delivered to the Oman government in 1976

The Bell 214A saw the basic UH-1 design being considerably uprated and re-engineered to produce a utility helicopter with a much improved payload capability and hot/high performance. An early customer for this version was the Imperial Iranian Army, whose first machine is illustrated here.

9422

FAV
N3912U
FUERZA AEREA VENEZOLANA

Thailand has also been a customer for the Model 214ST with two aircraft handed over to the Royal Thai Army in 1984.

Top left: The Bell 214C, similar in most respects to the A and B variants, entered service in relatively small numbers with the Imperial Iranian Air Force for the SAR/utility role.

Lower left: Probably the ultimate Huey development is the current production Bell 214ST, a stretched version of the earlier 214A with twin General Electric CT7 engines and other refinements. This aircraft is one of two delivered to the Venezuelan Air Force.

and another four entered service with the Dubai Air Force in 1981. Four also went to Iran as VIP aircraft, while others were purchased by the Ecuador, Philippine and Thai governments for specialist operation.

By 1978 Bell had begun developing a 'Stretched Twin' variant of the Model 214, designated the 214ST, and powered by two 1,625 shp General Electric CT7 engines driving a new fibreglass main rotor. The intention was that this new version would be developed and built in Iran, with production commencing in 1980 to meet an Iranian order for 350 aircraft. A flight test programme, using the modified third prototype Model 214A, N214X, was inaugurated on 15 March 1977 but the programme was terminated at the end of 1978 when the Iranian government defaulted on the advance payment schedule.

Instead Bell chose to continue Model 214ST development as a private venture. This led to the construction of three production prototypes at Fort Worth, the first of which (N214ST) first flew on 21 July 1979. These new aircraft further introduced a stretched and widened fuselage, to seat up to 18 passengers plus two pilots, a strengthened run-dry transmission and improved electrical and flight control systems to provide IFR capability. Subsequent modifications have taken the Model 214ST to 17,500 lb (7,942 kg) gross weight.

Production deliveries began in early 1982, but to date relatively few aircraft have entered military service. The largest orders have been six machines sold to the Peruvian Air Force in late 1983, and six to the Oman government in 1983-84. In early 1986 Bell was in the process of delivering 45 Model 214STs to the Iraqi Ministry of Transport.

Technical specifications

Helicopter Bell 214ST
Type Utility transport
Year 1979
Engine 2 × 1,625 shp General Electric CT7-2A
Rotor diameter 15.85 m (52 ft)
Fuselage length 15.24 m (50 ft)
Height 4.84 m (15 ft 10.5 in)
Empty weight 4,300 kg (9,481 lb)
Gross weight 7,938 kg (17,500 lb)
Maximum speed 256 km/h (159 mph)
Hovering ceiling IGE 1,950 m (6,400 ft)
Service ceiling 1,460 m (4,800 ft)
Range 813 km (505 miles)
Capacity 2 pilots + 18 passengers

Bell Model 406

Although the two-blade teeter rotor system has been a Bell trademark for some 40 years, the company began flying experimental four-blade systems as early as 1965, and this experience was put to good use in a 1981 proposal to the US Army for development of a near-term scout helicopter, using the OH-58A Kiowa as a basis for an Army Helicopter Improvement Program (AHIP) under the Bell Model designation 406.

On 21 September 1981 Bell was awarded a $151 million AHIP development contract, and this led to the conversion of five OH-58As to prototype AHIP/OH-58D configuration. The first of these made its initial flight on 6 October 1983, introducing a new four-bladed soft-in-plane main rotor with glassfibre composite blades which can be manually folded for air transportation or stowage. The two-bladed tail rotor is also of glassfibre construction. Power is provided by an uprated 650 shp Allison 250-C30R turboshaft, allowing an increase in maximum speed of some 10 mph (19 km/h) and a gross weight improvement of 1,500 lb (681 kg) over the original OH-58A.

The third OH-58D prototype introduced a mast-mounted sight, jointly developed by McDonnell Douglas Astronautics and Northrop's Electro-Mechanical Division and providing TV/FLIR pictures. Other avionics introduced on the AHIP included a new integrated multiplex cockpit control and display system developed by Sperry Flight Systems, datalink and secure voice equipment, laser rangefinder/designator, airborne target handoff subsystem, Doppler and strap-down Inertial Navigation System. Much of the avionics equipment is carried in the rear cabin area. Armament is confined to provision for two air-to-air self-defence missiles.

An initial contract for long-lead items to convert 16 OH-58As to production OH-58D standard, received in July 1983, has subsequently been followed by new orders covering the conversion of a further 100 aircraft between 1986-87. Deliveries of the first 16 OH-58Ds to the US Army began in late 1985. In service the AHIP is intended to provide scouting/aerial reconnaissance and surveillance support for both attack helicopter and ground forces. Successful deployment in these roles could lead to the conversion of 578 OH-58As to the new configuration by 1992.

Meanwhile, in 1984, Bell developed a private venture variant of the AHIP for the export market, known as the Model 406CS (Combat Scout). This new helicopter retained the OH-58D dynamics and four-blade composite main rotor but introduced a further uprated 735 shp Allison 250-C34R engine to maximise hot/high performance. Deleted was the specialised avionics and multiplex cockpit of the AHIP, while the mast-mounted sight was replaced by a roof-mounted TOW sight installation. Also noteworthy was a new skid undercarriage configuration, designed to permit semi-retraction for easy aerial transport and previously trialled by the US Army on the OH-58.

Model 406CS armament can comprise four TOW 2 anti-tank missiles, or a mix of 70 mm rockets, 7.62 mm or 12.7 mm machine guns, air-to-air missiles or other pylon mounted weaponry. A prototype Model 406CS, N2500B, first flew in June 1984 and subsequently carried out a demonstration tour through Europe, the Middle East and SE Asia. No orders had been announced at the end of 1985.

Opposite: Using the technology developed under the OH-58D AHIP programme, Bell has produced this Model 406 Combat Scout demonstrator, able to carry a variety of weaponry and with a roof-mounted sight. Note also the revised semi-retractable skid undercarriage, designed to improve air portability.

Technical specifications

Helicopter Bell OH-58D
Type 2-seat scout
Year 1981
Engine 650 shp Allison 250-C30R
Rotor diameter 10.67 m (35 ft)
Fuselage length 10.31 m (33 ft 10 in)
Height 2.59 m (8 ft 6 in)
Empty weight 1,285 kg (2,825 lb)
Gross weight 2,041 kg (4,500 lb)
Maximum speed 237 km/h (147 mph)
Hovering ceiling IGE +3,660 m (12,000 ft)
Service ceiling +3,660 m (12,000 ft)
Range 556 km (345 miles)
Capacity 2 crew

Bell-Boeing V-22 Osprey

The Bell-Boeing V-22 will be the first production application of the tilt-rotor concept. Prototype construction is now underway, with a first flight scheduled for 1987.

The V-22 Osprey is destined to become the first production application of over 30 years of tilt-rotor development by Bell, a vertical lift technology which offers higher cruising speeds and enhanced operating economics over conventional helicopters through the use of a tilting rotor system mounted on a stub-wing fuselage.

Bell originally proved the feasibility of the tilt-rotor concept with its experimental XV-3 on 18 December 1958, when one of two prototypes built carried out the first ever tilt-rotor transition in flight from vertical to forward flight and back again. A lack of power and technological limitations prevented any early capitalisation of this feat, and it was not until 1973 that Bell won sufficient funding to build two new tilt-rotor research aircraft for trials by the company and NASA.

Designated XV-15, the new aircraft introduced two 1,550 shp Avco-Lycoming LTC1K-4K turboshaft engines, mounted at the wingtips with a double ballscrew actuated redundant tilt mechanism driving 25 ft (7.62 m) diameter rotors, and interconnected to provide single-engine and fail safe capability. A twin-finned tail unit was mounted at the end of a conventional light alloy fuselage with provision for a nine-seat cabin, although the aircraft was only flown as a two-seat research vehicle.

The first XV-15, N702NA, made its initial hovering flight on 3 May 1977, and the first full transition was carried out by the second prototype, N703NA, on 24 July 1979. Since that time both aircraft have been used to explore the limits of tilt-rotor flight, both from an aerodynamic and operational viewpoint. In 1983, N702NA was evaluated by the US Navy and Marine Corps in the search and rescue and slung load roles, as well as nap-of-the-earth flying, simulated flight refuelling, air-to-air evasion and other manoeuvres designed to confirm the suitability of the tilt-rotor for naval multi-mission roles. The aircraft was also evaluated by the US Army.

Two Bell XV-15 tilt-rotor prototypes were built to prove the concept of this layout for future military and commercial rotorcraft. Here the first aircraft, N702NA, is seen during deck landing trials aboard the USS *Tripoli* off the coast of San Diego.

As a result of service interest, Bell had already schemed a scaled-up version of the XV-15 to meet future assault transport, search and rescue, cargo carrying and long range special operation needs of all three US military arms and, in mid-1982, teamed with Boeing Vertol to compete in the generic JVX (Joint Services Advanced Vertical Lift Aircraft) programme.

Although originally a tri-service competition, by early 1983 immediate US Army interest had waned and the US Navy assumed the lead role as executive service. On 26 April, a contract was issued to Bell-Boeing to cover preliminary design of the JVX over a two year period and in April 1985, two further contracts were placed to cover systems engineering, long-lead tooling, and construction of a full scale V-22 mock-up. By this time too Bell and Boeing Vertol had reached agreement on development and production responsibilities, with Bell taking the wings, nacelles, drive system and tilt-rotor assemblies and Boeing Vertol the fuselage and overwing fairing. Design and con-

struction of the tail unit was subcontracted to Grumman.

At the end of 1985 the construction of ten V-22 prototypes was planned, including four non-flying airframes. The first flight is scheduled for February 1988, with production deliveries due to begin in mid-1991. The initial customer will be the US Marine Corps, which anticipates ordering 552 MV-22A assault transport variants to replace Boeing Vertol CH-47 and Sikorsky CH-53 helicopters currently used in this role. Powered by two 6,000 shp class new technology turboshafts, the MV-22A specification includes the ability to carry 24 combat-equipped troops at 288 mph (463 km/h) over an operational radius of 230 miles (370 km), and to hover at 3,000 ft (914 m) at an ambient air temperature of 33°C (91°F). The US Army may also acquire up to 231 MV-22As to fulfil medevac and cargo carrying roles, using the aircraft to replace and expand its current STOL capability in these roles.

The US Navy plans to purchase 50 HV-22As to replace the current Sikorsky HH-3 in a combat search and rescue role. This variant of the V-22 is expected to operate over a 530 mile (852 km) radius, with the ability to hover mid-way at 7,000 ft (2,134 m) OGE and rescue up to four survivors. Finally the US Air Force requirement is for 80 CV-22A special operations aircraft, able to carry 12 combat troops or 2,880 lb (1,306 kg) internal cargo over an 806 mile (1,297 km) radius, with the ability to hover at 5,000 ft (1,524 m) OGE.

For shipboard operations, the entire wing and rotor system is designed to fold for stowage within 90 seconds, using a mix of blade folding, nacelle rotation, and wing swivelling to align the assembly fore and aft atop the fuselage. The V-22 will also be self-deployable over a range of 2,418 miles (3,892 km) and be able to carry external loads of up to 10,000 lb (4,536 kg). In VTOL mode gross weight will be some 47,500 lb (21,546 kg), but this may be increased to 55,000 lb (24,947 kg) if operating with a 20° forward tilt in the STOL mode. In such a configuration the estimated take-off run is under 500 ft (152 m).

Technical specifications

Helicopter Bell-Boeing MV-22A Osprey
Type Assault transport
Year 1988
Engine 2 × 6,000 shp Allison 501-M80C
Rotor diameter 11.58 m (38 ft)
Overall length 17.47 m (57 ft 4 in)
Height 5.28 m (17 ft 4 in) (6.63 m/21 ft 9 in with nacelles in vertical position)
Empty weight n/a
Gross weight (VTOL): 21,546 kg (47,500 lb)
Maximum speed 630 km/h (391 mph)
Hovering ceiling IGE n/a
Service ceiling n/a
Range n/a
Capacity 3 crew + 24 combat-equipped troops

Boeing Vertol V-107/CH-46

The Boeing Vertol Model 107 was originally developed in the late 1950s as a turbine-engined successor to the Piasecki line of piston-engined tandem-rotor helicopters then in service with the US military and several overseas operators.

First flown in April 1958, the Model 107 initially introduced two aft-mounted 877 shp Lycoming T53 turboshafts driving tandem three-bladed contra-rotating rotors. The engines were installed horizontally above the rear fuselage, thus allowing the introduction of a rear ramp entry for troops or small vehicles to the main cabin. The main undercarriage was carried by sponsons, which doubled as fuel tanks and afforded additional stability in the event of a water landing.

Under the designation YHC-1A, ten Model 107s, powered by 1,065 shp General Electric T58 engines, were ordered for the US Army in July 1958, but by the time the first machine flew in August 1959, this service was already focussing its interest on a larger variant, initially designated the YHC-1B but subsequently better known as the CH-47 Chinook. Evaluation of two YHC-1As was, however, carried out in 1960 by the US Marine Corps, which subsequently decided to adopt the type as its standard medium assault helicopter under the designation HRB-1 Sea Knight. A total of 50 such aircraft were initially ordered but, prior to the commencement of deliveries in October 1962, 46 were re-designated as CH-46As, and four had been reallocated to the US Navy for fleet replenishment duties as UH-46As. A further 20 UH-46As were subsequently built, while 114 CH-46As followed the original production batch. Some of the latter were subsequently converted for SAR operations, with Doppler radar and a rescue hoist, as the HH-46A, while one aircraft was modified to RH-46A configuration for mine-

The Boeing Vertol CH-46 Sea Knight has been operational with the US Navy as an assault transport and for vertical replenishment operations since 1962. This CH-46A was photographed aboard the USS *Springfield* in 1972.

sweeping trials. All production H-46As were powered by the 1,250 shp T58-GE-8B engine.

The designation UH-46B having been allocated to a proposed variant for the US Air Force, and CH-46C allocated to the three YHC-1A prototypes actually built, the next major production variant was the CH-46D. This introduced the uprated 1,400 shp T58-GE-10 engine and some minor improvements. From September 1966 all new aircraft were to this standard.

In its CH-46D form, the Sea Knight can carry 26 combat troops plus three crew, or an internal cargo payload of up to 10,000 lb (4,535 kg). Alternatively, an underslung load may be carried on the central hook. For defensive purposes during assault missions, a single 7.62 mm machine gun can be pintle-mounted in the starboard forward cabin door. The fuselage is watertight for emergency water landings. A total of 266 CH-46Ds were built for the USMC, while 10 UH-46D replenishment variants were added to the USN inventory. Both CH-46 and UH-46 versions saw service in Vietnam from March 1966, with over 100,000 combat hours logged by August 1968 and the 500th CH-46 delivered in June 1969.

Final new production for the US Navy comprised 174 CH-46F variants, delivered in the early 1970s and based on the CH-46D with an improved avionics fit. Total deliveries of the Sea Knight thus came to 624 aircraft.

In 1975, with a view to updating the fleet, two machines were modified by Boeing Vertol to CH-46E configuration. Changes included the adoption of uprated 1,870 shp T58-GE-16 turboshafts, crash attenuating pilot and co-pilot seats, a crash resistant fuel system and other modifications. The first of 273 production CH-46E conversions was completed by the US Navy in August 1977. Subsequently, the installation of glassfibre rotor-

US Marine Corps CH-46Es are now undergoing a Safety, Reliability and Maintainability (SR&M) modification programme to extend their life through the 1990s. The changes include 26 internal improvements to the airframe and systems, including the transmission and flight control system.

blades was added to the programme and, in 1980, the first contract was awarded for a further modification programme designed to reduce the operating costs of the HH-46 and CH-46 fleet beyond the year 2000. Known as the SR&M (Safety, Reliability and Maintainability) programme, the new improvements include upgrading electrical and avionics systems, dynamics, hydraulics, landing gear and airframe, all of which is supplied by Boeing Vertol as a retrofit kit. A prototype SR&M CH-46E was successfully test flown in November 1983 and delivery of production kits for installation by the US Navy began in mid-1985. A total of 345 aircraft are due to be thus modified, with the final kit being delivered in 1988.

In late 1985, 15 US Marine Corps squadrons were operational with the CH-46, while the HH-46 continued in US Navy service in the vertical replenishment role. Both variants are expected to remain in service into the next century.

Export sales of the Model 107 by Boeing Vertol began with a licence agreement with Kawasaki, which ordered ten aircraft powered by 1,250 shp General Electric CT58 turboshafts in 1962 prior to building the type under licence in Japan. The first locally assembled machine, designated the KV-107, flew in May 1962.

Military sales of the KV-107 have largely been confined to the local Defence Forces, for whom small scale production continues. Early deliveries included two KV-107II-3 mine countermeasures helicopters, equivalent to the RH-46A and fitted with long range fuel tanks and minesweeping towing gear for the Maritime SDF, 42 KV-107II-4 troop and cargo transports for the Ground SDF, and 19 KV-107II-5 SAR helicopters for the Air SDF. These latter machines also carried two 416 gall (1,891 litres) long range fuel tanks on either side of the fuselage, four searchlights, rescue hoist

The basic Model 107 has also been developed by Kawasaki for local and export military customers. Among the latter are the Royal Swedish Air Force and Navy, which currently operate some 20 examples on SAR/utility and ASW duties. The latter are the subject of an equipment and power-plant improvement programme.

and an extensive nav/com fit. Eight aircraft were also fitted with a Kawasaki-Boeing developed AFCS.

Subsequently the availability of the uprated 1,400 shp General Electric CT58-140-1 powerplant saw the introduction of the KV-107IIA in 1968, and later deliveries were to this standard, with the earlier aircraft being similarly reworked. Seven KV-107IIA-3, 18 KV-107IIA-4 and 27 KV-107IIA-5 had been delivered by early 1986.

Boeing Vertol Model 107 production for overseas military customers was confined to Sweden and Canada. Swedish aircraft, locally designated HKP-4 and powered by the 1,250 shp Rolls Royce Gnome H1200 licence version of the CT58, entered service with the Navy in the anti-submarine and minesweeping role and with the Air Force for SAR work. The first HKP-4 flew in April 1963 and a total of 14 were delivered from the Boeing Vertol production line. Subsequently, the Royal Swedish Navy took delivery of a further eight from Kawasaki. More recently Sweden has announced plans to upgrade its anti-submarine capability, with updating of the Navy HKP-4B and 4Cs and the transfer of Air Force HKP-4As to the naval inventory.

Deliveries to Canada of the Model 107 took place in 1963-65, when six CH-113 Labrador and 12 CH-113A Voyageur variants were delivered to the Air Force and Army respectively. Both versions were based on the CH-46A but the Labrador was configured for SAR duties. Later, the introduction of the CH-147 Chinook to provide Army support saw the CH-113As transferred to the SAR role, while from 1983 both variants were upgraded to a common SAR configuration featuring long range fuel tanks, external rescue hoists and new navigation avionics.

Technical specifications

Helicopter Boeing Vertol CH-46E
Type Tactical transport
Year 1975
Engine 2 × 1,870 shp General Electric T58-GE-16
Rotor diameter 15.24 m (50 ft)
Fuselage length 13.66 m (44 ft 10 in)
Overall length 25.70 m (84 ft 4 in)
Height 5.09 m (16 ft 8 in)
Empty weight 6,051 kg (13,342 lb)
Gross weight 10,569 kg (23,300 lb)
Maximum speed 270 km/h (168 mph)
Hovering ceiling IGE 2,560 m (8,400 ft)
Service ceiling 3,960 m (13,000 ft)
Range 370 km (230 miles)
Capacity 2 pilots + 26 troops

Boeing Vertol Model 114/CH-47 Chinook

Early variants of the Boeing Vertol Chinook are now becoming rare as operators take advantage of the manufacturer's upgrading programme. This is one of four CH-47As delivered to the Royal Thai Army.

Following design of the Model 107 in the mid-1950s to meet a US Army specification for a medium-transport helicopter, Boeing Vertol chose to scale up their proposal to better meet the requirement. The new design, drawn around two aft-mounted 1,940 shp Lycoming T55 turboshafts, featured a large box fuselage, with fuel and undercarriage attachments placed outboard within large sponsons. Transmission and rotor system were based on experience gained with the Model 107, which flew in August 1958 (page 61).

Initially the US Army ordered ten Model 107s under the designation YHC-1A for evaluation trials but, following acceptance of Boeing Vertol's new Model 114 proposal in March 1959, cancelled seven of the YHC-1As and ordered five of the new design instead. The first of these, designated YHC-1B, was rolled out in April 1961. The first YHC-1B to fly was the second prototype, 59-4983, on 21 September 1961, by which date the US Army had already ordered an initial production batch of HC-1B aircraft. Soon afterwards the name Chinook was adopted and the designation revised to CH-47A.

The first production CH-47A was handed over to the US Army in August 1962, powered by uprated 2,200 shp Lycoming T55-L-5 engines and introducing various detailed improvements. Later production CH-47As standardised on the 2,650 shp T55-L-7, grossing at 33,000 lbs (14,969 kg) and providing a maximum payload of 10,950 lbs (4967 kg) at sea level hover ISA. By April 1965 US Army CH-47As had accumulated 50,000 flight hours, including 14,000 logged in the Vietnam theatre, where the Chinook was instrumental in recovering many downed aircraft, as well as carrying out many resupply missions.

The last of 354 production CH-47As, which included a small number of aircraft diverted to the Thai Air Force and four machines modified as ACH-47A gunships, was delivered to the US Army in 1967, and was immediately followed by the CH-47B. This new version introduced 2,850 shp T55-L-7C engines, a blunted rear pylon with aft fuselage strakes, and redesigned rotor blades with cambered leading edges. Deliveries of 108 CH-47Bs, all for the US Army, began in May 1967 and most were shipped direct to the Vietnam

LC-001

RAAF

Top left: The CH-47C has been produced in some numbers by Agusta in Italy as well as by Boeing Vertol. LC-001 was the first of 20 Italian-built examples supplied to Libya.

Centre left: The Royal Australian Air Force operates a squadron of CH-47Cs in the heavy-lift and army support role.

Lower left: The Argentinian Air Force has two CH-47Cs on strength to support that country's scientific and other work in Antarctica. Both aircraft feature high visibility dayglo orange top surfaces.

Below The Royal Air Force is now a major Chinook operator, with 38 of the latest Model 414s on strength. This aircraft ZA675 of No 18 Sqdn was used to extract British civilians from Lebanon in 1983, hence the prominent Union Jack.

theatre, where they introduced improved lift and reliability to the local hot/high environment.

The next Chinook variant to appear was the CH-47C, first flown in October 1967 and designed to meet a new US Army requirement for a 15,000 lb (6,804 kg) slung load over a 30 nm (34.5 miles/55.5 km) radius in 95°F (35°C) at 4,000 ft (1,219 m). New 3,750 shp Lycoming T55-L-11C engines, matched to a transmission cleared to accept 6,000 hp, and increased internal fuel capacity, allowed the CH-47 to operate at a gross weight of 46,000 lb (20,866 kg) and hover with a 22,981 lb (10,424 kg) payload at sea level ISA, almost double the lifting performance of the original CH-47A. Production of the CH-47C for the US Army was to total 270 aircraft before finally ending in 1980.

A licence agreement signed with Agusta in 1968 led to a second production line being established in Italy, although local construction to meet initial orders of 26 CH-47C for the Italian Army

Left: Now entering service with the US Army in increasing numbers, the CH-47D is a re-work of older Chinook airframes with the latest standard of modifications, including composite rotor blades, uprated engines and new cockpit avionics.

and 16 for Iran did not begin until 1971. The first wholly Italian aircraft were delivered in 1974 and production of the CH-47C from this source has continued to date with further orders for Italy plus aircraft for Egypt, Greece, Libya, Morocco and Tanzania. Iran ordered a total of 95 CH-47Cs during the 1970s but the final 14 aircraft were embargoed in 1980 prior to delivery and were eventually transferred to the US Army inventory in 1985.

Boeing Vertol production for export customers began in 1973 to meet orders placed by the Australian and Spanish governments. These Chinooks, like five built later for Argentina, were essentially to CH-47C standard but with some improvement, including a new crashworthy fuel system. Also during 1973 Boeing Vertol received an order from Canada for eight Model BV-173 Chinooks, locally designated the CH-147. This new variant introduced a number of major improvements to the CH-47C configuration. Seating capacity was increased to 44 by introducing 11 centre aisle trooping seats, power drive was fitted to the rear ramp plus an inflatable water dam, and the CH-147 was the first Chinook cleared to a new gross weight of 50,000 lb (22,680 kg), with a 28,000 lb (12,701 kg) external load system and the transmission cleared to 7,200 hp. Avionics and the automatic flight control system were also updated.

In 1978 an order from the Royal Air Force for 33 Model BV352 Chinook HC Mk 1 gave Boeing Vertol the opportunity to further-develop the design, with a triple hook external load system, night capable cockpit lighting and revised avionics, a rotorbrake, windscreen and engine de-icing, and provision for new increased chord glassfibre rotor blades and a single-point pressure refuelling system.

The first Chinook HC Mk 1 made its initial flight on 23 March 1980 with standard metal rotor blades but, together with other early production aircraft, was later retrofitted with the new glassfibre blades. Deliveries of a further eight machines followed in 1984-86. These were powered by the T55-L-712 engine, with an emergency rating of 4,500 shp, chosen also for eventual installation in all RAF Chinooks. Six similar aircraft, fitted with nose-mounted weather radar, have since been ordered by Spain for delivery between May 1986 and April 1987.

On 11 May 1979, Boeing Vertol reflew an early CH-47A which had been extensively reworked under a US Army contract to the latest standard as one of three prototype CH-47Ds. The new configuration comprised 13 major improvements, including the installation of uprated 3,750 shp Lycoming T55-L-712 turboshafts, rotor transmission rating increased to 7,500 shp, composite glassfibre rotor blades, reconfigured cockpit layout and an advanced AFCS, night vision capability and a triple hook system.

Successful trials of the initial three CH-47D conversions has led to US Army contracts for 328 production modernisations to date with a further 108 conversions of earlier CH-47A/B and C aircraft expected to follow in the 1990s. Similar conversions are planned for the Italian Army CH-47C fleet, while other early export aircraft may also be partially upgraded.

The two latest Chinook production variants have been for Japan and Taiwan respectively. Three new-build CH-47Ds have been delivered via Kawasaki to the Japanese Ground and Air Self Defence Forces for evaluation prior to licence manufacture of an expected 55 aircraft from late 1986. Taiwan meanwhile has taken delivery of three utility layout Model 234 MLR Chinooks. Although basically a commercial version of the CH-47D, the aircraft have entered operation with the Nationalist Chinese Air Force in the heavy-lift and trooping role.

Technical specifications

Helicopter Boeing Vertol Model 114 (CH-47D)
Type Transport
Year 1979
Engine 2 × 3,750 shp Lycoming T55-L-712
Rotor diameter 18.28 m (60 ft)
Fuselage length 15.54 m (51 ft)
Overall length 30.17 m (99 ft)
Height 5.66 m (18 ft 7 in)
Empty weight 10,355 kg (22,784 lb)
Gross weight 22,680 kg (50,000 lb)
Maximum speed 295 km/h (183 mph)
Hovering ceiling IGE 2,316 m (7,600 ft)
Service ceiling 4,570 m (15,000 ft)
Range 390 km (242 miles)
Capacity 3 crew + 44 troops

Boeing Vertol XCH-62

Development of the Boeing Vertol XCH-62 began in 1971 as the BV301 project, aimed at meeting a US Army requirement for a heavy-lift helicopter able to move a 40,000 lb (18,140 kg) slung load over a radius of 23 miles (37 km) or 10,000 lbs (4,536 kg) over a 1,000 mile (1,610 km) radius. This capability, born out of Vietnam war experience, was intended to permit the CH-62 to move 70 percent of all US Army equipment, including the 16-ton M 551 Sheridan light reconnaisance tank, earthmovers, field hospitals etc.

In November 1970, proposals were issued to industry for development of the advanced technology components considered necessary for the project and soon afterwards Boeing Vertol was selected as the project leader. Research over the next four years included the design and testing of new composite fibreglass main rotor blades and titanium four-bladed rotor hubs. Also tested was a fly-by-wire control system with triple redundant wire runs, using a modified CH-47 Chinook. Meanwhile Allison received a contract to develop its 8,079 shp XT-701 turboshaft, three of which were to power the new helicopter via a combining gearbox with an output rating of 17,700 shp. The new dynamics system, with the torque transmitted across a single spiral-bevel gear mesh (exceeding any existing aircraft transmission by about 2 to 1), was tested for more than 100 hours in a ground rig between 1972 and 1974.

A contract to build a single XCH-62 prototype (72-2012) was awarded to Boeing Vertol on 29 January 1973. The first flight was scheduled for August 1975, but on 1 October 1974 funding problems caused cancellation of the project. At this point the XCH-62 was 95 percent complete and the decision was taken to mothball the aircraft in the hope that the project might be resurrected at a later date.

The sole XCH-62, 22012, was almost complete when funding was withdrawn in 1974. Since that time work has progressed as and when money has been available. Present plans are for the aircraft to be completed as a heavy-lift research vehicle (HLRV).

The overall size of the XCH-62 may be judged by this photograph of the prototype alongside a standard CH-47C Chinook.

In 1980 a contract received from NASA allowed some resumption of transmission development, using the aft and combiner gearboxes and drive systems and, by early 1983, some 50 hours at full power had been successfully completed. In August 1984 NASA, the US Army, DARPA and Boeing Vertol signed an agreement to complete and fly the XCH-62 as a heavy-lift research vehicle and, on 2 October 1984, the prototype re-entered the assembly shop for a survey and assessment.

As built, the XCH-62 is designed to be air transportable in a C-5A by removing the fixed undercarriage and, as well as its prime heavy-lift role, the aircraft can carry 35-55 troops, depending on seating density, in the main cabin. A minimum crew of three is planned, including a cargo operator in a rearward-facing position below the cockpit. Currently under consideration is the use of fly-by-light control technology instead of the fly-by-wire system, composite fuselage panels in place of the bonded honeycomb construction, and new rotor airfoil designs.

The revised first flight date for the resurrected aircraft has been set for 1988, followed by a 115 hour flight test programme. More recently, renewed funding problems have again affected progress. At one point in the programme the US Army envisaged purchasing up to 150 CH-62s, with a further 100 plus aircraft joining the US Navy and Marine Corps. In the event the latter opted for the Sikorsky CH-53E, but the US Army requirement is still unfulfilled.

Technical specifications

Helicopter Boeing Vertol XCH-62
Type Heavy-lift
Year 1975
Engine 2 × 8,000 shp Allison T701
Rotor diameter 28.04 m (92 ft)
Fuselage length 27.2 m (89 ft 3 in)
Height 12.20 m (38 ft 7.5 in)
Empty weight 46,720 kg (102,998 lb)
Gross weight 67,130 kg (148,000 lb)
Maximum speed n/a
Hovering ceiling IGE n/a
Service ceiling n/a
Range n/a
Capacity 3 crew + 18,140 (40,000 lb) slung load

European Industries EH 101

The ASW version of the EH 101 is on order for the British and Italian navies, with a first flight in December 1986.

By the early 1970s it was evident, not only to Sikorsky but also to both its British and Italian licensees, that a market might exist for an S-61 replacement, and in Europe this crystallised in the shape of separate studies by the Royal and Italian Navies into an anti-submarine helicopter to succeed their SH-3 Sea King variants.

In Italy Agusta worked in conjunction with naval staff to map out a design which included experience gained not only from production of the ASH-3H, but also from the development of the one-off tri-engined A 101 transport helicopter of the 1960s. This helicopter, powered by three 1,500 shp Rolls-Royce Gnome H1400 turboshafts, had grossed out at 28,466 lb (12,912 kg) but was abandoned in the early 1970s. In the UK initial design studies of various options developed into the Westland WG-34, also a tri-engined helicopter, which actually reached the prototype construction stage before being abandoned in 1980 following the consolidation of a joint Anglo-Italian initiative begun in 1979.

This initiative resulted from the realisation, by the two governments, that the degree of similarity between the two requirements was such that a common helicopter could be produced through a collaborative agreement between both countries. Accordingly in November 1979, a Memorandum of Understanding was signed by the two governments and in June 1980 Agusta and Westland formed a joint company, European Helicopter Industries, to pursue the new project.

Following a lengthy feasibility period, an agreement to jointly develop the new helicopter, now designated the EH 101, was signed between the participating parties in January 1984. By this date the design of three distinct variants had been initiated: a naval ASW aircraft with a folding tail unit, a commercial transport, and a civil/military utility version with a rear loading ramp and a consequently revised rear fuselage section. The work programme and costs were shared on as equal a basis as possible, with Agusta being responsible for the main rotor head, rear fuselage

At the 1985 Paris Air Show Agusta exhibited this full scale mockup of the EH101 utility variant, which features a modified fuselage with ramp access to the main cabin.

and tail unit, hydraulics, electrics, and the main transmission - with the latter sub-contracted to Fiat. Westland took responsibility for the nose section and main cabin, including the cockpit and AFCS, the engine installation, main rotor blades, undercarriage and fuel system.

The first of nine flight-test prototypes is due to fly in December 1986, powered by 1,725 shp General Electric T700-401 engines. Of these nine aircraft Agusta is constructing four, including a utility prototype, and Westland is building five, including a civil transport prototype. In addition Agusta has assembled a ground test vehicle.

The naval EH 101 is expected to have a gross weight of 28,660 lb (13,000 kg) with the ability to operate from frigate-size ships in high sea states and 58 mph (93 km/h) winds, and to remain on station for long periods with a full weapons load. Specialist ASW avionics will vary between two navies, but the aircraft will feature a chin radome capable of housing a 360 degree search radar, and carry fully integrated avionics management and mission systems. The Royal Navy variant will specifically carry the Ferranti Blue Kestrel radar, a GEC AQS-903 acoustic processor, MAD, a ring-laser gyro navigation system, and a single-pilot IFR duplex digital AFCS. In addition the cockpit will include an ergonomically designed layout, with CRT instrumentation and health and usage monitoring of all the aircraft systems. Initial orders for the naval EH 101 are split at 50 for the Royal Navy and 38 for the Italian Navy. The latter variant will differ from the RN version by carrying sonar rather than MAD equipment. Both variants will be able to carry an armament of up to four homing torpedoes or anti-ship missiles.

The utility EH 101 will be capable of carrying up to 28 combat-equipped troops or a cargo payload of almost six tons. The rear ramp is designed to give unrestricted access to the main cabin, which is just over 21 ft (6 m) long by 6 ft (1.83 m) high and 7 ft 10 in (2.39 m) wide at floor level. Loads of 15,000 lb (6,804 kg) can be carried on the external cargo hook. Performance and other characteristics of the utility EH 101 are expected to be in line with the naval version, but these could change with production aircraft if the new Rolls-Royce/Turboméca RTM322 powerplant is adopted. This engine, currently being promoted for the EH 101, produces some 22 percent more power than the T700 and is designed to replace the General Electric engine with minimal airframe changes.

Technical specifications

Helicopter European Industries EH 101
Type Multi-role helicopter
Year 1987
Engine 3 × 1,725 shp General Electric T700-GE-401
Rotor diameter 18.59 m (61 ft)
Fuselage length 15.85 m (52 ft)
Height 6.50 m (21 ft 4 in)
Empty weight 7,031 kg (15,500 lb)
Gross weight 13,000 kg (28,660 lb)
Maximum speed 278 km/h (173 mph)
Range 556 km (345 miles)
Capacity 2 crew + 28 combat-equipped troops/ equivalent cargo
Armament Naval/Military Utility versions: 4 torpedoes or anti-ship missiles and other weapons

Hiller UH-12/H-23

The origins of the current production Hiller UH-12 go back to the mid-1940s, when the original Hiller Company developed its Model 360 two-seat light helicopter using a unique Rotormatic rotor and flight control system designed by the company founder, Stanley Hiller.

The prototype Model 360, first flown on 11 November 1947, set the basic layout for all the future variants, with a bubble cockpit, a central engine platform and a narrow metal-covered tailboom. An exposed 178 hp Franklin piston engine drove a two-bladed main rotor, with its Hiller servo-paddle flight controls, while drive for the two-bladed tail rotor was taken via a diagonally mounted shaft from the main gearbox to the tail boom, and thence to the tail rotor.

Certificated in October 1948, the Model 360 attracted early attention from the French government which, in 1949, evaluated the type as an ambulance helicopter in Indo-China. This was followed by a production order, and then by a single example, 50-1254, for evaluation by the US Army for a similar role in Korea. Known in its initial production form as the Model UH-12A, but designated by the US Army as the H-23A Raven, the aircraft entered US service for battlefield evacuation duties in 1950. A total of 100 H-23As were delivered to the US Army, plus five to the Air Force for evaluation, before being superseded by the uprated H-23B/UH-12B powered by the 200 hp Franklin 6V4 engine and introducing a skid undercarriage. Concurrently the US Navy took delivery of 17 HTE-1 and 35 HTE-2 variants with dual controls and wheeled undercarriage for pilot training. In addition, another 20 HTE-2s were supplied to the Royal Navy, while 81 H-23Bs went via MDAP to other countries.

A total of 273 H-23Bs entered US Army service, many of them in the training role, before the type was superseded by the H-23C/UH-12C in 1955. This version retained the 200 hp Franklin engine but introduced a revised 'goldfish bowl' cockpit canopy with seating for three occupants, and all-metal rotor blades. In addition to deliveries to the US Army, the UH-12C also found popularity with a number of overseas air arms in the training and observation role.

The UH-12D, which first flew on 3 April 1956, was a new purely military version re-engined with the more powerful 250 hp Lycoming VO-435, a redesigned transmission with a 1,000 hr TBO, increased diameter main rotor blades, and a useful payload improvement of some 560 lb (254 kg). As the H-23D, later redesignated the OH-23D, 348 went to the Us Army between 1957 and 1963.

Meanwhile in 1958 Hiller rolled out the first UH-12E, based on the previous model but with the further uprated 305 hp Lycoming VO-540 powerplant. The UH-12E became the standard production version and, with some updating, is still in production today with total sales exceeding 2,000 aircraft. Whilst the UH-12E found much popularity in the commercial field, military sales continued. The US Army purchased 793 examples as the OH-23G, and others have gone to the Canadian forces as the CH-112, the Royal Navy, and a number of emerging countries. A few military sales have also taken place of the UH-

The Hiller UH-12, seen here in its H-23 version for the US Army, is still in production today as a light training and observation helicopter.

12E4/OH-23F variant, with a stretched cabin to seat four occupants, and the UH-12L4, which further introduced a new main rotor with a gyro-controlled stability augmentation system replacing the original servo-paddle control.

Also still available is a turbine-engined Soloy conversion of the UH-12E and UH-12E4, powered by a 420 shp Allison 250-C20B turboshaft derated to 301 shp to offer a considerable performance benefit in hot/high conditions.

While the UH-12E has remained in service for more than 25 years, the original Hiller company has not. The present Hiller Helicopters was formed only in April 1984, having purchased the assets of Hiller Aviation, which in turn had purchased the Hiller design rights and tooling etc from Fairchild in 1973. Fairchild had bought the original Hiller Aircraft Corporation in 1964.

Technical specifications

Helicopter Hiller UH-12E
Type Training/observation
Year 1958
Engine 340 hp Lycoming VO-540
Rotor diameter 10.80 m (35 ft 5 in)
Fuselage length 8.69 m (28 ft 6 in)
Overall length 12.40 m (40 ft 8 in)
Height 2.98 m (9 ft 9 in)
Empty weight 798 kg (1,759 lb)
Gross weight 1,270 kg (2,800 lb)
Maximum speed 154 km/h (96 mph)
Hovering ceiling IGE 3,290 m (10,794 ft)
Service ceiling 4,940 m (16,207 ft)
Range 676 km (420 miles)
Capacity Pilot + 2 passengers

Hiller FH-1100/RH-1100M

The Hiller Model 1100 was originally designed in the early 1960s as a competitor for the US Army Light Observation Helicopter (LOH) requirement and, in May 1961, was selected as one of three finalists for prototype manufacture and evaluation in competition with Bell and Hughes.

Allocated the designation OH-5A, five prototype 1100s (62-4207 - 4211) were ordered, with the first flight taking place on 26 January 1963. The new helicopter bore little apparent similarity to the successful UH-12 Series, although the main rotor system was similar to that used on the contemporary UH-12L4, with a two-axis stability augmentation system providing automatic pitch and roll stabilisation and all-metal blades of greater chord. Power was provided by a 250 shp Allison T63 turbine engine and accommodation was included for a pilot and three/four passengers.

In the event, the OH-5A and the Bell OH-4A lost the competition to the Hughes OH-6A, but in 1964 Hiller had been taken over by the Fairchild Corporation and it was decided to develop the aircraft for the commercial market under the revised designation, FH-1100. With an uprated 317 shp Allison 250-C18 engine and other minor changes, the FH-1100 went into production in 1966 and 240 were sold before manufacture ended in 1973. Unlike the Bell design which, reworked as the JetRanger found large military sales, the FH-1100 found very few military customers, being used only in small numbers as a para-military and utility machine in South America and SE Asia.

In 1980 a new Hiller Aviation company purchased the rights and tooling from Fairchild, with the intention of upgrading the FH-1100 design through the introduction of new main rotor blades, transmission improvements, and a more powerful 420 shp Allison 250-C20 powerplant. Before production could be relaunched however, the company collapsed and its assets were purchased by the Rogerson Corporation which set up a new company, Hiller Helicopters, in 1984.

Hiller Helicopters has since reworked the design still further, using its military origins to

The RH-1100M is currently being offered by the new Hiller organisation as a low-cost multi-mission helicopter, suitable for light attack and anti-armour duties. This is the full-scale mock-up, displayed at the 1985 Paris Air Show and converted from an old FH-1100 airframe.

The RH-1100M is closely based on the original FH-1100, which was developed from the Hiller entry in the 1960s US Army LOH competition.

develop a low-cost multi-mission variant, designated the RH-1100M Hornet. This new version, unveiled at the 1985 Paris Air Show in the shape of a full scale mockup, retains the new powerplant and dynamics but further introduces a chin-mounted TOW missile sight with stub pylons able to carry up to four TOW missiles or various interchangeable podded weapons systems. The aircraft also has provision for an autopilot, FLIR and an external cargo hook. Flight trials of the RH-1100M are expected to be dependent on future firm military interest

Technical specifications

Helicopter Hiller RH-1100M
Type Multi-mission
Year 1985
Engine 1 × 420 shp Allison 250-C20B
Rotor diameter 10.80 m (35 ft 5 in)
Fuselage length 9.08 m (29 ft 9.5 in)
Height 2.83 m (9 ft 3.5 in)
Empty weight 726 kg (1,600 lb)
Gross weight 1,406 kg (3,100 lb)
Maximum speed 204 km/h (127 mph)
Hovering ceiling IGE 5,180 m (17,000 ft)
Service ceiling 5,275 m (17,300 ft)
Range 990 km (615 miles)
Capacity Pilot + 4 passengers
Armament 4 × TOW anti-tank missiles or podded machine-guns, rockets, etc.

Hughes OH-6/Model 500M

The Hughes OH-6A entered service with a number of overseas air arms as the Model 500M. This is a Danish Army example, H-207, one of 14 currently in use as an observation/liaison helicopter.

The Hughes Model 500, also known as the Model 369, was originally designed in response to a 1960 US Army specification for a Light Observation Helicopter (LOH), able to carry out scouting, casualty evacuation and communications roles in the battlefield area and replacing the Bell H-13 and Hiller H-23 helicopters, and the Cessna 0-1 fixed-wing aircraft.

To meet the requirement, Hughes took as a basis their earlier two-seat Model 269A and designed a new compact five-seat helicopter, using semi-monocoque techniques to produce an egg-shaped crashworthy cabin and engine bay, with a slim all-metal tailboom and skid undercarriage. The four-bladed articulated main rotor system featured steel straps connecting opposing blades and providing the feathering and flapping movement, thus eliminating thrust bearings from the rotor head. Each blade consisted of an extruded light alloy spar, with a single sheet of wrap-around bonded light alloy forming the blade profile. Power was provided by a 317 shp Allison T63 turboshaft, de-rated to 252 shp. Originally only Bell and Hiller were selected as finalists in the LOH competition, but a controversial low pricing policy adopted by Hughes in anticipating of eventual orders for 4,000 plus aircraft, won the company a contract for five prototype Model 369s in early 1961. Designated the YHO-6, the first of these (62-4212) made its initial flight on 27 February 1963. Evaluation trials of the HO-6, along with its Bell and Hiller competitors, began at Fort Rucker in late 1963. Despite some criticism of its restricted cabin size, the HO-6 proved itself to be highly manoeuvrable and fast, later proven by establishing 23 world records in March-April 1966. In addition Hughes was quoting a price of under $30,000 per each unequipped airframe.

The choice of the Model 369 for the US Army was eventually announced in May 1965, with an initial order for 714 production OH-6As. Between 1965 and 1970, when the last OH-6A was delivered, 1,417 entered service with the US Army

Right: As the OH-6A, the Hughes Model 500 was much used by the US Army as an observation helicopter in the 1960s and 1970s, but is now relegated to the National Guard units.

12931
UNITED STATES ARMY

and many of these operated in Vietnam where the type was used in its observation role. Deliveries fell far short of the numbers originally envisaged however for, in 1968, the US Army re-opened its LOH competition and the OH-6A was superseded by the Bell OH-58.

Subsequently the US Army OH-6A fleet was dispersed to Air National Guard Units, which still operate the type, or put into reserve. A small number of OH-6As were also supplied to friendly countries, notably Argentina, Colombia, Dominica and Nicaragua. Several OH-6As have also been retained for experimental development, including 65-12917, which since December 1971 has been testing a no tail rotor (NOTAR) concept, and 68-17230, which is flight-testing a computerised higher harmonic control system designed to suppress fuselage vibration by up to 80 percent.

Concurrent with development of the OH-6A in the mid-1960s, Hughes built four commercial demonstrators powered by the 317 shp Allison 250-C18 de-rated to 278 shp, and introducing a 150 lb (68 kg) gross weight increase and a slightly improved fuel capacity. These led to an export equivalent of the OH-6A, designated the 500M or 369HM, which further introduced the ability to accommodate various mission kits. With the exception of the first four aircraft , which went to the Colombian Air Force in 1968, early deliveries were solely to Kawasaki in Japan, which had signed a licence agreement to produce the 500M for the Japanese Ground Self Defence Force. A total of 25 aircraft, unofficially known as the OH-6J, were supplied by Hughes to Kawasaki before the latter assumed full licence production, and 117 were eventually supplied to the JGSDF. Other customers for the 500M included Argentina, where the type was locally assembled by RACA, Brazil, Denmark and Italy, where BredaNardi signed a licence agreement with Hughes in 1971.

Fourteen 500Ms were also supplied to the Spanish Navy, these aircraft being fitted out with an AN/ASQ-81 magnetic anomaly detector on the starboard side of the fuselage and carrying two Mk 44 torpedoes between the skids for anti-submarine duties.

Improvements in the basic design during the late 1960s led to the one-off OH-6C and its 500C commercial equivalent, with the uprated 400 shp Allison 250-C20 engine for improved hot/high performance. This option was made available to military 500M customers. Some 270 500Ms were eventually manufactured by Hughes before the type was superseded by the new 500MD multi-role helicopter in 1975.

Technical specifications

Helicopter Hughes OH-6
Type Light observation
Year 1963
Engine 1 × 250 shp Allison T63 shaft-turbine
Rotor diameter 8.03 m (26 ft 4 in)
Fuselage length 6.48 m (21 ft 3 in)
Overall length 9.23 m (30 ft 3.5 in)
Height 2.48 m (8 ft 1.5 in)
Empty weight 483 kg (1,065 lb)
Gross weight 1,225 kg (2,700 lb)
Maximum speed 237 km/h (147 mph)
Hovering ceiling IGE 4,450 m (14,600 ft)
Service ceiling 5,575 m (18,300 ft)
Range 320 km (200 miles)
Capacity 2 crew and 4 fully-equipped soldiers seated on the floor
Armament 2 twin machine gun packs or 2 × M-75 grenade launchers, or a mixture of the two

ICA IAR-317

The IAR-317 marries the basic technology of the licence-built IAR-316B Alouette III with a new front fuselage to produce a low cost ground attack helicopter.

Following the licence-construction of some 180 Aérospatiale SA 316B Alouette IIIs over a ten year period from 1971, Intreprinderea de Constructii Aeronautice (ICA) in Romania began the development in the early 1980s of a new light attack and liaison helicopter which was to employ much of the SA 316B dynamics system and other components.

Designated the IAR-317 Airfox, the design changes in the new helicopter concentrated on the forward fuselage, which was re-engineered to form a slimmed down tandem-seat cockpit, with an elevated pilot position behind the weapons operator, and a solid nose. Entry to each cockpit is via jettisonable side doors which, like the other flat plate cockpit transparencies, are manufactured of toughened materials. Dual controls are fitted, as is a steerable nose wheel. The original SA 316 main undercarriage, rear fuselage and tail unit are retained, as is the 870 shp Turboméca Artouste IIIB powerplant. Intended armament, including podded machine guns, unguided rockets, or six anti-tank missiles, can be carried on stores pylons situated below the rear cockpit. In addition, a fixed armament of two 7.62 mm machine guns was built in, one on each side of the front cockpit.

The first prototype IAR-317 made its initial flight at the ICA Brasov factory in April 1984 and, by the time it was first shown publicly at the June 1985 Paris Air Show, had logged some 100 hours flight testing. Modifications to the aircraft during this period appear to have been relatively minor, and two further prototypes were under construction for completion by the years end. Production of an initial batch of IAR-317 for the Romanian Air Force is understood to have begun in early 1986, but the current status of the programme is unconfirmed.

Technical specifications

Helicopter ICA IAR-317 Airfox
Type Light attack/liaison helicopter
Year 1984
Engine 870 shp Turboméca Artouste IIIB
Rotor diameter 11.02 m (36 ft 1.25 in)
Fuselage length 10.84 m (35 ft 7 in)
Height 2.97 m (9 ft 9 in)
Empty weight 1,050 kg (2,315 lb)
Gross weight 2,200 kg (4,851 lb)
Maximum speed 220 km/h (137 mph)
Hovering ceiling IGE 2,000 m (6,560 ft)
Service ceiling 4,250 m (13,943 ft)
Range 525 km (326 miles)
Capacity 2 crew
Armament Two 7.62 mm machine guns + assorted weapons

Kaman Type 600/H-43 Huskie

The Kaman K-600 design was drawn up in the late 1940s as a growth variant of the naval HTK-1. The latter, introduced to service in the training role in 1952, used an original twin intermeshing rotor system with servo controlled cyclic and collective pitch, with the replacement of the tail rotor by a multi-finned tail unit.

The four/five-seat K-600 was successful in winning a 1950 US Navy competition for a transport/liaison helicopter. It retained the basic HTK-1 transmission system, but closed the gap between the two rotor heads by 6 in (0.14 m) and introduced the more powerful 600 hp Pratt & Whitney R-1340-48 piston engine. This was mounted behind the five-seat cabin and between a new twin-boom tail unit. Two prototype XHOK-1s (BuAer 125477 and -478) for the US Navy were followed by 81 production HOK-1 and 24 HUK-1, plus 18 of an H-43A variant for the US Air Force for crash rescue duties.

In September 1956 flight trials began of an experimental HOK-1, re-engined with an 825 shp Lycoming XT53 turbine engine mounted above the fuselage. In addition to providing extra power, this arrangement also allowed an extension of the cabin area into the former piston engine bay and the introduction of wide clamshell doors to give unobstructed access.

Early versions of the Kaman K-600 design were piston-engined, as represented by this HUK-1 146304 of the US Navy. This type is no longer in service.

The US Air Force operated the turbine-powered HH-43B as a base rescue aircraft worldwide, prior to introducting the improved HH43-F. This example, 59-1568, was the 50th production HH-43B.

Ordered for the USAF as a successor to the H-43A, the new version entered service as the H-43B (later HH-43B) in 1958, with the first of an initial batch of 16 aircraft (58-1841) being delivered that December. Subsequent H-43Bs, redesignated HH-43B in 1962, were powered by an uprated 901 shp T53 engine. A total of 198 HH-43Bs were eventually built, nearly all equipped for crash rescue duties with water/foam or compressed nitrogen firefighting kit, rescue winch and medical gear.

Many HH-43Bs were later re-engined with the more powerful 1,150 shp T53-L-11A turboshaft as the HH-43F. In addition 42 new-build HH-43F were completed for the USAF, including ten diverted to the Iranian Air Force. Other Huskies were delivered to Burma (12), Colombia (6), Morocco (4), Pakistan (10), and Thailand (3), as well as to the Iranian Army. Very few aircraft remain in service, although six Pakistani and some Iranian examples were still reported operational in 1985.

Few HH-43s remain operational today although a handful are still in service in the Middle East and Asia. This example, 62-4553, flies with the Pakistan Air Force. (L. T. Peacock).

Technical specifications

Helicopter Kaman HH-43B Huskie
Type Rescue
Year 1958
Engine 860 shp Lycoming T53-L-1B
Rotor diameter 14.33 m (47 ft)
Fuselage length 7.67 m (25 ft 2 in)
Height 4.74 m (15 ft 6 in)
Empty weight 2,027 kg (4,865 lb)
Gross weight 2,708 kg (5,970 lb)
Maximum speed 193 km/h (120 mph)
Hovering ceiling IGE 6,400 m (21,000 ft)
Service ceiling 7,620 m (25,000 ft)
Range 445 km (276 miles)
Capacity Pilot + 2 firefighters + 450 kg (992 lb) of firefighting equipment

Kaman K-20/H-2 Seasprite

In 1956 the US Navy put out to industry a requirement for a new high-speed utility helicopter, able to operate from small ships and over long distances on liaison and rescue missions.

Kaman entered the competition with a totally new design, owing little to its Huskie intermeshing blade ancestors. Designated the K-20 by the company, the new helicopter employed a more traditional dynamic layout, with a single roof-mounted 875 shp General Electric T58 turbine driving a four-blade metal main rotor and three-blade tail rotor. The semi-monocoque watertight fuselage featured a retractable main undercarriage and an interior layout for two crew and up to 11 passengers or four stretcher patients.

First flown on 2 July 1959 with the US Navy designation HU2K-1 Seasprite, the prototype (Bu Aer 147202) was followed by three similar trials aircraft, before deliveries began of an initial batch of 12 production HU2K-1s in late 1962. These and 72 similar aircraft were powered by uprated 1,250 shp T58 engines and entered service, redesignated as the UH-2A, in full IFR all-weather configuration. They were followed by 102 UH-2B variants, similar in all respects but initially completed to VFR standard only.

Trials with early UH-2s included evaluation of an armed gunship conversion by the US Army with twin machine gun turrets in the nose and stub weapons pylons, and high speed research

The initial Kaman H-2 conversion from a single to a twin-engined configuration was the UH-2C. This was the prototype conversion, 147981, modified from an early production UH-2A.

The SH-2D, represented here by converted UH-2B 150167, introduced a chin-mounted search radar, MAD gear, sonobuoy launchers and provision for two Mk 46 torpedoes to the basic Seasprite airframe to fulfil a shipborne LAMPS 1 anti-submarine role.

with an aircraft fitted with a General Electric J85 turbojet on one side of the fuselage. In addition, in 1963, Kaman received a US Navy contract to investigate the anti-submarine warfare potential of the basic design to succeed the unsuccessful Gyrodyne ASW remote piloted helicopter then in service. This led to consideration of a twin-engined variant, which first emerged as a conversion of UH-2A Bu Aer 147981, fitted with two 1,250 shp T58-GE-8 turboshafts in a redesigned rooftop housing but giving a combined output of only 1,685 shp due to transmission limitations.

Following a successful trials programme in 1965-66, 40 UH-2As and UH-2Bs were similarly converted to twin-engined configuration as the UH-2C, while six were further modified to an HH-2C combat rescue standard, with three 7.62 mm machine guns, self-sealing fuel tanks, crew armour, and a 200 ft (61 m) rescue hoist cable for operation in Vietnam. These were followed by 70 HH-2D Search and Rescue conversions with no armament or armour, but standardising on a four-blade tail rotor.

Meanwhile, the ASW programme had progressed to the trials stage. Several UH-2As and UH-2Bs were employed to evaluate equipment options, including dipping sonar, but it was eventually decided to opt for the installation of a Canadian Marconi LN-66 surface search radar in a ventral radome, with Texas Instruments magnetic anomally equipment and 15 DIFAR/DICASS sonobuoys for underwater detection, and two externally mounted torpedoes for submarine attack. This programme became identified as the US Navy Mk 1 LAMPS (Light Airborne

The current production version of the Seasprite is the SH-2F, which features an improved performance, simplified titanium rotor head and relocated tailwheel. This aircraft, 149750, was converted from a UH-2A but the SH-2F is also the subject of a new-build programme.

Multi-Purpose System), with the objective of giving the service its first small-ship ASW helicopter, able to operate from a variety of vessels including the FFG-7, DD-963, CG-26 and other classes of frigates, destroyers and cruisers. Initial production of the new Seasprite ASW variant, designated the SH-2D, was by conversion of 20 earlier UH-2 and HH-2 aircraft. The first of these flew on 16 March 1971 and operational deployment began in December 1971.

The SH-2D was followed by two YSH-2E prototypes fitted with upgraded search equipment to meet a Mk 2 LAMPS proposal, before Kaman completed the much revised SH-2F. This introduced a number of improvements over the SH-2D, including a strengthened undercarriage with a relocated tail wheel to improve deck edge clearance, uprated 1,350 shp T58-GE-8F engines, a modified '101' titanium main rotor head and updated avionics.

Almost all the earlier SH-2Ds were subsequently modified to SH-2F standard, while 88 UH-2s were also converted. Deliveries of the SH-2F to the US Navy began in May 1973, and the first shipboard unit deployed the following September. The last SH-2F conversion was completed in 1982. However, by 1980 attrition, together with the realisation that the planned replacement Sikorsky SH-60 Mk 3 LAMPS would be unable to operate from the smaller ships, caused the US Navy to consider re-opening the Seasprite production line to meet a need for an anticipated 90 additional aircraft. This led in 1981 to the ordering of 18 new-build SH-2Fs, with a further 36 ordered between FY 1983-1986. The availability of these extra aircraft

First flown in late 1984, the YSH-2G is the subject of a current trials programme for re-engining the SH-2F with two General Electric T700 engines.

enabled the formation of SH-2F Reserve Squadrons to begin in 1984, to supplement the active front-line units.

The SH-2 is currently scheduled to remain in US Navy service into the next century and consequently further updating can be expected. Already approved is the introduction of all-composite rotor blades from 1987 onwards, while currently under test is a YSH-2G prototype fitted with two 1,713 shp General Electric T700-GE-401 engines. Offering both performance and fuel efficiency improvements, the T700 also has the advantage of commonality with the US Navy's Sikorsky SH-60, and all SH-2Fs may be retrofitted in due course.

To date no Kaman Seasprites have entered service outside the US military, although the manufacturer has been actively promoting the SH-2F and SH-2G with various potential customers.

Technical specifications

Helicopter Kaman K-20 Seasprite (SH-2F)
Type Multi-purpose naval
Year 1966
Engine 2 × 1,350 shp General Electric T58-GE-8
Rotor diameter 13.41 m (44 ft)
Fuselage length 12.30 m (40 ft 4 in)
Overall length 16.03 m (52 ft 7 in)
Height 4.72 m (15 ft 6 in)
Empty weight 3,200 kg (7,055 lb)
Gross weight 5,810 kg (12,808 lb)
Maximum speed 265 km/h (165 mph)
Service ceiling 6,858 m (22,500 ft)
Range 680 km (422 miles)
Capacity 3 crew + 4 passengers or one passenger and LAMP equipment
Armament 2 × Mk 46 torpedoes

Ka-25 'Hormone'

The Ka-25, named 'Hormone' by NATO, was the result of 20 years development by the Kamov bureau of contra-rotating rotor systems, a design concept that lends itself well to shipboard operations – where a small rotor span, a short fuselage and the stability of this rotor layout (with no tail rotor) is a positive asset.

The principle of the Ka-25 design, with two three-bladed main rotors and a short, stubby fuselage culminating in a tail unit with large endplate fins, was first established in 1952 with the piston-engined Ka-15. This entered service with the Soviet Navy in 1955 and continued in production until the early 1960s. A slightly larger derivative, the Ka-18, did not enter military production.

The Kamov Ka-25 'Hormone' has been the standard Soviet Navy anti-submarine helicopter for over 20 years but is now being superseded by the more advanced Ka-27. This example was photographed operating with the Soviet Pacific fleet. Note the complex aerial display above the chin radome.

This Ka-25, flying alongside a 'Moskva' class helicopter cruiser in the Mediterranean, features doughnut flotation gear befitting its role at sea.

At the beginning of the 1960s, Kamov flew the prototype Ka-20, which introduced turboshaft powerplants to the basic Ka-18 rotor configuration, suitably scaled up to match the increased power, and with a new box fuselage fitted with a chin search radome and anti-submarine equipment. This prototype was first displayed to the public in July 1961 at Tushino airport, Moscow, during an Aviation Day flyover, carrying two dummy air-to-surface missiles on either side of the fuselage. The Ka-20 was soon followed by the definitive Ka-25, which differed only in relatively minor detail and entered production in 1966.

The initial production Ka-25 was powered by

two 900 shp Glushenkov GTD-3F turboshaft engines mounted on the fuselage roof forward of the main rotor gearbox and drive shaft. The rotor system features full de-icing equipment and automatic blade folding. The fuselage contains accommodation for two pilots side-by-side and a cabin capable of carrying up to 12 passengers, but normally fitted out for two/three systems operators for the ASW/missile targetting roles. Weapons, including torpedoes and depth charges, are carried in a ventral bay between the quadricycle undercarriage legs. A search radar is mounted forward of this weapons bay, under the nose, and dipping sonar is normally housed in a compartment aft of the bay, in the rear fuselage. Some aircraft, however, have been seen with an enlarged weapons bay extending aft into the sonar compartment area, believed to accommodate wire-guided torpedoes.

Aft of the main fuselage is a short tail section, culminating in a triple-finned tail unit. Each fin includes a large ventral area, and the two outer fins are toed inward with rudder control surfaces.

Three distinct variants of the Ka-25 are in Soviet military service, including the basic ASW version described above and known to NATO as 'Hormone-A'. This version operates from the Soviet Navy carrier fleet, each of which has about 20 machines on board, and from the larger battle cruisers.

In addition, the larger carriers and certain of the missile cruisers also operate the 'Hormone-B', a special electronics variant with datalink facilities, which is employed to provide over-the-horizon targeting and midcourse guidance for ship-launched long range missiles such as the SS-N-3, SS-N-12 and SS-N-19. 'Hormone-B' is identified by its larger under-nose radome and a small cylindrical radome in the sonar bay position.

Also in use is a utility variant, 'Hormone-C', which is operated on search and rescue and transport/external load missions by the Soviet Navy and with Aeroflot. About 460 Ka-25s were built before production ceased in 1975, including a small number exported to India, Syria and Yugoslavia. In Soviet service the type is now being replaced by the new, more powerful Ka-32.

Technical specifications

Helicopter Kamov Ka-25
Type ASW/general purpose
Year 1966
Engine 2 × 900 shp Glushenkov GTD-3
Rotor diameter 15.74 m (51 ft 8 in)
Fuselage length 9.83 m (32 ft 3 in)
Overall length 15.74 m (51 ft 8 in)
Height 5.37 m (17 ft 7 in)
Empty weight 4,400 kg (9,700 lb)
Gross weight 7,300 kg (16,093 lb)
Maximum speed 220 km/h (137 mph)
Service ceiling 3,500 m (11,485 ft)
Range 400 km (248 miles)
Capacity 2 pilots + 2/3 crew or 12 passengers
Armament 2 × ASW torpedoes or depth charges

Ka-26 'Hoodlum'

The Ka-26 is used in large numbers within the Soviet bloc as a light transport and agricultural support helicopter, able to operate either with a cabin attached, as seen here, or . . .

The Kamov Ka-26, identified by NATO as 'Hoodlum', was designed during the early 1960s as a partial replacement for the Ka-15 which, in addition to its naval duties, was used in the transport and other roles by Aeroflot.

The Ka-26 retained the contra-rotating three-blade rotor layout, although introducing composite blades, but featured an entirely new fuselage and powerplant layout. This comprised a basic two-seat side-by-side cockpit attached to a skeletal fuselage with a twin boom tail unit, quadricycle undercarriage and two outrigged 325 hp Vedeneev M-14V-26 piston engines mounted on stub wings. The area beneath the rotor system and main gearbox was thus free for the carriage of external loads or especially designed interchangeable payloads. These included a chemical hopper and associated agricultural spray equipment, a basic freight platform, or a six-seat passenger pod. As a flying crane the Ka-26 is able to sling load up to 1,100 kg (2,426 lb); in its passenger configuration this is reduced to 900 kg (1,984 lb).

Although most of the 600 plus Ka-26s built operate in civilian service, a number do fly with the Bulgarian and Hungarian Air Forces and, of course, the Aeroflot fleet are readily available for military operations. The aircraft is used in Soviet coastal waters for Search and Rescue, with a 150 kg (331 lb) capacity winch and inflatable flotation gear fitted, as well as operating from small ships on liaison and ice spotting duties. An ambulance version is also in service, with the passenger pod fitted out to carry two stretcher patients, two sitting wounded and a medical attendant.

... with the cabin deleted. This Hungarian example is fitted with crop spraying gear. Plans to replace the piston engines of the Ka-26 with a turbine powerplant are currently under consideration.

A turbine-engined conversion, the Ka-126, was developed in 1979 and test-flown but is not believed to have entered production.

Technical specifications

Helicopter Kamov Ka-26
Type Light general purpose
Year 1965
Engine 2 × 325 hp Vedeneyev M-14V-26
Rotor diameter 13.00 m (42 ft 8 in)
Fuselage length 7.75 m (25 ft 5 in)
Overall length -
Height 4.05 m (13 ft 3 in)
Empty weight 1,950 kg (4,300 lb)
Gross weight 3,000 kg (6,614 lb)
Maximum speed 170 km/h (105 mph)
Service ceiling 3,000 m (9,842 ft)
Range 400 km (248 miles)
Capacity Pilot + 6 passengers or 900/1,000 kg (1,984/2,204 lb)

Ka-27/Ka-32 'Helix'

The Kamov Ka-27, and its civil counterpart, the Ka-32, first became known in the West during 1981, when prototypes were seen aboard the Soviet guided missile destroyer *Udaloy* during an exercise in the Baltic in September of that year. Later in 1981 a Ka-32 was displayed at Minsk during a scientific conference on the use of aircraft in the national economy.

It rapidly became evident that the new helicopter, identified by NATO as 'Helix', was more than just a simple replacement for the Ka-25 'Hormone', since it was considerably more powerful and somewhat larger than its predecessor. In fact, the installed pair of 2,225 shp Isotov TV3-117V turboshaft engines offered over twice the power available to the earlier aircraft, giving it an external lifting capacity of 11,000 lbs (5,000 kg) over a range of about 115 miles (185 km) and an excellent engine-out performance for overwater SAR and ASW missions.

The basic layout of the Ka-27 follows that of the Ka-25, with two three-bladed contra-rotating rotors, a box cabin and a multi-finned tail unit, but close examination shows a number of improvements and changes. For example, the glassfibre rotors are of slightly greater diameter and display aerodynamic differences, while the cabin is larger, with accommodation for up to 16 seated passengers.

Three main variants of the Ka-27 have been in production since 1981 for the Soviet Navy. 'Helix-A' is the basic ASW version, with a chin-mounted radome, ventral weapons bay and a cabin arranged for two/three ASW operators. Provision for sonobuoys and MAD equipment is also made, and a sophisticated automatic flight control system permits night and all weather operation – a major improvement over the more restricted Ka-25.

The Kamov Ka-27 'Helix' is now in front-line service with Soviet naval units in the ASW and VERTREP role. Much more powerful than its predecessor, the Ka-27 is able to lift a 5,000 kg (11,000 lb) sling load.

With blades folded and access panels opened, a Ka-27 undergoes routine maintenance at sea aboard the aircraft carrier *Kiev* during a 1985 North Atlantic exercise.

'Helix-B' is a missile target acquisition and midcourse guidance version, which is replacing the 'Hormone-B' electronics variant and similarly introduces revised radome shapes, additional aerials and related equipment.

A third variant is common to the Ka-32, with additional long range tanks mounted on either side of the cabin, and a winch at the side door for the SAR and plane-guard role. This version is also the most suitable for vertical replenishment work and may be used in the future for commando assault missions. The civil Ka-32 is also used for SAR and vertrep work, based aboard the four nuclear-powered icebreakers, and is also in use to support offshore and onshore oil exploration and production as well as various construction projects.

All the 'Helix' variants feature electric blade and windscreen de-icing to permit all weather operation and the type has already set several official time-to-height records in the hands of an all-girl crew, including 6,000 m (19,685 ft) in 4 min 46.5 sec, as well as setting a record of 6,552 m (21,496 ft) for sustained height in level flight. To date the type has entered service only with the Soviet Navy and Aeroflot, but a number are shortly expected to be exported to India, where they will probably replace Ka-25s in service with the Indian Navy.

Technical specifications

Helicopter Ka-27
Type ASW and multi-mission naval helicopter
Year 1981
Engine 2 × 2,225 shp Isotov TV3-117V
Rotor diameter 15.90 m (52 ft 2 in)
Fuselage length 11.30 m (37 ft 1 in)
Overall length (rotors folded): 12.25 m (40 ft 2.25 in)
Height 5.40 m (17 ft 8.5 in)
Empty weight 6,000 kg (13,228 lb)
Gross weight 11,000 kg (24,250 lb)
Maximum speed 250 km/h (155 mph)
Hovering ceiling IGE 3,500 m (11,480 ft)
Service ceiling 6,000 m (19,685 ft)
Range 800 km (497 miles)
Capacity 3 crew + 16 passengers
Armament 2 × ASW torpedoes or ASV missiles, etc

Kamov 'Hokum'

Generall assumed to be a Kamov bureau design, the new 'Hokum' uses co-axial rotor technology, and probably the Ka-32 transmission and powerplant, to produce a high speed 'fighter' helicopter. This ilustration is believed to fairly accurately represent the new helicopter. (Herkenning).

Known at the present time only by its NATO reporting name, this new Kamov design is reportedly designed to meet an air to air anti-helicopter requirement for the Soviet Air Force, coupled with ground attack duties.

While it is possible that the aircraft was originally designed in competition with the Mi-28, current thinking suggests that Hokum is being developed to production status in its own right. Prototype flight trials began by June 1984.

In general appearance the new helicopter retains the co-axial rotor system developed by Kamov and may well use the basic dynamics of the Ka-27, including the twin 2,225 shp Isotov TV3 engines. The rotor diameter, however, has been reduced to some 46 ft (14 m) and airframe size and weight are also estimated to be less than those of the Ka-27. This would suggest an impressive performance and enhanced manoeuvrability. Other features evident from information available include a retractable tricycle undercarriage, a slim fuselage with possibly side-by-side crew seating and a triple-finned tail assembly. It may be presumed that the aircraft carries infra-red suppression equipment, armour and other survivability features, as well as rotor de-icing. Armament is primarily carried on stub-wing hardpoints, although a multi-barrel cannon is installed in the lower nose.

Technical specifications (estimated)

Helicopter Kamov 'Hokum'
Type Air-air combat
Year 1984
Engine 2 × 2,225 shp Isotov TV3
Rotor diameter 15 m (49 ft 3 in)
Overall length 14 m (46 ft)
Overall height 5.4 m (17 ft 8 in)
Empty weight 6,000 kg (13,228 lb)
Gross weight 9,977 kg (22,000 lb)
Maximum speed 350 km/h (217 mph)
Service ceiling 5,488 m (18,000 ft)
Capacity 2 + crew
Armament Air-to-air missiles, 23 mm cannon

McDonnell Douglas AH-64 Apache

Deliveries to operational US Army units of the McDonnell Douglas AH-64A Apache began in the spring of 1986 and this new attack helicopter is expected to be deployed to Europe sometime in 1987.

Following the failure of the 1966 US Army Advanced Aerial Fire Support System (AAFSS) competition, which was cancelled in 1969 when the selected Lockheed AH-56A Cheyenne helicopter failed to live up to expectations, the service evaluated its Vietnam experience with the Bell AH-1 Cobra and, in 1972, initiated a new Advanced Attack Helicopter (AAH) specification.

The new requirement, while less demanding than its predecessor, nevertheless represented a major advance over contemporary in-service anti-armour helicopters, calling as it did for an aircraft able to operate and survive from front-line field bases with a heavy weapon load by day or night in all weather conditions. In June 1973 the US Army selected two finalists in the AAH competition, Bell and Hughes, to build prototypes for evaluation. Bell's entry, the YAH-63, based on proven AH-1 and Model 214 technology, flew in October 1975 but was ruled out of the competition in December 1976.

The winning Hughes design, the Model 77 YAH-64, followed a traditional gunship layout, with tandem cockpits, nose-mounted sight and sensors and stub wing weapons pylons, but introduced a number of major changes over its

Above: Visible in this view of a production AH-64A is the ventral-mounted 30 mm Chain Gun and the nose-mounted sight and sensors. The pods on either side of the cockpit house the avionic and electronic systems of this complex helicopter.

Left: An AH-64A looses off 2.75-in air-to-ground rockets during desert armament trials. Each pod on the outboard underwing pylons contains 19 2.75-in rockets, while each inboard pylon carries four laser-guided Hellfire anti-tank missiles.

predecessors. Power was provided by two 1,536 shp General Electric T700 engines, shoulder-mounted with full IR suppression, and driving a four-bladed main rotor and 'quiet' four-blade tail rotor, both based on the successful 500MD design. The dynamics system was designed to withstand damage from 12.7 mm and 23 mm ammunition, as was the fuselage. The crashworthy undercarriage was designed to collapse progressively in the event of a forced landing and featured a tail wheel layout to protect the tail rotor from ground-strike damage. Planned avionics included TADS/PNVS, FLIR, AHRS, BITE fault detection, and helmet-mounted display systems.

Two YAH-64 prototypes, 73-22248 and 73-22249, were initially built, along with a ground test vehicle, and the first of these made its maiden flight on 30 September 1975. Manufacturer's trials were completed by May 1976, when both aircraft were handed over for US Army evaluation. This was completed in the December, when Hughes was awarded a full scale development contract, which included the construction of three further pre-production prototypes and the integration of avionics and weapons systems. The

Laid out before this Apache are the various alternative loads cleared for carriage on the underwing pylons, including 16 Hellfire anti-tank missiles, 76 2.75-in rockets in pod launchers, and auxiliary fuel tanks to provide a ferry range of more than 1,000 miles. Also shown are 1,200 rounds of 30 mm ammunition for the ventral Chain Gun.

latter included the adoption of the laser-seeking Rockwell Hellfire anti-armour missile instead of the originally intended TOW installation, and the selection of the new Hughes 30 mm XM230E1 Chain Gun.

The first pre-production aircraft flew in October 1979, introducing a new design tail unit with a low-mounted movable tailplane replacing the original fixed T-unit. Called a stabilator, the new tailplane was designed to move automatically to provide near level aircraft attitude during NOE flight manoeuvres, thus reducing pilot workload. Also standardised on the pre-production YAH-64 was an increased diameter tail rotor, a slight lengthening of the rotor mast and expansion of the forward avionics bays. Also during 1979 Hughes began development of new composite

main rotor blades with swept tips to replace the original all-metal version.

An order for initial production for the US Army of 11 AH-64As, now named the Apache, was awarded to Hughes in April 1982, and has since been followed by orders currently totalling 675 aircraft. Deliveries began in January 1984 and by early 1986, when the first machines became operational with the 6th Air Cavalry Combat Brigade at Fort Hood, Texas, some 85 AH-64As were in service.

The full production AH-64A, powered by uprated 1,696 shp T700-GE-701 engines, carries up to 16 Hellfire anti-armour missiles, or 76 2.75-in (69.8 mm) rockets, on four underwing hard-points together with a 1,200-round 30 mm Chain Gun mounted under the fuselage. The Martin-Marietta TADS provides target search, detection, FLIR and laser designation for the co-pilot/gunner, while a separate FLIR sensor provides PNVS imagery for the pilot. Both crew members are linked to the sensors by a Honeywell integrated helmet and display sighting system.

While some interest has been shown by overseas countries in acquiring the AH-64A, the unit cost has so far proved to be a major obstacle. Meanwhile the company, renamed McDonnell Douglas Helicopters since August 1985, is developing a marinised variant to meet potential US Marine Corps and Navy requirements for combat air patrol/escort, anti-shipping strike and over-the-horizon targetting roles. Modifications would include adoption of the navalised T700-GE-401 powerplant, folding main rotor blades and tail section with consequent relocation of the tail-wheel, and an underfuselage haul-down system. The Chain Gun installation would be deleted and replaced for air-to-air defence by two wingtip-mounted AIM-9L Sidewinder missiles. Other alternative armament would include TOW, Harpoon, Penguin or equivalent anti-armour and anti-shipping missiles. For surface search and target acquisition, McDonnell Douglas are proposing either a most or ventral mounted radar. Additionally under consideration is the OH-64B with an updated cockpit, composite main rotor system and more powerful engines.

An early AH-64, 28258, is also currently flying as a single-pilot testbed for the proposed US Army LHX (Light Helicopter Experimental) programme, with an advanced digital flight control system and integrated 'glass' front cockpit, the second cockpit being retained with a standard layout for a safety pilot.

Technical specifications

Helicopter McDonnell Douglas AH-64A
Type Two-seat attack
Year 1975
Engine 2 × 1,690 shp General Electric T700-GE-701
Rotor diameter 14.63 m (48 ft)
Fuselage length 15.06 m (49 ft 5 in)
Overall length 17.60 m (57 ft 9 in)
Height 3.83 m (12 ft 6 in)
Empty weight 4.662 kg (10,278 lb)
Gross weight 8.013 kg (17,665 lb)
Maximum speed 378 km/h (235 mph)
Hovering ceiling IGE 4,630 m (15,190 ft)
Service ceiling 6,250 m (20,500 ft)
Range 610 km (379 miles)
Armament 1 × 30 mm cannon + 16 × Hellfire missiles

McDonnell Douglas 500MD/ME

In the early 1970s a programme sponsored by the US Defence Department of the Advanced Research Project Agency (ARPA) led to the appearance of a modified OH-6A, 65-12968, nicknamed the 'Quiet One'. As the name suggests, the programme aim was to significantly reduce the noise level of the OH-6A, and this was primarily achieved by introduced a new five-blade main rotor and four-blade tail rotor, both with a reduced rotational speed, and an engine exhaust silencer. Flight trials of the 'Quiet One' began in early 1972 and subsequently led to a new version of the basic Model 500.

Designated the 500D and first flown in August 1974, the revised design featured an uprated 420 shp Allison 250-C20B powerplant, strengthened transmission, and a new five-bladed main rotor. It also introduced a new T-tail unit to improve flight stability at both high and low speeds and better handling characteristics in abnormal manoeuvres.

The first production commercial 500D was flown in October 1975 but meanwhile Hughes was already developing a military 500MD variant, using at least two OH-6As, including the 'Quiet One', as well as one of the early 500D prototypes as trials aircraft. Designed as a multi-role light helicopter the 500MD was structurally similar to the commercial model, but introduced self-sealing fuel cells, armour protection, and provision for an exhaust infra-red suppressor as well as the carriage of a variety of weaponry.

Weapons cleared for the initial 500MD Scout included a 7.62 mm Minigun with 2,000 rounds,

Development by Hughes Helicopters of the basic 500 design led to the Model 500D/TOW Defender which has found useful export sales with a number of military air arms. This aircraft, 518, is operated by the Kenyan 50th Air Cavalry.

The 500MD/ASW Defender, seen here in Taiwan Navy colours but with a pre-delivery civil registration, was developed by Hughes Helicopters (now McDonnell Douglas) to provide a lightweight anti-submarine/surface search system for shipboard operation.

fourteen 2.75-in (69.8 mm) rockets, 30 mm Chain Gun with 600 rounds or, in the ASW version, two Mk 46 homing torpedoes with ASW search radar and MAD gear. Subsequent development led to the 500MD (TOW) Defender. This installation comprised four TOW anti-armour missiles, mounted two each side on the weapons pylon, and a telescopic sight with associated firing controls built into the port side of the nose. Later a trial installation of a Hughes Aircraft mast-mounted sight was also cleared although no orders for this variant were received. The ultimate 500MD was the multi-mission Defender II, introduced in 1980 with all the earlier options included but additionally offering a quiet four-blade tail rotor, air-to-air defence missiles, FLIR night vision system, laser range-finder and radar warning equipment.

Orders for the 500MD came primarily from Kenya (30), Israel (30) and South Korea, where over 200 of both the Scout and TOW Defender versions have been assembled under licence by Korean Air Lines. Twelve examples of the ASW version are operated by the Taiwanese Navy.

In January 1982, Hughes began flight-testing a new basic variant of the 500 Series, the 500E. This introduced an elongated and more streamlined nose transparency, offering extra leg room and flight avionics space in the front cockpit. A lowered bulkhead and redesigned rear cabin structure provided additional space improvements for rear seat passengers. Primarily inten-

The newest military member of the Model 500 family is the MD 530MG, which marries the Model 530 airframe and powerplant improvements to the latest avionics and weapon systems technology. Here the prototype is equipped with mast-mounted sight, a chin FLIR installation and pylon-mounted weaponry.

ded for the civil market, the 500E has nevertheless been offered with the various 500MD military options as the 500MG Defender, with special emphasis on para-military-style operations. Standard 500Es are also in quasi-military service, including eight supplied to Kenya via the US Army Aviation Systems Command, and approximately 60 clandestinely sold to North Korea.

In October 1982, Hughes flew the prototype Model 530F, based on the 500E but introducing an uprated 650 shp Allison 250-C30 turboshaft and transmission to give a 50 shp increase in take-off power. To take advantage of the increased power, the main rotor diameter was increased by 12 in (30 cm), the diameter of the tail rotor increased by 2 in (5 cm), and the tail rotor drive shaft lengthened. Intended primarily for commercial external lift and hot/high operations, the 530F has also been sold to Iraq, which took delivery of 26 aircraft in 1986 for training, observation and communications work.

Military development of the 530F has concentrated to date on the 530MG Defender, which first flew in May 1984. The 530MG, available in both Scout and TOW versions, offers all the weaponry and systems alternatives of the earlier variants, including a mast-mounted sight, laser rangefinder, FLIR, TOW anti-armour missiles, podded 7.62 mm machine guns and 12-tube 2.75-in (69.8 mm) rocket launchers, but introduces a totally new integrated cockpit management system developed in association with Racal Avionics.

The heart of the new system is the Racal RAMS 3000 with its databus link concept. Navigation needs, communication, flight instrumentation, and weaponry control are all integrated and semi-automated to minimise crew workload and allow maximum head-up/hands-on flying. The result is a much simplified cockpit layout, with an instrument panel some two-thirds smaller than the earlier mechanical layout and a stowable weapons-aiming display.

Public demonstrations of the 530MG were first carried out at the 1984 Farnborough Air Display and since that time the aircraft has been on other demonstration tours in Europe and elsewhere. However, no orders for this version, or the 500MG have been announced.

In January 1984, Hughes Helicopters became a subsidiary of McDonnell Douglas and, on 27 August 1985, the company name changed to McDonnell Douglas Helicopters.

Technical specifications

Helicopter McDonnell Douglas 500MD
Type Multi-role light military
Year 1976
Engine 420 shp Allison 250-C20B turboshaft
Rotor diameter 8.05 (26 ft 5 in)
Overall length 9.30 m (30 ft 6 in)
Height 2.53 m (8 ft 3.5 in)
Empty weight 598 kg (1,320 lb)
Gross weight 1,360 kg (3,000 lb)
Maximum speed 258 km/h (160 mph)
Hovering ceiling IGE 2,745 m (9,000 ft)
Service ceiling 4,570 m (15,000 ft)
Range 482 km (300 miles)
Capacity Pilot + 6 passengers
Armament Provision for variety of weapons, including TOW missiles

MBB BO 105

The Bo 105 serves in both an observation/liaison and an anti-armour role with the West German Army. This is the PAM-1 variant, carrying six HOT anti-tank missiles.

Despite the dominance of the German helicopter in the early 1940s, it was not until the 1960s that the rebuilt industry began to re-establish its position as a manufacturer.

Beginning with the Bo 102 ground trainer, the Bölkow design team developed several alternative projects in an effort to find a marketable helicopter. In 1964 the decision was made to develop a four/five seat aircraft, designated the Bo 105 and powered by two 375 shp BMW 6022 engines, with a new rigid rotor system incorporating a titanium head with glassfibre blades. This design was accepted by the government as

Right: The Bo 105 is also built under licence by IPTN in Indonesia and operates with all three Indonesian military services in a variety of roles.

Below: A navalised version of the Bo 105 is also available for small ship patrol and attack duties. HMR151 is one of several currently operating with the Mexican Navy.

worthy of support and Bölkow duly received a 60 percent Ministry of Economics grant to cover development, plus an additional Defence Ministry grant for development of the rotor system.

Construction of three prototype Bo 105s began in 1965, with the first two intended to respectively flight test the airframe and rigid rotor system only, and the third incorporating the new engines with the new rotor system. Initial ground runs of the latter led to some problems establishing suitable testing techniques, and Bölkow therefore came to an agreement with Sud Aviation to assist in the test programme. Thus, on 24 January 1966, a three bladed version of the rigid rotor began flight trials in France, mounted on an SA 316C Alouette Astazou. (A subsequent attempt to develop the three-blade rigid rotor for the SA 341 Gazelle was abandoned, although Aérospatiale did sign a licence with Bölkow for glassfibre blade manufacture.)

The first prototype Bo 105 V1 (D-HAKO) began ground tests in September 1966, using Allison 250-C18 engines and a Westland Scout articulated rotor system, but was almost immediately destroyed as the result of intense ground resonance. Thus it was the Bo 105 V2 (D-HECA) that had to complete the ground tests, before being the first to fly, on 16 February 1967. This was followed by the BMW 6022-engined third prototype (D-HAJY) on 20 December 1967.

In mid-1968 Bölkow merged with Messerschmitt, and two further pre-production Bo 105s were laid down. At the same time plans were announced for the production of two versions, the Bo 105A powered by the Allison 250 engine, and the soon-to-be-abandoned Bo 105B, which would have used the BMW 6022.

With the imminent addition of HFB to the Messerschmitt-Bölkow group, and the creation of MBB, the Bo 105 V4 (D-HAPE) joined the trials programme on 1 May 1969, followed by the V5 (D-HAPI) later that year. Meanwhile, production was underway and, on 11 April 1970, the first definitive Bo 105A (D-HABV) made its initial flight. This aircraft introduced new 'droop-snoot' aerofoil main blades, but was otherwise similar to the final pre-production Bo 105s.

While initial sales of the Bo 105 were primarily in the civil sector of the market, including the ambulance, police and similar public service areas, the German Defence Ministry took delivery of three early aircraft (S2, S3 and S7) for a series of military trials aimed at meeting the growing needs of the Federal German Army. In particular, the Army had requirements for an observation/liaison helicopter and an anti-tank machine. Consequently, as early as 1972, one of the trials aircraft was flying with a HOT anti-tank missile installation and other armament options, including a ventral-mounted swivelling 20 mm cannon.

It was, however, the observation/liaison variant that was first ordered. In 1976 ten Bo 105Cs, with uprated Allison 250-C20 engines and a gross weight increase, were purchased for evaluation by a special Army unit at Celle. Later

Ordered by the Swedish Army is a Bo 105 variant modified to carry the TOW anti-tank guided missile system. Seen here is an early development Bo 105CB.

that year, an order for 227 similar Bo 105M (VBH) was placed, with deliveries commencing in 1979.

The anti-tank requirement proved more difficult to satisfy but, following trials in 1977-78 by two purpose-built prototypes (S315, S316), it was decided to order 212 Bo 105P (PAH-1) as an interim measure prior to the introduction of a more sophisticated anti-tank helicopter, the PAH-2. The Bo 105P standardised on an armament of six HOT missiles and a roof-mounted SFIM APX397 sight, and introduced a further uprated transmission to permit operation at 2,400 kg (5,291 lb) gross weight and to absorb tail rotor loads during automatic tracking. The first PAH-1s entered service in late 1979 and deliveries were completed in 1984.

In addition to meeting the Federal German Army requirement, MBB has also been involved in developing other military Bo 105 variants for export customers. These include a TOW missile anti-tank variant with the optional SAAB Helios sighting system, as ordered by the Swedish Army, a Search and Rescue version, and a naval variant with folding main rotor blades, radar and salt water protection for small ship operations.

Certain of these variants have been licence-assembled overseas. The Philippines Aircraft Development Corporation, for example, assembled 40 Bo 105s for local para-military use and re-export, while PT Nurtanio has built over 80 aircraft for the Indonesian Armed Services and

This trials Bo 105, D-HABV, has been used for development of a day/night mast-mounted sight system, intended for possible application to the proposed PAH-2.

other national organisations. The biggest co-production programme to date has, however, been with CASA in Spain, where 113 Bo 105s have been built for anti-tank, ground support and observation duties with the Spanish Army. CASA has also exported military Bo 105s to Iraq, at least 24 having been delivered by the end of 1984.

Total Bo 105 production has now exceeded 1,000 aircraft, over 600 of which are in military service around the world. Equipment updating and the ruggedness of the basic airframe, coupled with the advantages of the rigid rotor system and twin engines, means that the aircraft is still competitive on the battlefield. In addition, the introduction in late 1985 of a new basic variant, the Bo 105LS-4, which standardises on a stretched cabin and introduces the uprated 550 shp Allison 250-C28C powerplant to provide a much enhanced hot/high performance, is bringing new military sales. This version is being produced at a new facility in Canada set up jointly by MBB and Fleet Aircraft, and early orders include 12 aircraft for the Peruvian Air Force. Also planned is the Bo 105LS-5, which will introduce a new five blade composite main rotor system, together with new generation Pratt & Whitney (Canada) STEP engines.

Technical specifications

Helicopter MBB Bo 105M
Type General purpose
Year 1979
Engine 2 × 406 shp Allison 250-C20
Rotor diameter 9.82 m (32 ft 3 in)
Fuselage length 8.55 m (28 ft)
Overall length 11.86 m (38 ft 11 in)
Height 2.98 m (9 ft 9 in)
Empty weight 1,110 kg (2,447 lb)
Gross weight 2,300 kg (5,070 lb)
Maximum speed 270 km/h (168 mph)
Hovering ceiling IGE 2,715 m (8,907 ft)
Service ceiling 5,030 m (16,500 ft)
Range 656 km (407 miles)
Capacity 2 crew + 3 passengers
Armament 6 × HOT or 4 × TOW anti-tank missiles or podded rockets, machine-guns, etc.

MBB-Kawasaki BK 117

The design of the BK117 began in the early 1970s as a series of studies by MBB to develop a growth version of the successful Bo 105. From these studies, generically known as the Bo 107, came discussions in late 1974 with Boeing Vertol and Kawasaki. These two latter companies, who enjoyed a co-operation agreement involving the Vertol 107 tandem-rotor helicopter, had been considering a Japanese design, the KH-7, which was of similar size to the proposed Bo 107. In addition Boeing Vertol enjoyed a link with MBB via the rotor technology developed for the YUH-61A UTTAS prototypes.

It was therefore a natural progression for the three companies to agree a collaboration programme on a revised Bo 107/KH-7 design and, although Boeing Vertol withdrew during 1975 in order to concentrate on the H-61, MBB and Kawasaki continued discussions and in February 1977 signed a joint development agreement. Under this agreement Kawasaki became responsible for the front and centre fuselage, electrics and transmission, while MBB took responsibility for the main and tail rotor systems, tail section, hydraulics and undercarriage. Much of these latter components were closely based on those employed in the Bo 105.

Designated the BK 117, the first prototype D-HBKA was rolled out at the MBB Ottobrunn facility in 1979, first flying on 13 June. A second Kawasaki-assembled prototype JQ-0003 flew in Japan two months later on 10 August. Two other ground test prototypes were also built. In general appearance the BK 117 does enjoy a family resemblance to the Bo 105, with a similar four-bladed rigid rotor system and a box fuselage with rear clamshell access doors as well as sliding doors on each side of the cabin. The two 550 shp Avco-Lycoming LTS101 engines are similarly mounted atop the main fuselage. Between six and 11 passengers can be carried, depending on the seating layout, or the aircraft can be equipped for the casevac or cargo role.

Production BK 117s began to be completed in late 1981, following certification trials with JQ0003 and a German-built pre-production machine, D-HBKB. This latter aircraft deleted the ventral fin used on the original prototypes, in favour of revisions to the endplate fins on the tailplane. With civil certification granted in both West Germany and Japan in December 1982, customer deliveries began in early 1983. The majority of these to date have been to commercial operators, with particular success in the Emergency Medical Services (EMS) market. Other BK 117s have entered service with some police and para-military organisations, including the Venda Defence Force in South Africa.

In March 1985 a new version, the BK 117A-3, was certificated, with the gross weight increased

Shown at the 1985 Paris Air Show, the BK 117A-3M military prototype carried eight HOT missiles and mockups of a Lucas chin gun turret, mast-mounted sight and other military-orientated modifications.

from 6,283 lb (2,850 kg) to 7,055 lb (3,200 kg) and a new design tail rotor featuring twisted blades of wider chord and diameter. This was followed in June 1985 by the static display at the Paris Air Show of the multi-role A-3M, which was proposed as a military variant using the same basic airframe and clearance for a ventral Lucas gun turret, slaved to a helmet-mounted sight system.

Also offered on the A-3M was a choice of mast-mounted or roof-mounted weapons sight, together with stub pylons capable of carrying up to eight TOW or other anti-armour missiles and podded weaponry. The prototype shown, converted from the original pre-production BK 117 D-HBKB, additionally featured a Racal RAMS 3000 avionics management system with dual MIL-STD-1553B databus and multi-function cockpit displays.

In early 1986 no decision had been made to fly the A-3M in the above form, but MBB was building a simpler utility military model which was due to be flown later in the year.

Technical specifications

Helicopter MBB-Kawasaki BK 117A-3M
Type Multi-role military
Year 1985
Engine 2 × 550 shp Avco Lycoming LTS 101-650B-1 turboshafts
Rotor diameter 11 m (36 ft 1 in)
Fuselage length 9.98 m (32 ft 9 in)
Overall length 13 m (42 ft 8 in)
Height 3.84 m (12 ft 7.25 in)
Empty weight 2,560 (5,644 lb)
Gross weight 3,200 kg (7,055 lb)
Maximum speed 248 km/h (154 mph)
Hovering ceiling IGE 1,820 m (6,000 ft)
Service ceiling 1,370 m (4,500 ft)
Range 493 km (306 miles)
Capacity 2 crew + 10 troops or cargo
Armament Weaponry can include: TOW and HELITOW anti-tank missiles, air-to-air missiles, unguided rockets, machinegun pods, fixed forward-firing cannon, or 0.50 in (12.7 mm) machine gun.

Mi-1 'Hare'

The Mil Mi-1 is still in Soviet service as a basic trainer with some, like this example, allocated to State flying schools and similar institutions.

The Mil Mi-1 was designed soon after the Second World War to meet a general utility specification. Its layout followed conventional design practice of the period, as exemplified in the contemporary Bristol Type 171 and Sikorsky S-51, using a three-bladed main rotor and a tailboom mounted anti-torque rotor, with power supplied by an adapted 575 hp Ivchenko AI-26V radial engine.

The first of three prototypes made its initial flight in September 1948 and production began in late 1949, with service deliveries commencing in 1951. Initial variants were laid out to carry the pilot and three passengers, but payload problems restricted practical flight to two passengers and many early aircraft deleted the third seat. As the first helicopter to enter large scale Soviet service, the Mi-1 was quickly adopted for a wide range of missions, including Search and Rescue, liaison, training, and observation work.

In 1955 production was transferred to PZL at Swidnik in Poland, where the basic aircraft was redesignated the SM-1. The first locally-built machine flew in 1956 and was soon followed by the improved SM-1W, which introduced metal rotor blades and hydraulic controls, with the payload increased to cover three passengers. Also standardised was an early anti-icing system, which allowed for the continuous spraying of anti-freeze over the main and tail rotor blades and the windscreen.

Production of the Mi-1 family eventually ended in 1965, by which time several hundred had been delivered to the Soviet military and many more were operational with other Eastern Bloc and export customers. Designated 'Hare' under the NATO reporting name system, many of these remain in second-line service as training and utility aircraft.

In early 1986 first reports were received of the development of a two-seat successor to the Mi-1, designated the Mi-34 and powered by a 325 hp Vedeneyev M-14V-26 piston engine with a rigid-rotor layout.

Technical specifications

Helicopter Mil Mi-1
Type General purpose
Year 1948
Engine 575 hp Ivchenko Al-26V
Rotor diameter 14.35 m (47 ft 1 in)
Fuselage length 12.10 m (39 ft 8 in)
Overall length -
Height 3.30 m (10 ft 10 in)
Empty weight 1,880 kg (4,145 lb)
Gross weight 2,404 kg (5,300 lb)
Maximum speed 170 km/h (105 mph)
Hovering ceiling IGE -
Service ceiling 3,000 m (9,842 ft)
Range 580 km (360 miles)
Capacity Pilot + 3 passengers

Mi-2 'Hoplite'

The Mil Mi-2, which took the basic Mi-1 rotor and transmission and incorporated it in a new turbine-engined airframe, is widely used by the Soviet Union and other Warsaw Pact forces. These two aircraft were seen demonstrating at Tushino during the 1982 Soviet Air Force Day celebrations.

The Mil Mi-2 is a classic example of Soviet methods of technological progress, updating proven designs rather than introducing totally new technology.

In this instance, the Mil design team retained the basic rotor system and dynamics of the successful Mi-1, but introduced twin turboshaft engines mounted atop the fuselage and in front of the main gearbox. The Mi-1 tailboom was also retained but married to a new forward fuselage, with a redesigned cockpit and an enlarged cabin, with seats for up to eight passengers in the area previously taken up by the Mi-1 piston power-

plant. The resultant helicopter was only slightly larger than its predecessor, but showed a marked improvement in performance and payload.

Following a first flight in September 1961 and successful development trials with two Soviet-built prototypes, production of the Mi-2 was entrusted to PZL-Swidnik in Poland. The first Polish-built aircraft flew on 4 November 1965 and full production deliveries began the following year, when the type succeeded the Mi-1 on the Polish assembly line. Since that date, over 3,000 Mi-2s have been produced, with the majority entering military service with the Soviet Union and her allies. The type has been designated 'Hoplite' by NATO.

Several variants of the Mi-2 have been produced since 1966, including options with uprated 450 shp engines and/or glassfibre main and tail rotor blades. In addition, Mi-2s are in service in specialised ambulance, Search and Rescue, and training versions. Armed Mi-2s are also operational, carrying rocket pods or four 'Sagger' air-to-surface missiles on mid-fuselage pylons. Most military Mi-2s can also fit a swivel-mounted machine gun in the main cabin door area.

Production of the Mi-2 was continuing in 1985, although at a relatively low rate compared with the 300 per annum being built at the end of the 1970s. In addition, PZL was continuing development of a Westernised version, the Kania, powered by two 420 shp Allison 250-C20B engines and with a revised nose outline. To date, no military sales of the Kania are expected, this variant being intended only for the civil market.

Technical specifications

Helicopter Mil Mi-2
Type Light general purpose
Year 1961
Engine 2 × 400 shp Isotov GTD-350P
Rotor diameter 14.56 m (47 ft 9 in)
Fuselage length 11.94 m (39 ft 2 in)
Overall length 17.42 m (57 ft 2 in)
Height 3.75 m (12 ft 4 in))
Empty weight 2,370 kg (5,225 lb)
Gross weight 3,700 kg (8,157 lb)
Maximum speed 210 km/h (130 mph)
Hovering ceiling IGE 2,000 m (6,560 ft)
Service ceiling 4,000 m (13,125 ft)
Range 170 km (105 miles)
Capacity Pilot + 8 passengers or 700 kg (1,543 lb)
Armament Missiles or rockets; machine gun + unguided rockets or air-ground missiles

Mi-4 'Hound'

Just as the basic layout of the Mi-1 followed that of the contemporary Sikorsky S-51, so the design of the Mi-4 showed a striking similarity to that of the S-55 Whirlwind when it first appeared in 1952.

In truth, however, the Mi-4 was much closer to the later Sikorsky S-58 in terms of weights and payload, being powered by a 1,700 hp Shvetsov radial piston engine driving a four-bladed main wood/metal main rotor and a three-bladed tail rotor. With the nose-mounted powerplant and stepped-up cockpit, the whole of the rear fuselage was available for passengers and freight, and access to this area of some 16 m^3 (565 cu ft) was much enhanced by the use of clamshell doors under the tailboom. A ventral gondola under the cabin provided a navigation position in some variants.

Now largely disappearing from front-line service the Mi-4 'Hound' has operated in both the transport and the ASW role with a number of countries. This machine of the Soviet Navy features the chin radome and aft-stowed MAD gear of the ASW variant.

The prototype Mi-4, configured in a basic utility trooping role made its initial flight at the Mil plant in August 1952 and early production aircraft were first seen in public one year later. These machines carried up to 14 combat-equipped troops, small vehicles or up to 1,600 kg (3,528 lb) of supplies and entered service in large numbers with the Soviet Army. Subsequently, some aircraft also operated in the armed close-support role, fitted with a machine gun in an under-fuselage gondola and side-mounted air-to-surface rockets. Designated 'Hound-A' by NATO, this basic military Mi-4 also entered service with virtually all the Warsaw Pact air arms as well as being exported to a number of Soviet-friendly countries.

Two other production versions of the Mi-4 were also developed by Mil for Soviet military use. The first of these, known to NATO as 'Hound-B', was for anti-submarine duties with the Soviet Navy and introduced a chin-mounted search radar and a dipping sonar. Later machines also carried a towed MAD unit, stowed immediately behind the cabin beneath the tailboom. Sonobuoys were stowed on side-mounted racks below the cockpit and the aircraft could carry a limited selection of anti-submarine weaponry, including torpedoes.

'Hound-C' was the NATO reporting name given to an Electronic Counter-measures variant of the Mi-4, converted from the basic production aircraft with jamming equipment installed and recognisable by the additional lateral antennae. Three civil versions of the Mi-4 were also produced, for operation by Aeroflot in utility, passenger, ambulance and crop-spraying roles.

With more than 3,000 Mi-4s built during the 1950-1960s period, large numbers are still operational with second-line support units in the Soviet Union, as well as with a number of Warsaw Pact and other countries. The aircraft was the first helicopter to enter licence production in China, which built several hundered under the designation H-5 for her armed forces. The conversion of these to a turboshaft configuration, using American powerplants, has recently been considered but no go-ahead has yet been announced.

Technical specifications

Helicopter Mil Mi-4
Type Transport and general purpose
Year 1952
Engine 1,700 hp Shvetsov Ash-82V
Rotor diameter 21.00 m (68 ft 11 in)
Fuselage length 16.80 m (55 ft 1 in)
Height 5.18 m (17 ft)
Empty weight 5,268 kg (11,614 lb)
Gross weight 7,800 kg (17,195 lb)
Maximum speed 210 km/h at 1,500 m (155 mph at 4,920 ft)
Service ceiling 5,500 m (18,045 ft)
Range 250 km (155 miles)
Capacity 2 crew + observer, up to 14 combat-equipped troops, small vehicles or 1,600 kg (3,528 lb) of freight
Armament 1 × machine gun, air-to-surface rockets

Mi-6/Mi-10 'Hook/Harke'

Development of the Mil Mi-6 began in the early 1950s with the availability of suitable turboshaft power for large helicopters. The design followed the traditional Mil layout, with no attempt to move to tandem-rotor or other more exotic heavy-lift designs as was then being practised in the West.

A large five-bladed all-metal main rotor and four-bladed tail rotor were driven, via a heavy-weight transmission, by two 5,500 shp Soloviev D-25V engines mounted atop the forward fuselage. A virtually unobstructed 12 m (39 ft) long cargo bay terminated in clamshell doors beneath the tailboom at the rear, and a generous flight deck with extensive nose glazing at the front. A sturdy fixed tricycle undercarriage guaranteed rough-field operations and auxiliary stub wings were made available to offload the main rotor during missions which involved lengthy cruising flight.

The first of five prototype Mi-6s flew in the autumn of 1957, as the first turbine-powered Soviet helicopter and the largest helicopter in the world. These were followed in 1960 by a pre-production batch of 30 aircraft which were used for role evaluation and the setting up of 14 world records. These included a 100 km (62 mile) closed-circuit speed record of 183.67 knots (211 mph/ 335 km/h), which is still current, and the lifting of a 25,105 kg (55,345 lb) payload to an altitude of 2,840 m (9,317 ft).

As a heavy-lift helicopter, the Mi-6 introduced major tactical assault capability to the Soviet armed forces, being able to carry upwards of 60 equipped troops. The cabin floor is stressed to support a 2,000 kg/m^2 (4,409 lb/m^2) load and offers 2.5 m (8.2 ft) maximum height clearance inside the hold, allowing the internal carriage of armoured and other vehicles or complete missile units. In the ambulance role, the aircraft can carry 41 stretcher cases with two medical attendants, while in the pure heavy-lift role, 11,000 kg (24,255 lb) of cargo can be slung from the single-point hook.

Identified by NATO as 'Hook', more than 800 Mi-6s were built before production was terminated in the early 1970s, and all but about 30 entered service inside the Soviet Union, either with the Soviet military or with Aeroflot. The latter uses the type to support on-shore mineral exploration, construction projects and freight/passenger services in remote areas but, like all Soviet civil aircraft, these Mi-6s are readily available to meet military needs if required.

In 1961 a new variant of the Mi-6 appeared, introducing a much slimmer fuselage with a 28 passenger capacity, and an elongated heavy duty undercarriage designed to straddle large outsize loads. The dynamics of the standard Mi-6 were retained.

Until the advent of the Mi-26, the Mi-6 'Hook' was the largest helicopter in military service anywhere in the world and is still operational as a heavy lift transport. This machine is one of a small number still in Egyptian Air Force service.

By deleting much of the lower fuselage and introducing a revised undercarriage Mil succeeded in developing a crane-variant of the Mi-6, designated the Mi-10. Up to 60 airccraft are still in Soviet service.

Designated the Mi-10, (and by NATO as 'Harke') this version entered relatively limited production as a specialist flying crane, able to carry up to 8,000 kg (17,637 lb) as a slung load, with TV monitoring of both the load and the undercarriage. A special wheeled platform was designed to accommodate suitable freight loads, locked into position under the fuselage with hydraulic struts. This method of carriage could also be used for certain bulk items, such as prefabricated buildings or containers, and increased the payload capacity of the aircraft to 15,000 kg (33,073 lb).

The standard Mi-10, known to NATO as 'Harke', entered service with both the Soviet military and Aeroflot and was joined in 1966 by the Mi-10K. This version introduced a shorter undercarriage and lighter weight narrow chord tail pylon, together with an aft-facing crew station under the nose, complete with its own set of flying controls. The TV monitoring arrangement was deleted and the crew reduced from three to two. The Mi-10K was dedicated almost solely to underslung load work, although the cabin area was retained, and the lightening of the structure etc allowed an increase in the slung payload to 11,000 kg (24,255 lb).

Technical specifications

Helicopter Mil Mi-6
Type Heavy assault transport
Year 1957
Engine 2 × 5,500 shp Soloviev D-25V turbines
Rotor diameter 35.00 m (114 ft 10 in)
Fuselage length 33.18 m (108 ft 10 in)
Overall length 41.74 m (136 ft 11 in)
Height 9.86 m (32 ft 4 in)
Empty weight 27,240 kg (60,053 lb)
Gross weight 42,500 kg (93,695 lb)
Maximum speed 300 km/h (186 mph)
Service ceiling 4,500 m (14,764 ft)
Range 620 km (385 miles)
Capacity 5 crew + 65-90 passengers or 12,000 kg (26,455 lb), or 70 combat-equipped troops
Armament 1 × 12.7 mm machine gun

Technical specifications

Helicopter Mil Mi-10
Type Flying crane
Year 1961
Engine 2 × 5,500 shp Soloviev D-25V turbines
Rotor diameter 35.00 m (114 ft 10 in)
Fuselage length 32.86 m (107 ft 10 in)
Overall length 41.89 m (137 ft 5 in)
Height 9.90 m (32 ft 6 in)
Empty weight 27,000 kg (59,525 lb)
Gross weight 43,450 kg (95,790 lb)
Maximum speed 202 km/h (125 mph)
Service ceiling 3,000 m (9,840 ft)
Range 250 km (155 miles)
Capacity 2 pilots + 28 passengers; 11,000 kg (24,255 lb) slung load

Mi-8/Mi-14/Mi-17 'Hip/Haze'

Above: The Mil Mi-8, in widespread service with the Warsaw Pact, has also been successfully exported to a number of other countries where it serves as a troop transport and utility helicopter. 24512 is one of 10 Mi-8s in service with the Pakistan Army (L. T. Peacock).

Below: Designated 'Haze' by NATO, the Mi-14 is a naval variant of the Mi-8, especially configured for ASW and similar over-water operations. This machine is one of at least 100 in service with the Soviet Navy.

Relatively small numbers of Mi-14s have entered service outside the Soviet Union. This machine operates with the Polish Air Force in the ASW and SAR role.

Parallelling the success of the Mi-2 in 1961, which took the Mi-1 dynamics and married them to turboshaft engines and a new fuselage, the Mil design team attempted to repeat this exercise with the Mi-4 by introducing a 2,700 shp Soloviev powerplant and redesigning the main fuselage to provide much increased capacity. The new aircraft retained the tailboom, tail rotor and four-bladed main rotor of its piston-engined predecessor and, designated Mi-8, began flight trials in 1961.

Early tests, however, showed that the new design was underpowered and, in September 1962, a second prototype appeared with twin 1,500 shp engines replacing the single powerplant, while the first prototype was re-engineered to flight test a new five-bladed main rotor.

Thus modified, production of the Mi-8 got underway in 1964, against major orders from the Soviet and Warsaw Pact armed forces, with whom it entered service as their primary tactical transport helicopter. As a utility trooping aircraft, the Mi-8 carries up to 32 equipped soldiers, all of whom can exit rapidly through the rear clamshell doors. The latter also provide easy access for the loading of cargo or 12 ambulance stretchers, while 3,000 kg (6,614 lb) of freight can be carried underslung. Designated 'Hip-C' by NATO, this basic variant also features a forward passenger door with a winch overhead for rescue operations, and can carry a largely defensive armament of air-to-ground rockets mounted in racks on either side of the fuselage.

At least six other basic variants of the Mi-8 have also been identified, including the 'Hip-D' and 'Hip-G', which introduce additional antennae and other modifications for the airborne communications role. Similarly, the 'Hip-J' and 'Hip-K' are dedicated electronic countermeasures aircraft, with special antenna arrays and communications jamming equipment.

The 'Hip-E' is a heavily armed attack variant, carrying a triple stores rack on each side of the fuselage with up to 192 rockets in pods plus four 'Swatter' anti-tank missiles. In addition a 12.7 mm machine gun is fitted on a flexible mount in the nose. 'Hip-E' is in widespread Soviet military service and has an export equivalent, 'Hip-F', which carries six 'Sagger' missiles in place of the 'Swatter'.

Production of the Mi-8 had topped 8,000 by 1985, with some 1,600 in Soviet military service plus others with Aeroflot and the Warsaw Pact forces. The aircraft has also been successfully exported to a number of overseas air forces.

Some of these overseas customers, notably those in the Middle East and other hot/high areas, are considering the re-engining of their aircraft with the 1,800 shp Turboméca Makila engine. Feasibility studies have been carried out by the powerplant manufacturer, but no conversions have yet been undertaken.

Now entering service with several overseas countries, following deliveries to the Warsaw Pact nations, the Mi-17 is effectively a more powerful version of the Mi-8 for operation in hot/high environments. All Aeroflot helicopters incidentally are available for military use.

Meanwhile, production of a specialised anti-submarine version, the Mi-14, had also been initiated in 1973 to meet a Soviet Navy requirement. The Mi-14 introduced uprated 1,900 shp Isotov TV-3 engines, and an amphibious lower fuselage with a boat hull outline. In addition, the tail rotor was moved to the port side of the aircraft and the fixed undercarriage replaced by quadricycle retractable landing gear.

Operational equipment for the Mi-14 includes a chin-mounted search radome, a retractable sonar unit aft of the weapons bay, and a towed magnetic anomally detector stowed immediately aft of the cabin. Torpedoes and depth charges can be carried fully enclosed in the ventral weapons bay.

Known to NATO as 'Haze-A', the Mi-14 has now replaced the Mi-4 with Soviet Navy shore-based ASW units and some 100 are currently in service. Also operational is a mine countermeasures version, 'Haze-B', which deletes the MAD installation and features a fuselage strake and pod on the starboard side of the fuselage.

Limited numbers of Mi-14s have also been exported to Cuba and Libya, as well as to Warsaw Pact countries, and production is continuing.

In 1981, Mil introduced another new family development, the Mi-17, which married the uprated powerplants and improved dynamics system of the Mi-14 to the original Mi-8 transport fuselage. The resultant aircraft, known as 'Hip-H' to NATO, offers a substantially improved hot/high performance over the Mi-8, with a single-engine contingency rating of 2,200 shp. Apart from the changed tail rotor position, the Mi-17 is readily identifiable by its shorter engine nacelles, characteristic of the TV-3 powerplant installation.

Mi-17 production is being carried out to meet both Soviet and export requirements, with Cuba being the first overseas customer.

Technical specifications

Helicopter Mil Mi-8
Type Assault transport
Year 1962
Engine 2 × 1,500 shp Isotov TV2-117
Rotor diameter 21.29 m (69 ft 10 in)
Fuselage length 18.31 m (60 ft)
Overall length 25.24 m (82 ft 10 in)
Height 5.65 m (18 ft 6 in)
Empty weight 7,417 kg (16,350 lb)
Gross weight 12,000 kg (26,455 lb)
Maximum speed 230 km/h (143 mph)
Hovering ceiling IGE 1,320 m (4,330 ft)
Service ceiling 4,500 m (14,765 ft)
Range 360 km (224 miles)
Capacity 2 crew + 28 passengers

Helicopter Mil Mi-14
Type Amphibious anti-submarine
Year 1976
Engine 2 × 1,900 shp Isotov TV3-117 turbines
Rotor diameter 21.29 m (69 ft 10 in)
Fuselage length 18.15 m (59 ft 6 in)
Overall length 25.30 m (83 ft)
Height 6.90 m (22 ft 7.75 in)
Empty weight n/a
Gross weight 12,000 kg (26,455 lb)
Maximum speed 230 km/h (143 mph)
Hovering ceiling IGE 1,600 m (5,250 ft)
Range 200 km (124 miles)
Capacity 4 - 5 crew
Armament Torpedoes, depth charges

Mi-24 'Hind'

The Mi-24, better known worldwide by its NATO reporting name of 'Hind', was originally proposed by the Mil design bureau as a specialised escort and anti-tank gunship helicopter in the late 1960s, at a time when the US Army was already gaining such experience with the smaller Bell AH-1 Cobra in Vietnam, and had ordered large numbers of the disastrously unsuccessful heavyweight Lockheed AH-56 Cheyenne (cancelled in 1972).

The Soviet Defence Ministry, however, rejected the original proposal in favour of one which incorporated an assault troop capability. Mil then redesigned the basic layout around the dynamics of the Mi-8 to provide a cabin for eight combat-equipped soldiers plus a crew of four in an extensively glazed cockpit. Shoulder-mounted stub wings could carry a variety of weaponry for anti-armour and fire suppression in the assault zone, while a retractable tricycle undercarriage and deeper tailboom, culminating in a broad chord tail fin, minimised any resemblance to the Mi-8 origins.

Prototypes of the Mi-24 were probably flying by 1971, since pre-production aircraft (later designated 'Hind-B') were apparently in limited service with the Soviet forces in 1972. By early 1973 production Mi-24s, designated 'Hind-A' and introducing 16 degrees of anhedral to the stub wings together with additional weapon pylons, were in service alongside the 'Hind-B' with at least two units in East Germany. Their battle training experience soon proved the value of the aircraft in both the anti-tank and escort role, and the Mi-24 soon found itself also in an anti-helicopter role defending the troop-carrying Mi-8.

The 'Hind-A' armament included four AT-2 'Swatter' anti-tank missiles on rails under the wingtip endplate pylons, four underwing pylons for podded rockets, bombs or other stores, and a single 12.7 mm DShK machine gun in the nose, slaved to a chin-mounted sighting system.

The Mi-24 'Hind' has long been the epitome of Soviet attack helicopter philosophy, with close to 2,000 available to the Warsaw Pact forces and others exported farther afield. This Mi-24 'Hind-D' of the Polish Air Force displays its heavy armament and other equipment, including a dorsal-mounted IR jammer.

The 'Hind-E' is the latest identified Mi-24 variant, with modified wing-tip launchers for four AT-6 'Spiral' anti-tank missiles. The further modified 'Hind-E' seen here has the nose gun turret replaced by a twin-barrel 23 mm cannon mounted on the starboard side of the front fuselage.

With the availability of the more powerful 2,200 shp TV3-117 engines to replace the original 1,700 Isotov TV2-117 powerplants, the Mil bureau was able to improve the performance and, at the same time, moved the tail rotor from the starboard

to the port side of the tailfin. Late production 'Hind-As' standardised on this layout, as did the 'Hind-C', which further deleted the nose gun and the wingtip missile rails. It was a special version of the 'Hind-C', known as the A-10, which set up a series of world records from 1975 onwards, including the current overall helicopter speed record of 198.9 knots (228.9 mph/368.4 km/h).

The improvement in power also enabled Mil to produce a new, more heavily armoured variant, optimised for the gunship role while still providing a transport capability. Based on the late production 'Hind-A', the new version featured a completely new nose section, with stepped tandem cockpits for the pilot and weapons operator, and a chin turret multi-barrel 12.7 mm machine gun installation slaved to an undernose sighting system. Also introduced under the nose was a radar and sensor pack, necessitating a slightly lengthened nosewheel leg to ensure adequate ground clearance. Armouring the aircraft against small arms fire from the ground involved the replacement of aluminium by steel and titanium to protect critical components, including the crew, and the introduction of glassfibre skinned rotor blades instead of the original metal blade pocket design.

Eventually, the 'Hind-D' superseded the earlier marks on the Arsenyev and Rostov assembly lines, with over 1,000 aircraft in service by 1985. This includes a growing number of 'Hind-E' variants with modified wingtip launchers for four AT-6 'Spiral' anti-tank missiles and an enlarged undernose sensor pod. Also in operation is a modified 'Hind-E', with the nose gun turret replaced by a twin-barrel 23 mm cannon mounted in a semi-cylindrical fairing on the starboard side of the front fuselage. Some sources designate this version the Mi-25.

'Hind-D/E' production in 1985 was continuing at the rate of some 15 per month to meet Soviet and export demand, with overseas operators including Algeria, Iraq, Libya and Cuba. The aircraft has also been operated since December 1979 by Soviet forces in Afghanistan.

Technical specifications (estimated)

Helicopter Mil Mi-24 (Hind-A)
Type Assault
Year 1971
Engine 2 × 2,200 shp Isotov TV3-117 turbines
Rotor diameter 17.00 m (55 ft 9 in)
Overall length 17.00 m (55 ft 9 in)
Height 6.50 m (21 ft 4 in)
Empty weight 8,400 kg (18,520 lb)
Gross weight 11,000 kg (24,250 lb)
Maximum speed 320 km/h (199 mph)
Service ceiling 4,500 m (14,750 ft)
Capacity 4 crew + 8 combat-equipped troops
Armament 1 machine gun, 4 anti-tank missiles + rockets; weapon load: 1,275 kg (2,810 lb)

Mi-26 'Halo'

Development by Mil of the Mi-26 heavy-lift helicopter began in the early 1970s to provide an updated successor to the Mi-6 for day/night operation and with increased capability.

Although superficially similar to the Mi-6, and following the Soviet tradition of building on success rather than leapfrogging into untried technology, the Mi-26 offers considerable advantages over the earlier aircraft. In particular the new helicopter was designed to meet a specification that included a gross weight of 56,000 kg (123,458 lb), making it the heaviest production helicopter yet flown anywhere in the world, but with an empty weight not exceeding half this figure.

In order to achieve this requirement without jeopardising reliability, the Mil team concentrated initially on improving the Mi-6 dynamics, in particular the main rotor system and gearbox. The latter, designed in-house, was engineered to save weight and at the same time to absorb up to 20,000 hp from the new 11,400 shp Lotarev D-136

turboshaft engines. The main rotor hub was manufactured of titanium, again to save weight, but introduced two extra blades, making a total of eight. Blade construction was of fibreglass over a one-piece tubular spar, with built-in twist and taper in thickness towards the tip, and leading edge anti-icing elements. Rotor diameter was reduced slightly compared with the Mi-6. Similar construction techniques were employed for the five-blade tail rotor.

Since its public debut in the early 1980s, the Mi-26 has entered service both with the Soviet military and Aeroflot on heavy lift operations. As yet this impressive helicopter has not been reported in service outside the Soviet Union.

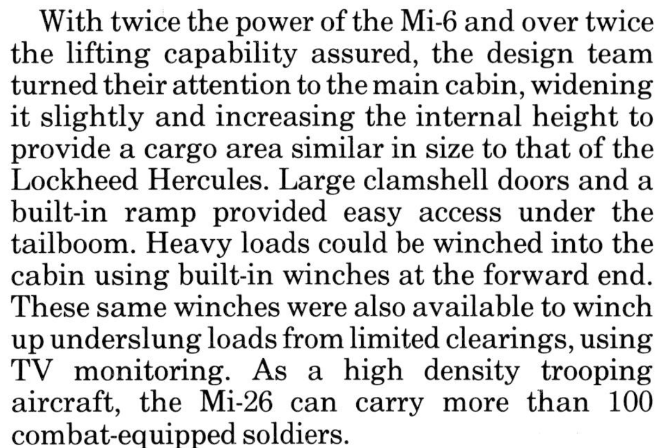

With twice the power of the Mi-6 and over twice the lifting capability assured, the design team turned their attention to the main cabin, widening it slightly and increasing the internal height to provide a cargo area similar in size to that of the Lockheed Hercules. Large clamshell doors and a built-in ramp provided easy access under the tailboom. Heavy loads could be winched into the cabin using built-in winches at the forward end. These same winches were also available to winch up underslung loads from limited clearings, using TV monitoring. As a high density trooping aircraft, the Mi-26 can carry more than 100 combat-equipped soldiers.

Forward of the cabin was a four-seat passenger compartment, behind a revised flight deck layout, which placed the navigator and flight engineer behind the pilot and co-pilot and above a solid nose housing the weather radar and other avionics. Finally, the undercarriage retained a tricycle layout but with the main wheels tucked in close to the fuselage and with a kneeling ability to facilitate operations from minimally prepared sites in the Soviet outback.

The first of several prototype/pre-production Mi-26 flew on 14 December 1977 and, by the time the aircraft was first shown to the public at the 1981 Paris Air Show, the flight test programme was virtually complete. Production began soon afterwards and the first aircraft were confirmed in service, probably with a single Soviet air force trials unit, in early 1983. Meanwhile, in February 1982, a Mi-26 set five world helicopter payload-to-height records, including 25,000 kg (55,113 lb) to 4,100 m (13,451 ft) and 56,768.8 kg (125,156 lb) to 2,000 m (6,562 ft).

In 1985 the aircraft, identified by NATO as 'Halo', was in production to meet Soviet military and Aeroflot orders, with several dozen in service, including some operational with Soviet forces in Afghanistan.

Technical specifications

Helicopter Mil Mi-26
Type Heavy transport
Year 1977
Engine 2 × 11,400 shp Lotarev D-136 turbines
Rotor diameter 32.00 m (105 ft)
Fuselage length 33.72 m (110 ft 7 in)
Overall length 40.025 m (131 ft 3.75 in)
Height 8.05 m (26 ft 5 in)
Empty weight 28,200 kg (62,170 lb)
Gross weight 49,500 kg (109,128 lb)
Maximum speed 295 km/h (183 mph)
Service ceiling 1,800 m (5,900 ft) hovering
Range 800 km (500 miles)
Capacity 5 crew + 90 combat-equipped troops, or 70-100 passengers, or 5,000 kg (11,023 lb)

Mi-28 'Havoc'

The Mi-28, known under the reporting name of 'Havoc' by NATO, was designed by the Mil bureau in the late 1970s as a dedicated ground and air-to-air attack helicopter, using experience gained with the Mi-24 but with much improved manoeuvrability and a greatly reduced cross-section as a result of the deletion of a trooping role.

Prototype aircraft were flying by 1984, revealing an external layout similar to that of the US Army AH-64 Apache but with decidedly stepped tandem cockpits as on the Mi-24. The five blade main rotor is believed to have been developed from the Mi-24 system, but possibly with a new titanium head. The power is provided by two new front-drive turboshafts, shoulder-mounted and producing an estimated 1,350 shp apiece. Estimated gross weight of the Mi-28 is 7,100 kg (15,653 lb), heavier than the Apache, but with a better payload capability in the region of 1,200 kg (2,646 lb) plus fuel.

Nose-mounted systems appear to give the Mi-28 day/night vision and radar sensor and sighting capabilities, while armament includes a ventrally-mounted 23 mm gun turret and a mix of AT-6 'Spiral' anti-tank and SA-14 air-to-air missiles on four stub wing pylons.

Initially the production status of the Mi-28 was unclear and the prototypes were believed to have been participating in competitive evaluation against the Kamov 'Hokum', which also appeared to be optimised for nap-of-the-earth anti-armour and anti-helicopter warfare. More recently however the Mi-28 has entered production as a successor to the Mi-24 in the anti-armour role.

Technical specifications (estimated)

Helicopter Mi-28
Type Attack
Year 1984
Engine 2 × 1,350 shp
Rotor diameter 17.00 m (55 ft 9 in)
Fuselage length 17.40 m (57 ft 1 in)
Overall length n/a
Height n/a
Empty weight n/a
Gross weight 7,100 kg (15,653 lb)
Maximum speed 300 km/h (186 mph)
Hovering ceiling IGE n/a
Service ceiling n/a
Range 240 km (149 miles)
Capacity 2 crew
Armament Anti-tank and air-to-air missiles, 23 mm gun turret

Seen so far only on trials in Afghanistan, the new Mi-28 is expected to succeed the 'Hind' as the Soviet Union's main attack helicopter.

32

Schweizer-Hughes TH-T55/ Model 300

Also known as the Model 269, the current Hughes 300 Series originated in September 1955 as a simple two-seat light helicopter, powered by a 180 hp Lycoming HIO-360 piston engine and using a three-bladed main rotor system taken directly from one end of the one-off 1951 McCulloch MC-4 tandem-rotor design.

As a commercial helicopter the prototype Model 269, N78P, first flew in October 1956 and, by the years end, had been demonstrated to a US Army military evaluation team, which was considering the design as a light observation helicopter in competition with the Sud Aviation Djinn and the Brantly B2. In 1957-58 examples of all three types were ordered by the US Army for military trials, with five improved Model 269As being subsequently delivered to Fort Rucker under the designation YHO-2-HU.

In the event, the US Army decided not to pursue the light observation helicopter specification, but Hughes used the trials data and experience to further improve the design, leading to civil production of the Model 269A as a utility and pilot training machine. In 1964, after some 300 examples had been produced, there was renewed US Army interest in the aircraft for the basic pilot training role, and this crystallised in an order for 20 Model 269As later that year.

Designated the TH-55A Osage, the first aircraft (64-18001) was delivered to Fort Rucker in November 1964. Subsequently a total of 792 TH-55As entered US Army service between 1964 and March 1969, and the type is still in use as the Army's primary trainer.

Meanwhile Hughes continued development of the basic design, including the three-seat Model 269B and leading to the improved Model 269C or 300C in August 1969. This introduced a more powerful 190 hp Lycoming HIO-360-D1A engine, and changes to the dynamic system to accommodate increased diameter main and tail rotors. Payload was increased by 45 percent over the earlier versions.

Overseas military sales of the Model 269/300 family have included 38 aircraft for the Japanese Ground Self Defence Force, licence-built by Kawasaki, while others have been sold direct to Algeria (8), Brazil (20), Colombia (6), Ghana (6), India (10), Spain (17), and a number of other countries. In addition, a licence to manufacture the type is held by BredaNardi in Italy.

The Hughes TH-55A has been the US Army basic trainer since 1966 and continues in service supported by the new Schweizer manufacturing organisation.

Above: The improved Schweizer-Hughes Model 300C continues in production for both military and civil customers. These three aircraft were the first of 24 being delivered to Thailand in 1986.

In 1983, as part of a reorganisation of Hughes and its subsequent amalgamation with McDonnell Douglas, the US production rights for the 300C were sold to Schweizer Aircraft of New York. The first Schweizer-built aircraft flew in June 1984 and this company is continuing to market and produce the 300C for military and civil use, as well as providing support and spares for the earlier machines.

Technical specifications

Helicopter Hughes Model 269A
Type Trainer/general purpose
Year 1960
Engine 180 hp Lycoming H10-360-A1A
Rotor diameter 7.71 m (25 ft 3 in)
Fuselage length 6.80 m (22 ft 4 in)
Overall length 8.80 m (28 ft 10 in)
Height 2.66 m (8 ft 9 in)
Empty weight 474 kg (1,045 lb)
Gross weight 757 kg (1,669 lb)
Maximum speed 144 km/h (90 mph)
Hovering ceiling IGE 2,895 m (9,500 ft)
Service ceiling 4,460 m (14,630 ft)
Range 480 km (298 miles)
Capacity Pilot + 2 passengers

Sikorsky S-55

The S-55 was originally developed by Sikorsky in the mid-1940s as a 12-seat utility helicopter, powered by the proven Pratt & Whitney R-1340 radial piston engine, and designed to meet a US Air Force requirement.

The aircraft adopted the classic Sikorsky rotor layout, with a three-blade main rotor and two-blade tail rotor at the end of a narrow boom, but mounted the powerplant at a 45 degree angle in the nose, with a canted driveshaft connecting it to a main gearbox installed above the cabin roof and behind the raised two-seat cockpit. A quadricycle fixed undercarriage provided ground stability. This layout provided a boxy main cabin with easy access, and proved an almost instant success.

Ordered by the USAF, the first of five prototypes (49-2012 – 2016), designated the YH-19, made its initial flight on 21 November 1949. These were followed by an order for 56 H-19As with the uprated 600 hp R-1340-57 engine and other production improvements. Concurrently ten similar HO4S-1 and 60 HRS-1 variants were ordered by the US Navy for transport and Marine assault duties.

The introduction of the 700 hp Wright R-1300 radial engine led to the H-19B in 1952, 266 of which were built for the USAF including some for transfer to friendly countries. A further 291 were built for the US Navy as the HO4S-3 and HRS-2/HRS-3. Some of these were also transferred to overseas operators.

The type also entered service in the early 1950s with the US Army, the H-19C Chickasaw being the equivalent of the H-19A and the H-19D introducing the Wright powerplant. A total of 373 in total were delivered to the US Army before production ended. In all Sikorsky built 1,067 S-55s for military customers, while a further 547 were built by overseas licensees. These included Westland in Great Britain, which developed a turbine-engined variant for the Royal Air Force, the Whirlwind Mk 10, powered by the 1,050 shp Rolls Royce Gnome turboshaft, and an export/commercial equivalent, the WS-55 Series 3. This was later followed by S-55T turboshaft conversions in the United States.

The large number of S-55s built, and their ready availability following retirement from the US services, has led to the type still being offered for sale by specialist overhaul and rebuild companies such as Orlando Helicopters in Florida, while small numbers of UH-19s remain operational with several Third World military operators.

Technical specifications

Helicopter Sikorsky S-55 (H-19C)
Type Transport and general purpose
Year 1952
Engine 608 hp Pratt & Whitney R-1340-57
Rotor diameter 16.15 m (53 ft)
Fuselage length 12.85 m (42 ft 2 in)
Overall length 19.07 m (62 ft 7 in)
Height 4.066 m (13 ft 4 in)
Empty weight 2,245 kg (4,950 lb)
Gross weight 3,266 kg (7,200 lb)
Maximum speed 162 km/h (100 mph)
Hovering ceiling IGE 1,950 m (6,397 ft)
Service ceiling 3,218 m (10,558 ft)
Range 650 km (400 miles)
Capacity 2 crew + 10 troops or 1,296 kg (2,857 lb)

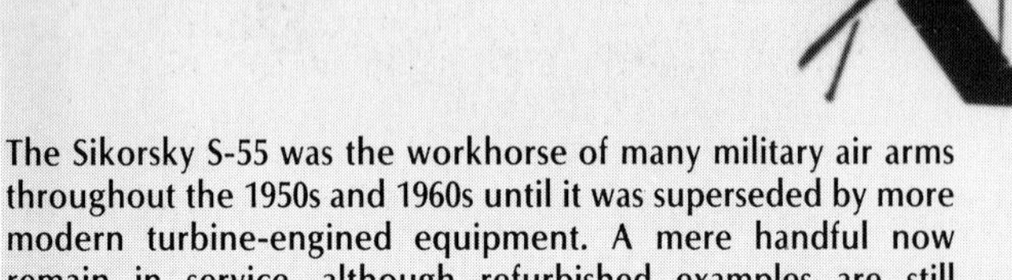

The Sikorsky S-55 was the workhorse of many military air arms throughout the 1950s and 1960s until it was superseded by more modern turbine-engined equipment. A mere handful now remain in service, although refurbished examples are still available on the market.

ARINES
HMR-161
HR-11

Sikorsky S-58

Sikorsky built large numbers of their S-58 for the US military, including the Army H-34. Many of these subsequently found their way to other air arms under US aid schemes or by resale.

Early trials by the US Navy with the Sikorsky S-55 in the anti-submarine warfare role quickly showed the need for a larger and more powerful aircraft to meet the potential search and attack capability of the helicopter in this role.

The new requirement was issued to the industry in 1952 and Sikorsky met the challenge by stretching the basic S-55, and introducing the more powerful 1,525 Wright R-1820 piston engine driving an upgraded transmission with four-bladed main and tail rotors. Other changes included the adoption of a tailwheel tricycle undercarriage and additional fuel capacity. The basic cabin layout provided room for up to 18 passengers or eight stretchers.

Designated by Sikorsky as the S-58, but initially ordered by the US Navy as the XHSS-1, the first of three prototypes (BuAer 134668) made its initial flight on 8 March 1954, with the first production HSS-1 Seabat following only six months later on 20 September. A total of 215 HSS-1s were built for the US Navy to serve in an anti-

With the availability of the turboshaft engine, Sikorsky was able to develop the S-58T variant, built by conversion of earlier aircraft and marketed today by California Helicopters. This machine is one of 18 in Thai military service. (A. Balch).

submarine role, with two systems operators in the main cabin. In this role the aircraft could carry two Mk 44 homing torpedoes in addition to the crew of four and the necessary ASW avionics. The HSS-1 entered operational US Navy service in August 1955 and was subsequently followed by 156 HSS-1Ns, which introduced automatic stabilisation and other equipment to provide a day-night IFR and auto-hover capability. In 1962 all HSS-1 and HSS-1N aircraft were redesignated SH-34G and SH-34J respectively, by which time these variants were being superseded in US Navy service by the Sikorsky Sea King.

The cabin size of the S-58 made it ideal for a number of other military tasks, including trooping and SAR work, and resulted in major orders from the US Marine Corps (HUS-1/UH-34D) and the US Army (H-34A Choctaw), and smaller orders from the US Air Force, US Coast Guard and a number of overseas military customers. In total Sikorsky built 1,887 S-58s in various versions, while the type was also built under licence by Sud Aviation in France and, in an anglicised form with turbine powerplant as the Wessex by Westland in the UK.

With its retirement from US military service, large numbers of surplus H-34s became available for refurbishing and resale to existing and new overseas operators. In addition the certification of a US turboshaft conversion, the S-58T in April 1971, using the Pratt & Whitney Canada PT6T-6 TwinPac, offered a new version with a much enhanced performance which has been taken up by the Indonesian and Royal Thai Air Forces. Since December 1981 this latter variant has been marketed and supported by California Helicopter Inc, which has acquired all S-58T rights from Sikorsky.

By 1986 very few piston-engined S-58s remained in military service, but the S-58T variant is likely to remain operational for several years yet.

Technical specifications

Helicopter Sikorsky S-58 (HSS-1, HUS-1)
Type Utility transport
Year 1954
Engine 1,525 hp Wright R-1820-84
Rotor diameter 17.07 m (56 ft)
Fuselage length 14.25 m (46 ft 9 in)
Overall length 20.00 m (65 ft 7 in)
Height 4.86 m (15 ft 11 in)
Empty weight 3,815 kg (8,410 lb)
Gross weight 6,040 kg (13,316 lb)
Maximum speed 198 km/h (123 mph)
Hovering ceiling IGE 1,495 m (4,905 ft)
Service ceiling 2,896 m (9,500 ft)
Range 290 km (180 miles)
Capacity 2 pilots + 16/1,350 kg (2,976 lb)

Sikorsky S-61

The Sikorsky S-61 family incorporates a number of variants as well as others built under licence. Denmark operates the original S-61A on SAR and utility work.

The development of helicopter anti-submarine operations during the early 1950s was inevitably frustrated by the relatively poor payload of such types as the S-55 and S-58, which prevented the realistic carriage of sensors and weaponry over any distances, and the major disadvantage of operating over water in the hover on a single air-cooled engine.

Thus the advent in the mid-1950s of the first turboshaft engines for rotary-wing use was bound to revolutionise design and operation of helicopters in the ASW role. In fact the US Navy contracted with General Electric in 1956 for the development of a suitable turboshaft, the T58, and this began test-flying in a Sikorsky HSS-1F in January 1957. The twin installation quickly demonstrated that it could offer almost twice the power of the previous single piston engine plus a considerable weight saving and immediately led to a US Navy specification for a new ASW helicopter able to carry dunking sonar, an 840 lb (381 kg) weapon load, sufficient fuel for 4 hours endurance and full all-weather/night avionics.

Sikorsky entered the resultant competition with the S-61, a new design which built on dynamics experience gained with earlier Sikorsky helicopters, but otherwise introduced many fundamental changes. The new T58 engines were mounted atop the fuselage, in front of the main gearbox and rotorhead, thus allowing the cockpit to be positioned in the nose with a capacious main cabin immediately behind and extending to the tail section. The main and tail rotors followed conventional Sikorsky practice but were five-bladed, while the main undercarriage could be retracted into outrigger sponsons. Together with a boat hull lower fuselage this arrangement provided the design with a limited amphibious capability.

On 24 December 1957 Sikorsky received a development contract from the US Navy for seven YHSS-2 prototypes, a political designation for the S-61 aimed at suggesting that the new helicopter was simply a variant of the earlier HSS-1 (S-58). The differences no doubt became more apparent when the first YHSS-2, BuAer 147137, flew on 11 March 1959. The early prototypes were all powered by two 1,050 shp General Electric T58-GE-6 engines and during the initial trials programme were able to demonstrate a performance and payload capability comfortably in excess of the 1957 specification. No major aerodynamic problems were encountered, no doubt due to the 12 months experience already gained with the smaller S-62, which bore a strong scaled-down resemblance to the S-61, and the powerplant also benefitted from the two years flight testing already amassed in the HSS-1F.

Trials therefore concentrated on proving the operational equipment intended for the production HSS-2, including a new Bendix AN/AQS-10 dunking sonar and automatic transition to the hover and stabilisation systems, and these were continued in a service environment by the early production aircraft, the first of which rolled off the Sikorsky line in December 1960. Initial deliveries were to US Navy Squadron VHS-1 at Key West in Florida in May 1961 and these were followed by the first operational deliveries, to VHS-3 at Norfolk VA and VHS-10 at San Diego CA, in the September. Soon afterwards Sikorsky used a company development aircraft to set up a new world speed record of 210.6 mph (339 km/h), the first official record over 200 mph (322 km/h).

Only the initial production batch of 20 HSS-2s, now named the Sea King, retained the T58-GE-6 powerplant, as development of this engine rapidly led to the improved 1,250 shp T58-GE-8 becoming available. Also, in 1962, the aircraft designation was standardised under a revised US Navy nomenclature system as the SH-3A.

A total of 245 SH-3As were eventually built for the US Navy, including three examples modified as CH-3B transports for US Air Force offshore support of radar platforms in the Atlantic Ocean. Three further CH-3Bs were later built from scratch, as were eight VH-3A VIP variants ordered in 1961 and allocated to the joint US Marine/Army Executive Flight Detachment in

The SH-3D variant of the Sea King introduced uprated engines and improved sonar, but only 72 production machines were built for the US Navy before it was superseded by the SH-3G. This SH-3D, 152709, was photographed aboard the USS *Enterprise* with HS-2 squadron during the evacuation of Saigon in 1975.

Agusta has supplied a number of SH-3D and SH-3H variants, fitted out with Italian avionics and weapons systems. This is one of several ASH-3s supplied to Peru in recent years.

Washington. A ninth VH-3A was converted from a standard SH-3A. Nine other SH-3As were modified in 1964 into RH-3A mine-countermeasures aircraft with equipment to sweep for moored mines in Vietnam waters, while in 1970 twelve aircraft were converted by the US Navy to HH-3A configuration to carry out armed long-range SAR missions in Vietnam.

With the Sea King established in US Navy service, Sikorsky also began offering the type for export as the S-61A (transport version) and the S-61B (ASW variant). The latter was ordered by Canada as the CHSS-2/CH-124, with 41 being delivered from May 1963, while the S-61A was purchased by the Royal Danish Air Force for SAR/trooping and by Malaysia as the S-61A-4 Nuri. The type has also been built in some numbers under licence in Italy and Japan.

Meanwhile on 17 June 1963, Sikorsky flew the privately-funded S-61R, a more specialised tactical transport variant which resulted in part from design work undertaken in 1959 for a subsequently cancelled US Marine Corps requirement. The S-61R introduced major revisions to the fuselage aft of the cockpit, with an extended cabin terminating in a full-width rear ramp door, and the introduction of a slimmed down tailboom with a new fin and tailplane to ease cabin access and overcome aerodynamic changes. Power was provided by two uprated 1,300 shp GE T58-GE-1 turboshafts, fed from bladder fuel tanks under the cabin floor. Also new was the undercarriage layout, with a semi-retractable twin nose-wheel unit replacing the earlier tail wheel and new enlarged stub wing sponsons housing the main gear. Internally a 2,000 lb (907 kg) capacity winch was installed in the main cabin to ease the loading of up to 5,000 lb (2,268 kg) of cargo. Alternatively, the aircraft could carry up to 25 armed troops. A number of reliability and maintenance modifications were also incorporated, to ease field deployment away from base servicing facilities.

Although the prototype S-61R, N664Y, was company-owned, by the date of its first flight an order from the US Air Force for an initial 22 production aircraft, designated the CH-3C, was already four months old. The first of these, 62-

12577, made its first flight during the late summer of 1963. Deliveries to the USAF at Tyndall AFB in Florida began with 62-12580 on 30 December.

A total of 75 CH-3Cs were eventually built for the USAF before this variant was superseded in 1966 by the CH-3E. This introduced the more powerful 1,500 shp GE T58-GE-5 engines, which enabled the cabin accommodation to be increased to 30 passengers and enhanced hot/high performance. A total of 45 new-build CH-3Es were produced and most of the earlier CH-3Cs were also converted to the new standard.

Further updating during the same period resulted in the HH-3E, developed during 1965-66 to meet an urgent demand for combat-rescue helicopters in Vietnam. Modifications to meet this need included self-sealing fuel tanks, an in-flight refuelling probe, jettisonable long-range fuel tanks, armour protection and provision for limited defensive armament. Gross take-off weight was increased to 22,050 lb (10,002 kg). Fourteen HH-3Es were ordered by the USAF, although six were subsequently cancelled, and a number of CH-3C/CH-3E airframes were also modified to HH-3E configuration. The type entered service with the USAF Aerospace Rescue and Recovery Service in Vietnam during 1966 and was soon nicknamed the 'Jolly Green Giant' in deference to its camouflage colour scheme and ability to travel long distances over jungle terrain, like the advertisement cartoon character of the day.

The CH-3 and HH-3E family did not feature the waterproof lower fuselage developed for the SH-3, but this was included in the HH-3F variant ordered in 1965 by the US Coast Guard. Also new was an offset nose radar and the deletion of the defensive and in-flight refuelling modifications adopted by the HH-3E. A total of 40 HH-3Fs were built for the USCG, with deliveries beginning in 1968. In addition this variant has also been built under licence by Agusta, which to date has delivered over 20 examples as the AS-61R to the Italian Air Force for coastal rescue duties.

Meanwhile Sikorsky had continued development of the original S-61B/SH-3A anti-submarine variant and this led, in 1966, to the improved SH-3D for the US Navy. This standardised on the 1,400 shp GE T58-GE-10 engine, with an uprated main gearbox to handle up to 2,500 hp, which greatly improved the single-engine performance.

Popularly known as the 'Jolly Green Giant', the HH-3E was an armed rescue version of the S-61R, with external fuel tanks and a telescopic refuelling probe among the modifications. This example, 65-12782, was one of a number converted from the earlier CH-3C for the US Air Force.

In addition gross weight was increased to 20,500 lb (9,299 kg) with accompanying structural strengthening. Other changes principally involved improving the operational capability. AN/AQS13A sonar and AN/APN-182 Doppler replaced the earlier models, an AN/ASN-50 heading reference system was added, and the cockpit instrument layout revised. In addition the range was improved by incorporating an extra fuel tank.

A prototype YSH-3D (BuAer 52139) was followed by the first of 22 for the Spanish Navy and 72 production machines for the US Navy. In addition two SH-3As were converted to SH-3D configuration, while a number were exported as the S-61D-4 to the Argentine and Brazilian Navies.

The SH-3D also became the basis of licence-production agreements with Agusta in Italy and Westland in the UK. The latter anglicised and modified the basic aircraft quite considerably (page 170), while Agusta primarily confined changes to the avionics and weapons system. Italian production began in 1967 against an initial order from the Italian Navy for 24 aircraft, designated the ASH-3D, deliveries of which began in 1969. Modifications included the adoption of the 1,500 shp GE T58-GE-100 powerplant, and the introduction of an improved tail plane and some structural strengthening.

Operational development of the ASH-3D led to further changes to fit the aircraft out as a fully integrated all-weather ASW/ASV weapon system, able to operate independently of surface

vessels. Modifications included the adoption of a ventral-mounted SMA/SPS 360 degree search and targetting radar, nose-mounted search radar, and provision for the carriage of homing torpedoes and either medium or long-range air-to-surface missiles.

Orders from the Italian Navy were subsequently followed by several export contracts, in particular for the Imperial Iranian Navy and South American customers. In addition further development by Agusta led to the SH-3D/TS VIP transport for the Italian Air Force and the AS-61A-4 export equivalent which was delivered in small numbers to Iran, Libya and Saudi Arabia.

Sikorsky production of the SH-3 ended in the early 1970s, but conversion programmes ordered by the US Navy subsequently saw 105 SH-3A and SH-3Ds being converted to long-range utility transports as the SH-3G, and 163 being updated to SH-3H standard. This latter configuration involved the installation of new ASW equipment, including MAD and active/passive sonobuoys, ESM gear, and a Canadian Marconi LN66HP search radar under the fuselage to provide a multi-purpose capability. Initial SH-3H conversion contracts were placed with Sikorsky in 1971 and the programme continued into the early 1980s.

The various operational versions of the Sea King currently in service are likely to be largely superseded over the next decade by the new generation of helicopters now appearing, in particular the Sikorsky Seahawk and the European Industries EH 101. However, the availability of new electronic systems and the proven reliability and usefulness of the basic S-61 airframe will ensure it being in service into the next century.

The HH-3F variant was built for the US Coast Guard and the Argentine Air Force by Sikorsky, while others have been produced under licence by Agusta. Seen water-taxying is one of 26 HH-3Fs ordered by the Italian Air Force for the SAR role.

Technical specifications

Helicopter Sikorsky S-61 (SH-3A)
Type Twin turbine anti-submarine
Year 1960
Engine 2 × 1,250 shp General Electric T58-GE-18
Rotor diameter 18.90 m (62 ft)
Fuselage length 16.69 m (54 ft 9 in)
Height 5.13 m (16 ft 10 in)
Empty weight 5,647 kg (12,450 lb)
Gross weight 9,299 kg (20,500 lb)
Maximum speed 267 km/h (166 mph)
Hovering ceiling IGE 3,200 m (10,500 ft)
Service ceiling 4,480 m (14,700 ft)
Range 1,000 km (620 miles)
Capacity 2 pilots + 2/3 operators
Armament 381 kg (840 lb) weapon load -175a

Helicopter Sikorsky S-61R (HH-3F)
Type Amphibious rescue
Year 1965
Engine 2 × 1,500 shp General Electric T58-GE-5
Rotor diameter 18.90 m (62 ft)
Fuselage length 19.05 m (62 ft 6 in)
Overall length 22.25 m (73 ft)
Height 5.51 m (18 ft 1 in)
Empty weight 5,295 kg (11,673 lb)
Gross weight 9,990 kg (22,024 lb)
Maximum speed 264 km/h (164 mph)
Hovering ceiling IGE 2,960 m (9,710 ft)
Service ceiling 4,145 m (13,600 ft)
Range 800 km (497 miles)
Capacity 3 crew + 25 troops or 15 stretchers

Sikorsky S-62

The Sikorsky S-62 married the S-55 dynamics to a single General Electric T58 turboshaft and a new amphibious fuselage. The type is still in service in Japan and the USA on SAR duties, as illustrated by this Coast Guard HH-52A.

The design of the Sikorsky S-62 was initiated in the mid-1950s soon after the arrival of the General Electric T58 turboshaft, which began flight tests in an S-58 airframe in 1956.

Despite its scaled-down visual similarity to the S-61, the S-62 was actually much more closely allied to the well-established S-55 and in fact the first flight of the S-62 prototype, N880, on 14 May 1958, preceded that of the S-61 by ten months. The new helicopter essentially used the dynamic components of the S-55, including the three-bladed main rotor, married to a single 1,050 shp T58 engine derated to 730 shp and mounted horizontally in front of the main gearbox and atop the forward cabin. This arrangement was not only lighter and less bulky than the S-55 piston engine installation, but also allowed the cockpit to be positioned in the nose of the helicopter. Other S-55 components employed included parts of the flying control and hydraulic systems, and the tail rotor pylon, attached to a new rear fuselage section. The centre fuselage contained a main cabin area some 14 ft (4.27 m) long by 5 ft 4 in (1.62 m) wide by 6 ft (1.83 m) high, able to accommodate 8-11 passengers and with direct access to the cockpit. Entry to the cabin was obtained via a large sliding door on the starboard side. The bottom of the fuselage was designed as a watertight structure, with suitable strengthening for water landings and a boat hull layout. In conjunction with this the semi-retractable main undercarriage was installed in outrigger floats, designed to stabilise the aircraft on water. A fixed tailwheel completed the undercarriage arrangement. The resultant helicopter was some 160 lb (72 kg) lighter than the S-55 but with 130 more horsepower available.

Although initially developed and flown as a commercial venture, the S-62 raised some interest among military operators as a potential Search and Rescue and transport helicopter, and this eventually crystallised in 1960 with an order for two examples for the Indian Air Force under the designation S-62C. This sale was the first of several arranged in association with Mitsubishi, which negotiated a licence agreement with Sikorsky and subsequently delivered further S-62Cs to the government of Thailand and the Japanese Air Self-Defence Force. The latter eventually took delivery of a number of S-62Cs, under the designation S-62J, for search and rescue duties.

Meanwhile, evaluation by the US Coast Guard Service in the early 1960s proved the value of the S-62 as a replacement for the HH-34s then in use. The USCG was particularly impressed with the amphibious capability and the result was an order for a new variant, initially designated the HU2S-1G but subsequently known as the HH-52A.

This version introduced the uprated 1,250 shp T58-GE-8 turboshaft, auto-stabilisation, towing equipment and a 4 ft (1.22 m) extending platform that folded out from the cabin door to ease the recovery of survivors during water operations. The first three HH-52As were handed over to the USCG in January 1963 and deliveries eventually totalled 99 aircraft. Twenty years later some 78 were still operational but in 1985 the type began to be superseded in service by the Aérospatiale HH-65A Dolphin and present plans see the HH-52A being totally retired from service by the mid-1990s.

Technical specifications

Helicopter Sikorsky S-62
Type Amphibious Search & Rescue/Transport
Year 1958
Engine 1,250 shp General Electric T58-GE-8 turboshaft
Rotor diameter 16.16 m (53 ft)
Fuselage length 13.58 m (44 ft 6.5 in)
Height 4.33 m (14 ft 2 in)
Empty weight 2,204 kg (4,860 lb)
Gross weight 3,583 kg (7,900 lb)
Maximum speed 148 km/h (92 mph)
Hovering ceiling IGE 5,425 m (17,800 ft)
Service ceiling 2,010 m (6,600 ft)
Range 743 km (462 miles)
Capacity 2 crew + 8-11 passengers

Sikorsky S-64

The development of the Sikorsky S-64 was a natural outcome of the obvious benefits of employing a basic rotary-wing dynamics system as a powerful airborne crane, with minimal excess weight allowing the maximum payload to be carried. The design was also an unusual example of a two-way trans-Atlantic transfer of technology.

In 1955 Westland Helicopters, the UK Sikorsky licensee, began development of their WS-56 Westminster, a proposed transport helicopter which employed the rotor system of the 1953 Sikorsky S-56 Mojave married to an entirely new fuselage. In particular the weighty piston engines of the S-56, two 2,100 hp radials mounted in pods outboard of the main fuselage, were replaced by two 2,900 shp Napier Eland turboshafts mounted atop the forward fuselage ahead of the main gearbox. Originally intended only as a ground rig, the prototype Westminster with a skeletal fuselage structure first flew on 15 June 1958. A second prototype followed in 1959 and the two Westminsters carried out a successful trials programme, including tests of an experimental six-bladed main rotor for Sikorsky, before the project was eventually abandoned in late 1960.

Meanwhile, in March 1959, Sikorsky flew the one-off S-60, which retained the dynamics and powerplants of the S-56 but introduced a simplified spinal fuselage with a three-seat cockpit which included a rearward seating position to permit the monitoring of external loads. During two years of flight testing the S-60 was demonstrated to the US Army and the West German government, both of whom expressed much interest in a projected turboshaft-powered variant. With the experience thus amassed by Westland and Sikorsky, the development of the larger and more powerful S-64 was fairly straightforward and an initial company-sponsored prototype, N325Y, first flew on 9 May 1962.

Designated the S-64A, N325Y followed the basic skeletal form of the S-60, but introduced a nose-wheel undercarriage layout to ease the positioning of bulky loads under the centre fuselage, and a revised cockpit design. Power was provided by two 4,500 shp Pratt & Whitney JFTD12-4A turboshafts, mounted atop the front fuselage and driving a six-bladed main and four-bladed tail rotor system à la Westminster. Trials with N325Y were carried out by the US Army during 1963, and meanwhile Sikorsky built two

CH-54A Tarhes with the 478th Aviation Company in Vietnam rapidly proved their worth to the US Army by recovering many crashed aircraft for repair. Today the type serves only with the US Army National Guard.

further prototypes for evaluation by the West German Army. In the event, the latter opted for the S-65 instead but US Army interest crystallised in the form of an order for six pre-production S-64 helicopters, designated YCH-54A Tarhe.

The first YCH-54A, 64-1402, was delivered in late 1964 and in April 1965 the type set up three new world altitude records, including a climb to 29,341 ft (8,943 m) with a payload of 2,204 lb

Although used primarily as a flying crane, the CH-54A can also carry troops and other equipment in a specially designed fuselage pod. Here the S-64 prototype, N325Y, demonstrates its use.

(1,000 kg). The maximum underslung payload was 20,000 lb (9,080 kg). American involvement in Vietnam, and the need for a helicopter to recover downed aircraft and move heavy equipment, rapidly led to the confirmation of a production contract for the CH-54A following evaluation of four YCH-54As in that theatre during 1965.

Also ordered as a result of the operational trials were 21 universal pods, delivered complete with communications, ventilation and lighting systems and with wheels to simplify ground handling. During the trials up to 87 combat-equipped troops were carried in this manner, thus allowing the CH-54 to double as a transport helicopter. More normal pod loads were 45 troops or 24 ambulance litters; alternatively the pods could be adapted for various other uses, including field command posts, surgical units etc.

A total of 54 production CH-54As were eventually produced for service with US Army heavy-lift units and these were followed by an order for 37 upgraded CH-54Bs, which introduced more powerful 4,800 shp JFTD-2-5A turboshafts, a strengthened transmission, new profile main rotor blades, and twin-wheel main undercarriage units. These modifications increased the gross weight from 42,000 lb (19,050 kg) to 47,000 lb (21,319 kg), giving a useful increase in lift capacity to 12.5 tons and enhancing hot/high performance.

With the end of the Vietnam war, the need for the CH-54 as a front-line aircraft slowly diminished and by the mid-1980s the aircraft remained in service only with the Army National Guard. Despite its uniqueness the type was not sold to any other military operator and is expected to be withdrawn from use once the Boeing Vertol CH-47D becomes widely available.

Technical specifications

Helicopter Sikorsky S-64A 9CH-54A)
Type Flying crane
Year 1965
Engine 2 × 4,500 shp Pratt & Whitney JFTD12-4A
Rotor diameter 21.95 m (72 ft)
Fuselage length 21.41 m (70 ft 3 in)
Overall length 26.97 m (88 ft 6 in)
Height 7.75 m (25 ft 5 in)
Empty weight 8,732 kg (19.250 lb)
Gross weight 19,068 kg (42,037 lb)
Maximum speed 203 km/h (126 mph)
Hovering ceiling IGE 3,230 m (10,600 ft)
Service ceiling 2,743 m (9,000 ft)
Range 370 km (230 miles)
Capacity 3 crew + 9,080 kg (20,000 lb) external load

Sikorsky S-65

The S-65 was specifically developed by Sikorsky in the early 1960s for the heavy assault role with the US Marine Corps, and proved to be a logical progression from the S-64 flying crane and the smaller S-61R/CH-3 transport helicopter.

In some respects it resembled the S-61R, with a fully enclosed fuselage, side sponsons and rear ramp loading, but it was closely allied to the S-64 with the basic dynamics system of this heavy-lift helicopter married to the new fuselage. However, the powerplant arrangement was original, with a Solar T62T-12 turbine, acting as hydraulic engine-start system, located atop the front fuselage in a faired cowling, and the two 2,850 shp General Electric T64-GE-6 turboshafts thus displaced outboard in shoulder mounted positions. In addition the main rotor blades and tail unit featured power-folding and the bottom fuselage was made watertight, to better suit ship-based operations.

From a go-ahead authorised in August 1962, it was just over two years before the first of two S-65 prototypes, 151613, built under a US Navy contract as the YCH-53A, made its initial flight on 14 October 1964. Full production for the USMC began the following year, with a first order for 15 CH-53A Stallions and deliveries began in mid 1966 with an operational deployment to the Vietnam war theatre in January 1967. The initial order was rapidly followed by further contracts leading to the eventual production of 139 CH-53As for the Navy and Marine Corps before this variant was superseded by the improved CH-53D in 1969.

The CH-53D introduced a number of refinements to the original Sikorsky CH-53A, including uprated engines and automatic blade folding. 157132 was one of 126 built for the US Marine Corps and is seen here in service with HMM-164 squadron aboard the USS *Juneau* in mid-1974.

The HH-53 was developed for the US Air Force to provide a long-range combat rescue helicopter for the Vietnam war. This HH-53C shows the long range fuel tanks and retractable flight refuelling probe of the HH-53 series.

All except the initial 32 CH-53As had provision for towed minesweeping gear, and 15 were transferred to the US Navy, re-engined with the 3,925 shp T64-GE-413 powerplant and used for mine countermeasures duties as RH-53As. Another seven CH-53As were transferred to the US Air Force, which in September 1966 had ordered eight new HH-53B variants for its Aerospace Rescue and Recovery Service. These were powered by 3,080 shp T64-GE-3 turboshafts and featured a retractable flight refuelling probe, jettisonable auxiliary fuel tanks, rescue hoist and provision for defensive armament. The first HH-53B flew on 15 March 1967 and deliveries began the following June. A follow-up order was subsequently cancelled in favour of 44 HH-53Cs, which introduced the uprated 3,925 shp T64-GE-7 engine and provision for an external load hook of 20,000 lb (9,070 kg) capacity. The first HH-53C was delivered on 30 August 1968. Later the USAF also took delivery of 20 CH-53Cs for use in the pure transport/freighting role.

The completion of the CH-53D, the first of which was handed over to the USMC on 3 March 1969, saw several further improvements being introduced. These included the uprated engines and a consequent increase in payload, with up to 64 troops being carried in a high-density configuration. A total of 126 CH-53Ds were built, including two converted to VH-53D staff transports. In addition the US Navy took delivery of 30 RH-53D mine countermeasures variants, with provision for air refuelling and light defensive armament, and later retrofitted with 4,380 shp T64-GE-415 engines; six further RH-53Ds were delivered to Iran.

The basic CH-53D was also sold to Israel, which eventually received some 35 examples, including two S-65-Oe variants originally operated by the Austrian Air Force as alpine rescue aircraft. However, the largest export customer for the CH-53 to date has been West Germany, whose Army evaluated two CH-53Ds in 1969 before taking delivery of 110 similar CH-53Gs assembled under licence by VFW-Fokker.

Meanwhile a new specification had been issued by the US Marine Corps, calling for a helicopter able to lift up to 16 tons over a distance of at least

84 01

MARINES

Above: With toned down markings this production CH-53E shows off the third engine and canted tail unit that readily identify the variant, while moving an obsolete F-101 Voodoo.

Top left: No less than 112 CH-53Gs were built for the West German Army, the majority by VFW-Fokker. 84+01 was the first of two aircraft supplied direct by Sikorsky.

Left: The CH-53E for the US Marine Corps, the current production version of the S-65, is a major growth version with a third engine, extra main rotor blade and many other improvements. The result is a helicopter able to handle 93 percent of a Marine infantry division's equipment.

58 miles (93 km), to accommodate the CH-53 and other heavier aircraft and weaponry then entering the inventory. Sikorsky's answer was to substantially upgrade the CH-53 by installing a third engine, increasing the main rotor diameter and adding an extra main blade. To handle the extra power the transmission was uprated and, at the same time, the opportunity was taken to improve survivability, maintainability and flight control.

Designated the YCH-53E, the first of two prototypes, 159121, flew on 1 March 1974, less than 12 months after being ordered. Trials were delayed when it was destroyed in a ground accident in September 1974, but were able to resume when the second prototype achieved flight status in January 1975. Both these early prototypes featured a new tail unit with a low-set

The MH-53E was originally developed by converting this early production CH-53E 159877 as an aerodynamic prototype. Noteworthy are the much enlarged fuel tank sponsons and the outrigged rear view mirrors for the mine countermeasures role.

tailplane, but this was replaced by a weight-saving gull-wing stabiliser on the first pre-production aircraft when it flew in December 1975. Funding delays meant that it was February 1978 before an initial production contract for six CH-53Es was placed with Sikorsky, and December 1980 before the first production aircraft rolled off the line.

Despite the family relationship to the CH-53D, the new variant is substantially different. The three 4,380 shp General Electric T64-GE-416 turboshafts, with the third engine installed behind the rotorhead, generated via the uprated transmission and new main rotor double the lift capacity of the earlier machine for only 50 percent more power. Also new was a digital automatic flight control system, half the weight and size of the CH-53D installation and with a continuous double computer fail-safe capability, and a 6.5 ft (2 m) stretch in the fuselage.

Internally the CH-53E can carry 55 troops in simple fold-up seats, or seven standard cargo pallets. The maximum internal payload, over a 115 mile (185 km) radius, is 30,000 lb (13,610 kg). For the carriage of external loads both single and dual point suspension systems are available. The normal operating range of 300 miles (483 km) can be extended to more than 1,000 miles (1,609 km) by use of auxiliary tanks for self-ferrying, or even further by air-refuelling. Operational deliveries of the CH-53E to the US Marine Corps began in

June 1981, by which time 35 aircraft were on order, including one for US Navy minesweeping trials. Redesignated MH-53E, this variant introduced modified electrical, hydraulic and envrionmental control systems, and expanded flight control computers able to automatically maintain a preset cable skew angle and tow tension for the minesweeping hydrofoil sled. Much enlarged sponson fuel tanks, able to carry an additional 1,000 galls (4,546 litres) fuel, were also introduced to increase endurance.

An aerodynamic prototype MH-53E, converted from an early CH-53E, 159877, began flight testing on 23 December 1981 and was followed by the production prototype in September 1983. Current multi-year procurement contracts allow for the delivery of 29 MH-53E Sea Dragons to the US Navy between FY1986-1989, with eventual orders for this customer expected to reach at least 57 aircraft. In addition the same basic variant is to be evaluated by the Japanese Maritime Self-Defence Force.

CH-53E Super Stallion orders for the US Marine Corps have meanwhile reached 93 aircraft, with deliveries stretched out to FY1989 and total orders expected to eventually exceed 300. By 1986 the type was in service with four USMC squadrons, together with one US Navy unit, at Sigonella in Sicily to provide a vertical on-board delivery and other services for the US Mediterranean fleet.

Sikorsky is currently looking at further upgrading the CH-53E/MH-53E by introducing an all-composite main rotor head and rotor blades, which would improve the hover performance and provide a 3,000 lb (1,361 kg) payload increase. Also planned are uprated T64-418 engines, CRT cockpit layout, Omega navigation system and improvements in night visition, self-defence, crashworthiness, cargo-handling and other areas. Such modifications are expected to allow the aircraft to keep pace with future US Navy and Marine Corps operational needs, thus ensuring continued production into the next century.

Technical specifications

Helicopter Sikorsky S-65A (CH-53A)
Type Tactical transport
Year 1965
Engine 2 × 2,850 shp General Electric T64-GE-6B
Rotor diameter 22.02 m (72 ft 3 in)
Fuselage length 20.47 m (67 ft 2 in)
Overall length 26.90 m (88 ft 3 in)
Height 7.60 m (24 ft 11 in)
Empty weight 10,662 kg (23,505 lb)
Gross weight 15,875 kg (39,760 lb)
Maximum speed 315 km/h (195 mph)
Hovering ceiling IGE 4,084 m (13,400 ft)
Service ceiling 5,660 m (18,570 ft)
Range 415 km (258 miles)
Capacity 3 crew + 37 troops

Helicopter Sikorsky S-65 Super Stallion (CH-53E)
Type Tactical transport
Year 1965
Engine 3 × 4,380 shp General Electric T64-GE-416
Rotor diameter 24.08 m (79 ft)
Fuselage length 22.50 m (73 ft 10 in)
Overall length 30.02 m (98 ft 6 in)
Height 8.46 m (27 ft 9 in)
Empty weight 14,550 kg (32,077 lb)
Gross weight 31,667 kg (69,813 lb)
Maximum speed 315 km/h (195 mph)
Hovering ceiling IGE 3,627 m (10,718 ft)
Service ceiling 3,780 m (12,400 ft)
Range 500 km (310 miles)
Capacity 3 crew + 55 troops

Sikorsky S-70/H-60 Black Hawk

In the mid-1960s the US Army began to assemble a requirement for a replacement for the Bell UH-1, then in service in large numbers as the standard assault and medical evacuation transport as well as for other duties.

Defined as a Utility Tactical Transport Aircraft System (UTTAS), the specification called for a helicopter able to carry 11 combat-equipped troops and three crew at an altitude of 4,000 ft (1,219 m) and a cruise speed of 201 mph (322 km/h), powered by two General Electric T700 engines and featuring a wheeled undercarriage and various defensive and survivability measures. In addition, the aircraft was to be easily air-transportable in the C-130 Hercules, with six able to be loaded aboard the C-5A transport.

Initial submissions from the US helicopter industry were narrowed down in 1972 to entries from Boeing Vertol and Sikorsky, from whom prototypes were ordered under the designations YUH-61A and YUH-60A respectively for competitive evaluation. Each company built four flying prototypes plus ground test examples, with initial roll-outs taking place in late 1974.

The first YUH-60A, 73-21650, made its first flight on 17 October 1974, beating its rival into the air by some five weeks. In general appearance both designs shared a number of similarities, in particular a low squat fuselage with a close-mounted main rotorhead to meet the air-transport ability need, manually-folding four-bladed main rotor, shoulder-mounted powerplants, large fin and tailplane area, duplicated critical components and crashworthiness contruction features. Yet

The Sikorsky UH-60A Black Hawk is rapidly replacing the UH-1 'Huey' as the US Army's standard tactical transport.

The UH-60A is able to deliver slung loads up to a weight of 8,000 lb (3,630 kg) into the battle area or can combine a smaller external load with a cabin full of combat troops.

there were also several fundamental differences. The YUH-61 for example featured semi-rigid rotor technology, based on the MBB Bo 105 system, and a nosewheel undercarriage, as opposed to the Sikorsky choice of a more traditional articulated rotor system and a tailwheel undercarriage.

Competitive evaluation of the two designs began in March 1976 and Sikorsky was announced as the winner on 23 December, with an initial order for 15 production UH-60As being placed by the US Army soon afterwards. The first of these, 77-22714, flew on 17 October 1978. The production UH-60A Black Hawk differed in a number of respects from the original prototype, notably in the installation of uprated engines and the introduction of an extended rotor mast. The initial US Army order was rapidly followed by additional multi-year contracts, which by 1986 totalled 1,107 aircraft.

Service introduction of the UH-60A began in 1980 and the type is now deployed with the US Army throughout the world, with over 700 aircraft operational. Later machines carry hardpoints for the installation of an external stores support system (ESSS), which provides four removable pylons for the carriage of long-range fuel tanks to allow self-deployment over a distance of 1,323 miles (2,130 km) without refuelling. The same pylons can be used to carry assorted armament pods, rockets, or Hellfire anti-armour missiles. Also now being introduced is an improved IR engine heat suppressor system and revised exterior and interior lighting systems, compatible with night vision goggles.

The basic design of the Black Hawk has proved suitable for the development of several derivatives, including the SH-60 Seahawk (described separately). In October 1980, Sikorsky began work on a YEH-60A variant fitted with four dipole antenna below the fuselage plus a retractable whip antenna. First flown on 24 September 1981 the YEH-60A also carried internal electronic countermeasures equipment to enable it to intercept, monitor and jam enemy communications. Trials were followed by a production contract in October 1984, placed with Tracor Aerospace, to convert 40 UH-60As to EH-60A 'Quick Fix' configuration. The first of these ECM/ESM conversions was completed in April 1986. Current US Army plans envisage the eventual acquisition of 132 EH-60As.

Also test flown during 1981 was a prototype YEH-60B, intended to meet a US Army stand-off target acquisition (SOTAS) requirement. This involved the installation of an extendable 19 ft (6 m) rotating radar antenna beneath the fuselage, with a modified long-stroke main undercarriage, which was designed to swing back to clear the antenna during operation. This programme was shelved in September 1981.

Meanwhile the designations HH-60D and HH-60E were allocated to proposed all weather combat rescue versions for the US Air Force, designed to supplement and replace the HH-53 fleet. The level of sophistication called for by the USAF eventually resulted in cancellation of the proposals in 1984 on cost grounds. Meanwhile, to make up the shortfall in rescue helicopters, the USAF took delivery of 11 UH-60As in 1982-83, ten of which entered service with the 55th ARRS in Florida. The eleventh was allocated for conversion to a prototype HH-60A Night Hawk, intended as a less costly answer to the USAF combat-rescue requirement.

Initially flown on 4 February 1984 with new external and internal long-range fuel tanks, an air-to-air refuelling probe, some additional avionics and a rescue hoist, the aircraft completed initial USAF evaluation trials and was then further modified with the installation of new mission avionics. These included FLIR, multifunction cockpit CRT displays, a MIL-STD-1553B multiplex databus, advanced navaids, secure communications and defensive equipment. Thus updated it resumed USAF trials in late 1985.

HH-60A procurement plans by the USAF called for the purchase of 90 aircraft, powered by uprated

The HH-60A Night Hawk has recently been the subject of US defence cuts and is now unlikely to enter service in its original configuration. The prototype, seen here, features long range fuel tanks and retractable refuelling probe plus specialised mission avionics.

1,690 shp T700-GE-401 engines with transmission and some other components common to the SH-60 Seahawk, but the programme again ran into funding problems in 1986 and has been shelved.

Interest in the basic UH-60A has also extended to the US Marine Corps, which has a requirement for nine VH-60As to replace Bell VH-1Ns on VVIP flight duties, and to several overseas customers. Exported as the S-70A, the basic Black Hawk is in service with the Philippines Air Force, while the very similar S-70C, powered by 1,625 shp General Electric CT7-2C engines, is in service with the Republic of China Air Force and on order for other overseas customers. One S-70C is also currently acting as a flight test vehicle for the new 2,100 shp Rolls Royce-Turboméca RTM322 turboshaft which, together with other improvements, is being considered for a future UH-60 variant.

Technical specifications

Helicopter Sikorsky S-70 (UH-60A Black Hawk)
Type Tactical transport
Year 1978
Engine 2 × 1,543 shp General Electric T700
Rotor diameter 16.35 m (53 ft 8 in)
Fuselage length 15.26 m (50 ft)
Overall length 19.76 m (64 ft 10 in)
Height 5.13 m (16 ft 10 in)
Empty weight 4,950 kg (10,913 lb)
Gross weight 7,470 kg (16,468 lb)
Maximum speed 360 km/h (224 mph)
Service ceiling 5,790 m (19,000 ft)
Range 600/1,060 km (373/659 miles)
Capacity 2 crew + 11 troops or 1,200 kg (2,645 lb)

Sikorsky S-70/SH-60 Seahawk

The SH-60B Seahawk, developed by Sikorsky from the basic UH-60A, introduced specific avionics and armament modifications to fulfil the LAMPS 3 role for the US Navy. This aircraft, BuAer 161169, is one of five prototypes built.

Right: In US Navy service the SH-60B has adopted a grey overall colour scheme, as shown in this view of a production aircraft hovering over the flight deck of the guided missile frigate USS *Crommelin.*

Following the realisation in the early 1970s that the Kaman SH-2D Seasprite, which won the original light airborne multi-purpose system (LAMPS) programme, would be unable to meet planned mission improvements (LAMPS Mk II), the US Navy decided to issue a new requirement to meet a revised LAMPS Mk III specification.

The avionics portion of this was awarded to IBM Federal Systems Division in 1974, but the airframe decision was delayed until 1977, pending the results of a fly-off competition between navalised versions of the Boeing Vertol YUH-61 and the Sikorsky UH-60. Both the competing prototypes were modified UTTAS contenders, with the Sikorsky aircraft having its tailwheel repositioned further forward but with other changes being demonstrated only in mockup form.

The success of the UH-60 in the US Army UTTAS competition much influenced its subsequent selection by the Navy for the LAMPS III programme, since the high degree of commonality offered useful cost savings, and the construction of five YSH-60B prototypes was authorised in 1977. The first of these, 161169, flew on 12 December 1979. Apart from the repositioned and strengthened tailwheel, this aircraft introduced a number of other major changes to the basic S-70 design. These included electric main blade folding, a rotorbrake, stub pylons for the carriage of torpedoes and MAD gear, and a revised tail unit with outer sections to the stabilator and the pylon folding to facilitate shipboard stowage. Centre and front fuselage modifications included deletion of most of the main cabin windows and the port cabin entry door, with local structural changes to incorporate a port side sonobuoy housing, ventral

radome, chin-mounted ESM pods, flotation gear, rescue hoist, and DAF Indal RAST haul-down gear to allow rough weather small ship operations.

Subsequent prototypes trialled the chosen ASW and avionics systems, including secure communications and datalink equipment, acoustic processor, digital computer and search radar. In total the changes added some 2,866 lb (1,300 kg) to the basic S-70 empty weight, but this was countered in the SH-60B by the introduction of uprated and marinised 1,690 shp General Electric T700-GE-401 turboshafts, allowing a maximum gross weight increase to 21,884 lb (9,926 kg).

By mid-1982 the five prototypes had logged almost 3,000 flying hours, including extensive shipboard trials, which were followed by a launch order for 18 aircraft for the US Navy. Subsequently, orders have been increased to cover a planned requirement for 204 machines. The first production Seahawk flew on 11 February 1983 and, like all subsequent aircraft, was despatched to IBM for avionics integration before being handed over to the US Navy. Operational deployment of the SH-60B began in 1984, with plans to eventually base the aircraft on 106 'Oliver Hazard Perry' class frigates and 'Spruance' class destroyers.

In March 1985 the US Navy authorised full-scale development of an SH-60F Seahawk variant, intended as a replacement for the SH-3H Sea King and designed to operate from aircraft carriers to defend the inner zone of a carrier battle group from submarine attack. Known as the 'CV-Helo', the SH-60F introduces the Bendix AQS-13F dipping sonar rather than the sonobuoy, with MAD carried only as an option. The new variant will also carry out the role of SAR plane guard during carrier fixed-wing operations. The stated US Navy requirement for the SH-60F covers 175 aircraft, 76 of which are so far optioned or on firm order. The first production SH-60F is due to fly in late 1986 and service entry is expected in mid-1987. Currently under consideration is a utility version of the SH-60F to replace HH-3s of the US Coast Guard.

Export sales of the Seahawk family to date include six SH-60Bs for the Spanish Navy and eight for the Royal Australian Navy, the latter fitted with the MEL Super Searcher radar and designated the S-70B-2. In addition two Seahawk airframes have been delivered to Mitsubishi in Japan for the installation of locally developed electronic and mission systems to meet a Japanese Maritime Self Defence Force requirement for an SH-3 replacement. Provisionally designated XSH-60J, the first of these prototypes is due to fly in 1987, with production deliveries commencing in the early 1990s.

Technical specifications

Helicopter Sikorsky S-70L (SH-60B Seahawk)
Type Multipurpose naval/anti-submarine
Year 1979
Engine 2 × 1,690 shp General Electric T700
Rotor diameter 16.35 m (53 ft 8 in)
Fuselage length 15.26 m (50 ft)
Height 5.23 m (17 ft 2 in)
Empty weight 6,191 kg (13,650 lb)
Gross weight 9,908 kg (21,843 lb)
Maximum speed 249 km/h (155 mph)
Service ceiling 5,790 m (19,000 ft)
Range 1,100 km (683 miles)
Capacity 2 pilots + 2 operators
Armament 2 × Mk 46 torpedoes

Sikorsky S-76

The H-76 Eagle, introduced at the 1985 Paris Air Show, is a beefed-up variant of the S-76B powered by PT6B-36 engines and is being offered both in anti-armour and naval versions.

Designed in the early 1970s, the S-76 was initially developed as a twin-engined helicopter specifically for the civil market, in particular aiming at the expanding offshore support and corporate sectors.

Construction of four prototypes was initiated by Sikorsky in May 1976, with the intention of producing an aesthetic looking aircraft incorporating dynamics experience and other features culled from the concurrent S-70 Black Hawk programme. This background showed itself in such areas as the rotorhead and rotorblade design. The chosen powerplant for the S-76, two 650 shp Allison 250-C30 turboshafts, was installed atop the fuselage, above a large baggage bay and behind the rotorhead, while the four-door cabin layout afforded room for up to 14 occupants including the crew. The streamlined fuselage used a mix of composite and metal construction, with a fully retractable tricycle undercarriage, and a tail section culminating in a prominent streamlined fin with a four-blade tail rotor mounted above the port stabiliser. IFR avionics was installed from the outset.

The first S-76 to fly was the second prototype, N762SA, on 13 March 1977 and this was successively followed by the remaining prototypes and three pre-production aircraft. Full production deliveries to commercial customers began on 28 February 1979 and initial military interest was restricted to para-military and EMS sales, in particular to the Jordanian government, which took delivery of 18 S-76As between 1979 and 1983.

Meanwhile a downturn in the civil market prompted Sikorsky to develop a more specific military variant, designated AUH-76 and intended as an armed/utility helicopter. The prototype for this version was N5435X, the 161st production S-76A airframe first flown in April 1982. This aircraft introduced sliding main cabin doors and a cargo floor as standard, with a fixed undercarriage, crash-resistant fuel tanks, armoured crew seats, troop seats, cargo hook, rescue hoist, engine air particle separators, auxiliary fuel tank and fixed fittings for stretcher carriage among the available options. Armament trials subsequently cleared the AUH-76 for the carriage of TOW missiles or alternative rocket pod and similar weaponry on a multi-purpose pylon system, plus a 7.62 mm machine gun pintle-mounted in the doorway. Twelve AUH-76s configured for light attack and trooping support were subsequently delivered to the Philippines Air Force in 1983, along with two VIP, one transport and two SAR configured aircraft.

This initial AUH-76 variant suffered, however, from being underpowered, a factor which also affected some potential sales of the commercial S-76. Accordingly in 1983 Sikorsky re-engined an S-76 airframe with two 960 shp Pratt & Whitney PT6B-36 engines for a 200-hour ground running programme, completed in April 1984. This was followed on 22 June 1984 by the start of a flight test programme, using a second aircraft, N3123U, designated the S-76B. Subsequently two further prototypes were built, including N3124G, which was completed in spring 1985 as the definitive basic military H-76 variant, the Eagle.

The PT6B-36 installation in the S-76B/H-76 called for a distinct redesign of the engine nacelles and local structure, with the powerplants mounted farther outboard on shoulder stubs and with well separated exhaust ducts. Other airframe modifications included a 15 percent reduction in the fin area of the tail rotor pylon, and an increase in chord and aerodynamic changes to the tailplane, while the H-76 further introduced an increase in fuselage skin thickness to withstand missile launch blast. The 48 percent increase in take-off power conferred by the PT6B-36 engines also saw dynamic modifications on the H-76, to allow the rating to improve to 1,500 shp and maximum gross weight to climb by 1,100 lb (499 kg). The main rotor hub and shaft were strengthened, the main, intermediate and tail rotor gearboxes were upgraded, and tail rotor blade chord increased.

These improvements allow the H-76 to carry a substantial weapons load, such as 16 TOW missiles, together with optional equipment including a mast-mounted sight, laser rangefinder and an integrated weapons management system. As an assault transport, the aircraft can carry up to ten fully equipped troops or 3,300 lb (1,498 kg) on the external hook. Other proposed developments include an air-to-air defence variant with up to 16 AAMs or a mixed missile/cannon armament backed by self-protection radar warning, jamming and chaff dispensing systems, AFCS and a high clearance landing gear.

Also under development is the H-76N, designed for anti-ship surveillance and targetting, anti-submarine warfare, surface attack and similar naval operations operating from frigate-sized ships. Basic modifications for this role include a strengthened high-clearance undercarriage, fold-

The original S-76 military variant, the AUH-76, is in service as a utility transport with the Philippine Air Force. The aircraft is also able to carry out an anti-armour role fitted with TOW missiles, as shown in this view of the development prototype N5415X.

ing main rotor blades, and provision for deck securing, while other options include a dual digital AFCS-coupled hover capability tactical navigation system, hover in-flight refuelling and data link. Surface warfare H-76Ns are offered with a chin-mounted 360 degree radar installation and air-to-surface missiles, while the ASW version is offered with dipping sonar, processing suite, and two torpedoes. The H-76N will also be offered with a choice of the PT6B-36 engine installation or the new 735 shp Allison 250-C34S, which retrofits into the original S-76A engine bay.

Although no orders for the H-76 or H-76N had been announced by early 1986, Sikorsky was heavily promoting military sales among the smaller European countries such as Sweden and Belgium and also in SE Asia where requirements existed for this size helicopter.

Technical specifications

Helicopter Sikorsky H-76 Eagle
Type Armed utility helicopter
Year 1985
Engine 2 × 960 shp Pratt & Whitney Canada PT6B-36 turboshaft
Rotor diameter 13.41 m (44 ft)
Fuselage length 13.22 m (43 ft 4.5 in)
Height 4.52 m (14 ft 9.75 in)
Empty weight 2,545 kg (5,610 lb)
Gross weight 5,171 kg (11,400 lb)
Maximum speed 269 km/h (167 mph)
Hovering ceiling IGE 2,560 m (8,400 ft)
Service ceiling 4,725 m (15,500 ft)
Range 713 km (433 miles)
Capacity 2 crew + 10 passengers
Armament 16 × TOW missiles or machine gun and rocket pods, 2 torpedoes.

Westland Army Lynx

The Westland Army Lynx AH 1 has now assumed an anti-armour role with the Army Air Corps, with provision for eight TOW missiles plus spare rounds carried in the cabin. A night firing capability is now being incorporated.

The WG-13 Lynx programme was the first product of the amalgamated British helicopter industry, drawing particularly on the experience of the Saunders-Roe Scout/Wasp and the Bristol Sycamore and Belvedere programmes of the late 1950s, to meet a British Army requirement for an 8,000 lb (3,629 kg) gross weight utility helicopter to replace the Whirlwind, Sycamore, Scout and Wasp helicopters.

In 1967 the programme became part of the Anglo-French helicopter agreement under which the Lynx, along with the Aérospatiale Gazelle and Puma, were to be jointly developed for the British and French armed forces. Lynx variants proposed under this agreement included a general purpose utility version for the UK Army Air Corps, a dedicated tandem-seat gunship version for the French ALAT (cancelled in 1969) and naval marks for both Fleet Air Arms.

The first prototype WG-13, XW835, first flew at Yeovil on 21 March 1971 and was followed by four similar aircraft, all based on the utility design with a skid undercarriage and box cabin. Power was provided by two 700 shp Rolls-Royce BS360 turboshafts, then still under development, mounted side by side atop the fuselage and aft of the rotorshaft. The main gearbox, mounted ahead of the rotorshaft, introduced conformal gearing to save weight and size which, combined with a one-piece titanium semi-rigid rotor hub, gave the helicopter a relatively low profile.

Lynx development continued throughout the first half of the 1970s, with eight pre-production aircraft (including six naval prototypes) following the original four WG-13s. Specific Army development machines were XX153 and XX907, used for equipment and role trials, including the development of an automatic flight control system combining automatic transition to and from hover with autostabilisation and autopilot. In June 1972 XX153 was used to set up new world speed records over a 15/25 km (9.3/15.5 mile) straight line (199.92 mph/321.74 km/h) and the 100 km (62.1 mile) closed circuit flights (197.909 mph/318.50 km/h). This aircraft also became the first Lynx to be rolled in flight later the same year.

By 1974 Rolls-Royce had increased the power of the BS360 engine, now named the Gem, to 900 shp and orders were placed for 111 aircraft, including 50 utility machines for the Army Air Corps and another 13 for the Royal Air Force. This latter order was, however, cancelled before the first production utility AH Mk 1, XZ170, flew in February 1977. Service entry with the Army Air Corps took place later that year and the type became operational with BAOR Germany at Detmold in August 1978.

During the same period comparative trials were carried out with HOT and TOW anti-tank missile installations, using roof-mounted sights and pylon launchers on either side of the cabin. Following selection of the TOW configuration, 60 AAC Lynx helicopters were fitted with the necessary sighting system and hardware, and these began entering service in the anti-tank role in February 1981 with No 654 Sqdn at Detmold. In the assault role the aircraft can carry up to ten armed troops or three-man mobile anti-tank teams with missiles and launchers.

By January 1983 100 Lynx AH Mk 1s were in British Army service with 14 due to follow. Some of these, all TOW-equipped, were allocated to No 3 Commando Brigade Air Squadron Royal Marines, following a decision not to go ahead with a hybrid Army/Navy Mk 6 variant designed specially for the beach assault role. Meanwhile, the final AH Mk 1, ZD285, was in fact completed as the first AH Mk 5 (Interim) with an uprated transmission but standard engines, and delivered to the Royal Aircraft Establishment. A second, similar, aircraft followed, with both machines being dedicated to trials of new avionics and other equipment intended to enhance future versions.

The first definitive AH Mk 5, ZE375, was flown on 23 February 1985. It standardised on the uprated transmission matched to two 1,120 shp Gem 41-1 turboshafts, an improvement already previously incorporated three years earlier in the naval variant. Eight Mk 5s were ordered for the Army Air Corps but only two were actually completed to this standard, the others being subsequently integrated in a new order, placed by the Army Air Corps in mid-1985 for five new Lynx AH Mk 7.

Based on the Mk 5, the first AH Mk 7 flew in early November 1985. It standardised on the more powerful 1,120 shp Rolls-Royce Gem 41-1 engines with a three-pinion main gearbox and uprated transmission, and further introduced the reverse-direction composite tail rotor from the Westland 30 programme. With the extra power available, this improves the Lynx ability to hover for extended periods at the new 10,750 lb (4,880.18 kg) gross weight, as well as reducing noise. Together with a new digital core cockpit management system under development, the changes are designed to improve the aircraft in the anti-tank role, and some earlier Army Lynx may be updated to the new AH Mk 7 standard as part of a mid-life overhaul programme.

Export sales of the Army Lynx have been confined to just three basic aircraft for policing duties in Qatar, despite extensive tours by a specially built demonstrator G-LYNX. A major order, including licence production, was negotiated with Egypt in the mid-1970s, with up to 700 aircraft being mentioned, but was subsequently cancelled.

Technical specifications

Helicopter Westland Lynx AH Mk1
Type Multi-purpose
Year 1976
Engine 2 × 900 shp Rolls-Royce BS 360 Gem
Rotor diameter 12.80 m (42 ft)
Fuselage length 11.66 m (38 ft 3 in)
Overall length 15.16 m (49 ft 8 in)
Height 3.66 m (12 ft)
Empty weight 2,658 kg (5,847 lb)
Gross weight 4,763 kg (10,478 lb)
Maximum speed 282 km/h (175 mph)
Hovering ceiling IGE 2,950 m (9,678 ft)
Range 676 km (420 miles)
Capacity 2 crew + 10 troops or 1,360 kg (3,000 lb) external load
Armament 8 × TOW missiles or podded machine-guns, rockets etc

The newest Lynx version is the AH Mk 7, which introduces uprated engines and a reverse-direction W30 tail rotor.

Westland Navy Lynx

The Navy Lynx is operated by several NATO air arms and other services in the ASW, SAR and ASV roles. This machine, an HAS Mk 3 of the Royal Navy, is carrying Sea Skua anti-ship missiles.

Developed in parallel with the Army Lynx (page 160) from the five common WG-13 prototypes of the early 1970s, the Navy Lynx initially differed only by the adoption of a tricycle landing gear with sophisticated oleo shock absorbers, but subsequently became more specialised to meet the needs of small-deck anti-submarine and anti-shipping operations for a number of navies around the world.

The initial naval prototype, XX469, first flew at Yeovil on 25 May 1972 and was allocated to deck landing trials both in the UK and in France. Its loss in a mechanical accident later that year accelerated completion of a second prototype, XX510, first flown on 5 March 1973, which was subsequently followed by four further naval prototypes. These included two aircraft, XX904 and XX911, especially dedicated to French naval equipment trials as part of the shared development programme.

First production orders for the type were confirmed in mid-1972, being 30 HAS Mk 2 for the Royal Navy and 18 HAS Mk 2 (FN) for the French Aéronavale, the fundamental difference between the two variants being in their avionics, ASW equipment and armament.

Royal Navy production began with XZ227, first flown in February 1976 but retained for trials work. The aircraft standardised on a modified nose, containing Ferranti Seaspray search and tracking radar, folding main rotor blades and tail cone, flotation gear and three-axis autostabilisation. Deck operations were enhanced by the introduction of a hydraulically actuated harpoon deck lock system and toe-out main wheel units with sprag brakes to prevent uncontrolled movement in heavy seas. Negative thrust available from the main rotor could be employed to increase stability on deck after touchdown. Power was provided by two 900 shp Rolls-Royce Gem 2 engines, permitting a maximum gross weight of 3,676 kg (8,104 lb).

Among overseas air arms operating the Navy Lynx is the Brazilian Fleet Air Arm. Note the toed-in main wheels, characteristic of the naval variant.

Following a period of operational trials and training, the HAS Mk 2 entered front line service with the Royal Navy in January 1978, with the first sea deployment taking place on 8 February on a 'Leander' class frigate, HMS *Phoebe*. Subsequently the type became standard equipment aboard some 40 RN ships, replacing in many instances the obsolescent Westland Wasp.

The initial batch of 30 HAS Mk 2s was followed from early 1979 by a further 30 aircraft, before production switched to 23 HAS Mk 3s with 1,120 shp Gem 41-1 engines and an uprated transmission to permit an increase in gross weight to 10,500 lbs (4,767 kg). The last of these was delivered in April 1985. A number of aircraft were fitted with MAD gear in an extended sponson during the early 1980s, following operational tests, and the standard torpedo and depth charge armament was expanded in 1982 with the clearance of the Sea Skua anti-shipping missile.

French HAS Mk 2 (FN) service began with the delivery of 261 to St. Raphael in September 1978, the first production aircraft having been retained for trials. The initial order for 18 machines was followed by further contracts covering a total of 26 Mk 2 (FN).

In 1982 deliveries began of the HAS Mk 4 (FN), featuring the uprated engines and transmission also introduced in the HAS Mk 3 and the last of 14 HAS Mk 4s (FN) was handed over to the Aéronavale in early 1984.

In service the French Navy Lynx operates with four front line squadrons, deploying from bases on the Atlantic and Mediterranean coasts aboard various fighting ships. Equipment includes Alcatel DUAV 4 dipping sonar operated via a hydraulic winch and an automatic flight control system which provides transition to the hover and automatic Doppler hold in the hover.

A total of nine other countries have also purchased variants of the Navy Lynx, mostly for small-ship operations in the ASW/ASV role, but also including six HAR Mk 25 Search and Rescue aircraft for the Royal Netherlands Navy and six SAR/surveillance HAR Mk 86 for the Royal Norwegian Air Force. By the end of 1985 a total of 189 Navy Lynx helicopters had been built by Westland, with outstanding orders for a further ten aircraft. These include seven HAS Mk 8s for the Royal Navy, a new variant featuring an improved transmission with a three-pinion main gearbox, the more powerful 1,120 shp Gem 41-2 powerplant, and a further increase in gross weight to 10,750 lbs. (4,880 kg). These changes enable the introduction of a 360 degree Seaspray Mk 3 radar, a Racal Central Tactical System and other improvements. Deliveries of the HAS Mk 8

will begin in 1987 and earlier Royal Navy aircraft may be upgraded to a similar standard.

Meanwhile Westland is offering an Advanced Navy Lynx as an option to the HAS Mk 8. The proposed new variant is offered with the Gem 41-2 or the 1,260 shp Gem 60 engine, married to a new transmission with an 1,840 shp rating and a composite reverse direction tail rotor, all taken from the Westland 30 programme and matched to new BERP composite main rotor blades and a new bolted rotorhead. The payload benefits offered by these modifications would allow structural reinforcement, undercarriage and flotation gear improvements, and other changes to be adopted.

Technical specifications

Helicopter Westland Lynx Mk3
Type Multi-purpose ASW/ASV
Year 1979
Engine 2 × 1,120 shp Rolls-Royce BS 360 Gem 41-1
Rotor diameter 12.80 m (42 ft)
Fuselage length 11.66 m (38 ft 3 in)
Overall length 15.16 m (49 ft 8 in)
Height 3.66 m (11 ft)
Empty weight 3,101 kg (6,836 lb)
Gross weight 4,767 kg (10,500 lb)
Maximum speed 270 km/h (168 mph)
Hovering ceiling IGE: 2,950 m (9,678 ft)
Range 630 km (390 miles)
Capacity 2 crew + 10 troops or 2 torpedoes or 2 depth charges

Westland Lynx 3

The Westland Lynx 3 was developed in the early 1980s as a stretch version of the standard Lynx family by essentially marrying the growth technology of the Westland 30 Lynx derivative (page 184 to in-service Lynx experience and development.

As with the earlier aircraft both Army and Navy variants have been projected, although to date only a single anti-armour prototype has been built. This machine (ZE477) flew for the first time on 14 June 1984, using a strengthened W30 tail section and composite tail rotor (rotating in the opposite direction to that on the original Lynx), married to a Lynx forward fuselage with a 30 cm (11.81 in) plug to increase the cabin volume. Gross weight is some 27 percent greater than the Lynx and power is provided by two 1,115 shp Rolls-Royce Gem 60 engines, with a transmission based on that installed in the W30. Revised lateral air intakes incorporate particle filters. A standard Lynx main rotor fitted on the prototype would be replaced on the production version by new BERP composite rotor blades, claimed to increase rotor efficiency by 40 percent, and a lighter bolted titanium semi-rigid head.

The Army Lynx 3 features a wheeled tricycle undercarriage incorporating the latest crash absorption system designed to survive descent rates of 20 ft (6.10 m) per sec, with side-by-side crew seating with armour protection and shock absorbing struts. Weaponry could include 25 mm cannon, machine gun pods, rockets and anti-tank missiles mounted on stub pylons on either side of the main cabin. The latter is large enough to carry eight spare missiles or up to ten troops. The aircraft can also be equipped with full day/night vision sensors, roof or mast-mounted sight, and the latest cockpit management systems technology.

The Navy Lynx 3 proposal introduces a folding tail cone, with a repositioned tailplane and the deletion of endplate fins to facilitate stowage, folding main rotor blades and a navalised undercarriage with flotation gear. The harpoon deck lock and main rotor negative thrust features, introduced on the Navy Lynx to simplify deck operations, would be retained. Proposed avionics include a chin-mounted 360 degree radar, MAD, dunking sonar, and active and passive sonobuoys. Armament could include up to four torpedoes, depth charges or anti-ship missiles.

Although the Lynx 3 prototype has carried out a

number of sales demonstrations as part of its evaluation programme, no orders had been announced by April 1986, although some interest had been shown by several potential customers.

Technical specifications

Helicopter Westland Lynx 3
Type Anti-armour/multi-mission helicopter
Year 1984
Engine 2 × 1,115 shp Rolls-Royce Gem 60
Rotor diameter 12.80 m (42 ft)
Fuselage length 13.79 m (45 ft 3 in)
Overall length 15.47 m (50 ft 9 in)
Height 3.30 m (10 ft 10 in)
Empty weight n/a
Gross weight 5,896 kg (13,000 lb)
Maximum speed 306 km/h (190 mph)
Hovering ceiling IGE
Service ceiling n/a
Range 620 km (385 miles)
Capacity 2 crew + 10 troops
Armament 8 × HOT, TOW or Hellfire anti-tank missiles, air-air missiles, 20 mm cannon, podded machine-gun or rockets etc. (Naval version can carry 2 × Mk 44, Mk 46 or Sting Ray torpedoes, depth charges, or 4 × Sea Skua anti-ship missiles etc)

Right: First flown on 14 June 1984 the Lynx 3 marries the front end of the standard Lynx with the improved dynamics and rear fuselage of the Westland 30. The prorotype, ZE477, features the crashworthy undercarriage and other modifications intended for the Army variant.

Left: So far in mockup form only, the Naval Lynx 3 would feature a folding tailfin with a revised low-set tailplane and 360-degree search radar. The BERP main rotor is being considered for all Lynx variants.

Westland Scout

The Scout AH1 is still in front line service with the British Army Air Corps in Hong Kong, although it has been largely replaced by the Lynx in the UK and West German theatres.

With the arrival of the first generation of relatively small and powerful turboshaft engines in the mid-1950s, Saunders-Roe began looking at using such a powerplant in a growth version of their piston-engined Skeeter helicopter, then just entering service with the British Army Air Corps as a two-seat aerial observation post.

Initial schemes envisaged retaining the Skeeter transmission and tailboom, married to a new four-seat front fuselage, modifying the three-bladed main rotor system to a four-blade configuration, introducing a skid undercarriage, and installing a Blackburn-Turboméca Turmo engine, suitably de-rated to 325 shp. These schemes led to a detailed design project in early 1958, designated the P 531, and the construction of a private venture prototype G-APNU, which first flew at their Eastleigh facility on 20 July 1958.

Following construction of a second prototype, G-APNV, which introduced new main rotor blades, a full-span tailplane and other improvements, UK military interest in the P531 initially concentrated on developing a naval version (page 176). Development of an Army variant retaining the skid undercarriage was, however, close behind and this led to the P 531-2 in 1959, the year Saunders-Roe was taken over by Westland.

The first P 531-2, G-APVL, first flew on 9 August 1959, powered by a 650 shp Blackburn Nimbus engine. It was followed by a second example in May 1960, laid down by Saunders Roe, but completed by the Fairey division of Westland at Hayes in Middlesex, to where all P 531 Series development was moved. This second prototype, G-APVM, was experimentally powered by a derated 1,050 shp de Havilland Gnome turboshaft

In the 1982 Falklands conflict the Scout was used for casevac and also for ground attack, using its SS 11 missiles to clear Argentinian trenches in the absence of armoured targets.

(developed from the General Electric T-58), but was subsequently re-engined with the Nimbus, which was adopted as the standard powerplant.

During 1960 both P 531-2 prototypes, together with a third example XP165, were taken on charge by the UK Defence Ministry for trials, prior to the adoption of the type for the Army Air Corps. Seven further pre-production aircraft followed during 1961 before deliveries of the full production version, designated the Scout AH Mk 1, began in 1962. The first two orders for the Army Air Corps, for 12 and 28 aircraft respectively, were completed by the end of 1963, by which time the Scout was in service with Advanced Rotary Wing Flight (ARWF) at Middle Wallop and operational with No 651 Squadron in the newly created battlefield support role. Subsequently, a total of 139 Scouts were delivered to the British Army, including a number armed with the SS.11 anti-tank missile and fitted with a roof-mounted sight. Others were used primarily for observation, liaison and patrol work and the type proved to be a rugged performer throughout its career. Superseded by the Westland Lynx in the late 1970s, the type was eventually withdrawn from BAOR service in West Germany in the early 1980s, but has remained in front line operation in the Falklands and Hong Kong, where its relative simplicity is still an advantage when so far from UK spares depots.

Despite its popularity with the Army Air Corps, the Scout found few overseas customers. Two were delivered to the Royal Australian Navy in 1961 for survey work on HMAS *Moresby* and three entered service with the Royal Jordanian Air Force in 1963. The Bahrain Police also took delivery of two Scouts during 1965, followed by two for the Uganda Police in 1966. All the export aircraft had been destroyed or withdrawn from use by 1975.

Technical specifications

Helicopter Westland Scout AH Mk 1
Type 5-seat general purpose
Year 1961
Engine 968 shp Rolls-Royce Bristol Nimbus Mk 503 turbine
Rotor diameter 9.83 m (32 ft 3 in)
Fuselage length 9.24 m (30 ft 4 in)
Overall length 12.29 m (40 ft 4 in)
Height 3.56 m (11 ft 8 in)
Empty weight 1,465 kg (3,230 lb)
Gross weight 2,405 kg (5,300 lb)
Maximum speed 211 km/h (130 mph)
Service ceiling 4,075 m (13,370 ft)
Range 510 km (317 miles)
Capacity Pilot + 4 passengers
Armament 4 × SS 11 missiles

Westland Sea King/Commando

The current Royal Navy version of the Sea King is the HAS Mk 5, which carries updated avionics and a MEL Sea Searcher search radar in an enlarged dorsal radome.

The origins of the Westland Sea King, developed in the UK from the Sikorsky S-61D far beyond simple licence production, date back to the early 1960s, when the company considered building a civil derivative under the designation WS-61 Wiltshire. Although this idea was to be abandoned, the experience was used to advantage in 1965 when the Royal Navy called for tenders for a new anti-submarine helicopter to replace the Westland Wessex. Westland tendered both a home-grown design, the tandem-rotor WG11, and a licence-version of the US Navy Sikorsky SH-3D, which won the competition both on cost grounds and the shorter development time-scale. The latter was of particular importance to the Royal Navy, which was faced with a rapidly growing submarine threat. As a result, an immediate order for 60 Sea Kings was placed on 27 June 1966, leading to the importing by Westland of four Sikorsky SH-3D airframes to carry out urgent initial development work while anglicising of the design proceeded.

The first of the SH-3Ds flew into the Westland factory on 11 October 1966 and, serialled XV370, was used for initial handling and AFCS trials. Meanwhile, the three other airframes were shipped from Sikorsky as major assemblies, and built up by Westland with Rolls-Royce Gnome engines (developed from the General Electric T58), British avionics and other equipment. The last of the four prototypes joined the flight test programme on 31 May 1968 to carry out vibration and ASW equipment trials.

With the anglicisation of the drawings well advanced, construction of the first British-built aircraft, XV642, was initiated during 1968 and, designated the Sea King HAS Mk 1, made its first flight on 7 May 1969. Allocated for cold weather tests, it was subsequently joined in the trials programme by the second production aircraft, which carried out weapons trials. Apart from the conversion of the basic airframe design to meet British standards and the introduction of the 1,500 shp Gnome powerplants, the real differences between this first UK version of the Sea King and the SH-3D revolved around the Royal Navy tactical requirement. Unlike the US Navy this called for a self-contained ASW system, able to search for and attack submarines quite independently of a parent ship.

Thus the Sea King HAS Mk 1 introduced an Ecko AW 391 search radar mounted in a dorsal radome, dunking sonar positioned in a floor well and a Doppler navigation system - all feeding into a tactical plotting display in the rear cabin, which provided a constant update of the helicopter's exact position relative to surface and underwater contacts. A Newmark automatic

Some early Mk 2 Sea Kings have been modified to carry aerial early warning radar in a semi-retractable radome on the starboard side of the fuselage. This AEW version serves with the Royal Navy aboard its 'Invincible' class carriers.

flight control system, based on that developed for the Wessex HAS Mk 3, allowed all weather day/night ASW operation, with automatic transition to and from the hover, coupled hover and turns to pre-selected heading. The standard armament comprised four torpedoes or depth charges.

Initial deliveries to the Royal Navy began with six aircraft supplied to an Intensive Flying Trials Unit at RNAS Culdrose. Over a ten month period from August 1969, these Sea Kings logged some 2,900 hours flying, including 2,000 hrs of reliability tests, providing useful experience prior to the operational deployment of the first front line squadron, No 824, aboard the aircraft carrier HMS *Ark Royal* In June 1970. The final HAS Mk 1 was delivered in June 1972 and by March 1973 seven RN squadrons were equipped with the type.

Meanwhile Westland had been developing further variants to meet overseas interest. One of these was the Mk 41 for the West German Navy, based on the Mk 1 but developed for the Search and Rescue role, with the sonar equipment deleted and the rear cabin bulkhead moved back 5 ft 8 in (1.73 m) to provide room for up to 21 passengers and two crew in the main cabin. Extra bubble windows and fuel tanks were also incorporated and a rescue winch permanently positioned over the starboard door. A total of 22 Mk 41s were ordered and, following an extensive trials and training programme, deliveries began in July 1973. After 13 years' service in the SAR role, the Mk 41 is now the subject of a modification programme to enable it to fulfil an ASV role, armed with the BAe Sea Skua missile and fitted with the Ferranti Seaspray Mk 3 radar system and datalink to provide over-the-horizon targetting.

Preceding the Mk 41 on the production line was the Mk 42 for the Indian Navy. Basically similar to the HAS Mk 1 but with a different avionics fit, the first Mk 42 flew in October 1970 and the initial order for six was completed in 1971, subsequently being followed by six more in 1974.

After the initial batch of Mk 42 came ten Mk 43 SAR variants, similar in layout to the Mk 41, and delivered to the Norwegian Air Force in 1972-73. These were later joined by a single Mk 43A, produced to a later mod. standard. Westland developed a new troop-carrying version of the basic SAR Sea King to meet an urgent Egyptian requirement. Designated the Commando Mk 1, five such aircraft were delivered from October 1973, with seating for 21 troops and deletion of the SAR role modifications.

The final Sea King variant based on the Mk 1 was the Mk 45 for Pakistan, which introduced the necessary modifications to allow the carriage of two AM 39 Exocet missiles in the anti-shipping role. Six Mk 45s entered service in 1977, following some 30 months of trials and modifications to perfect the system.

Meanwhile, proposals to improve the payload and performance of the basic Mk 1 Sea King were accelerated in 1972, when the Royal Australian Navy placed an order for ten HAS Mk 50s, to be powered by uprated 1,660 shp Gnome H1400-1 engines, with a strengthened transmission and a sixth blade added to the tail rotor. Gross weight rose by 500 lb (227 kg) to 21,000 lb (9,524 kg), and a Bendix AN/AQS-13B replaced the Plessey 195 sonar. The first Mk 50 flew on 30 June 1974 with deliveries of an initial eight aircraft commencing the following January. Twelve Sea Kings, including two Mk 50A attrition replacements, were eventually built for the RAN and the survivors are due to be replaced in the prime ASW role by the S-70B Seahawk over the next few years.

Conclusion of the uprating trials now cleared the way for completion of the Egyptian order for a further 19 Commandos, and a second order for six ASW Sea King Mk 47s. Whilst the latter were essentially similar to the Mk 50, the new Commandos introduced a fixed main undercarriage layout, with stub weapons pylons replacing the sponsons of the earlier version. A total of 17 Commando Mk 2s were delivered in 1975-76, while two others were handed over as VIP aircraft. Also delivered during this period were three Commando Mk 2As and one VVIP Mk 2C for Qatar.

The next Sea Kings to be built were for Belgium, which ordered five SAR Mk 48s in March 1974, with an interior layout similar to that of the Mk 41, but with the uprated dynamics of the Mk 50. Then in November 1974, the decision was taken by the Royal Navy to take advantage of the uprating programme with an order for 13 new HAS Mk 2s. This variant retained much of the avionics fit from the Mk 1 but introduced the Mk 50 dynamics modifications, some local airframe strengthening and an improved fuel jettison system. Later a further eight new Mk 2 and the conversion of 46 Mk 1s was authorised, so that by early 1980 the original Sea King had disappeared from front line Royal Navy service.

The Commando version of the Sea King, identifiable by its revised main undercarriage, serves with the Royal Navy and the Egyptian and Qatari military. QA20 is one of four Mk 2s in service with Qatar.

Egypt operates four Commando Mk 2Es in the early warning electronic countermeasures role, with additional avionics equipment aboard. This is the first aircraft, carrying a British civil registration for the ferry flight.

In between production of the new Mk 2s Westland also built three other Sea King variants, in particular 15 HAR Mk 3s for the Royal Air Force SAR units and four Commando Mk 2E aircraft for an airborne electronic countermeasures role with the Egyptian Air Force. Also delivered were three new Mk 42As for India, the A suffix designating the uprated airframe with deck hauldown gear for frigate operations.

Continuing design development led in September 1979 to the first flight of the Sea King HC Mk 4, based on the Commando Mk 2, but retaining the tail pylon and main rotor folding of the Sea King to permit use by the Royal Navy for Marine assault operations. This new version entered service in December 1979 and 37 have been ordered to date to replace the veteran Wessex Mk 5. Also now in service are two hybrid Mk 4Xs, which retain the Sea King sponsons and dorsal radome for UK government equipment trials, and eight Commando Mk 3 for Qatar, which feature a similar airframe layout but further introduce new hot/high Gnome engines and Exocet missiles for the ASV role.

Further advances in ASW detection and the development of new electronic equipment led, on 2 October 1980, to the first flight of another new variant for the Royal Navy, the HAS Mk 5, 30 of which were ordered with the new digital MEL Sea Searcher radar in an enlarged radome, provision for MAD, a lightweight acoustic processing and display system, passive sonobuoy stowage, and navigation updates. In addition to new-built Mk 5s the majority of the Mk 2s were also subsequently converted to the new configuration.

Also produced by conversion of the Mk 2 has been the Mk 2(AEW), which was introduced in 1982 as a result of the Falklands crisis, to fulfil a Royal Navy aerial early warning need. This variant carries a Thorn-EMI Searchwater radar, with the antenna housed in an inflatable and semi-retractable radome mounted on the starboard side of the cabin. Eight such aircraft are currently in service, operating from the RN carrier fleet to give early warning coverage and

target direction over a range of more than 100 miles (161 km).

The current Westland Sea King production variant is the Mk 42B for India, also referred to as the Advanced Sea King. This latest version reverts to a five-bladed tail rotor but introduces composite main and tail rotor blades, developed by Westland for new and retrospective application to all S-61 variants, together with upgraded avionics, MEL Super Searcher radar, and provision for the carriage of the BAe Sea Eagle radar-guided anti-shipping missile. The first of 20 Mk 42Bs first flew in May 1985, but deliveries are not expected to commence before early 1987. Unconfirmed is another Indian Navy order for three Mk 42C transport variants for VERTREP work.

Interest in the Advanced Sea King is also being shown by several other potential customers, including the Royal Navy, which may combine the airframe modifications with new avionics and operational equipment under the designation Sea King HAS Mk 6. Meantime, total orders for the Westland Sea King family had reached 306 by early 1986 and the type will certainly remain in service beyond the year 2000.

The latest Sea King is the Mk 42B, currently under development for the Indian Navy and featuring composite main rotor blades and other airframe and avionics improvements, plus the capability to carry the BAe Sea Eagle anti-ship missile.

Technical specifications

Helicopter Westland Sea King Mk 42B
Type ASW helicopter
Year 1985
Engine 2 × 1,660 shp Rolls-Royce Gnome H.1400-1 turboshafts
Rotor diameter 18.90 m (62 ft)
Fuselage length 17.01 m (55 ft 9.75 in)
Height 5.13 m (16 ft 10 in)
Empty weight 6,201 kg (13,672 lb)
Gross weight 9,525 kg (21,000 lb)
Maximum speed 208 km/h (129 mph)
Hovering ceiling IGE 1,525 m (5,000 ft)
Range 1,230 km (764 miles)
Capacity 4 crew
Armament 4 homing torpedoes or 4 depth charges; able to carry BAe Sea Eagle long-range anti-ship missiles

The Westland Wasp is now being phased out of service with the Royal Navy, which has used it since the mid-1960s to pioneer small-ship ASW operations. This machine is operating from HMS *Aurora* in 1966.

Westland Wasp

The naval Wasp was one of two helicopters developed in the late 1950s from the Saunders-Roe P 531, a turbine-engined four/five-seat derivative of the Skeeter AOP helicopter then in service with the British Army Air Corps.

When Westland absorbed the Saunders-Roe company in 1959, two P 531s were already flying and the second of these was under evaluation to meet a Royal Navy requirement for a frigate-based anti-submarine helicopter. In October 1959, together with two further navalised P 531 prototypes, this aircraft entered service with a Fleet Air Arm trials unit, as a result of which a more definitive version was developed. This was ordered by the Royal Navy in September 1961.

Designated the Wasp HAS Mk 1, the prototype of the new variant was first shown to the public at the 1962 Farnborough Air Show, several weeks prior to its first flight on 28 October. Noteworthy changes from the experimental P 531 included: the adoption of a specially developed quadricycle undercarriage, designed to maximise operations in high sea states; an offset tailplane to allow folding of the tail unit; folding main rotor blades; altered cabin contours to improve space and visibility; and standardisation of a 710 shp Bristol-Siddelly (later Rolls-Royce) Nimbus turbo-shaft, mounted on a platform behind the main rotor shaft and gearbox.

Intended to operate as an extension of the frigate's weapons system, the Wasp was designed to carry two Mk 44 torpedoes or depth charges under the fuselage, relying on the parent ship to provide sonar contact and guidance to the attack area. XS463 was followed by a second pre-production prototype later in 1962 and both aircraft carried out extensive deck landing trials in all sea conditions prior to the introduction to service of an initial batch of 30 production Wasps.

These began entering service at RNAS Culdrose in mid-1963 and the first were issued to 'Leander' class frigates in early 1964. Subsequently, a second production order for 30 aircraft was authorised by the Royal Navy, which eventually took delivery of 96 machines before production terminated. Some later aircraft were fitted with roof-mounted sights and provision to carry two AS.12 air-to-surface missiles to fulfil an anti-shipping role. More than 50 Royal Navy ships operated the Wasp at the peak of its career, but with the introduction of the more sophisticated Westland Lynx, the Wasp began to be replaced as a front-line aircraft. Nevertheless in 1986 it was still operated by a number of frigates and other vessels, including the survey ships HMS *Hecate, Herald* and *Hydra* and the ice patrol vessel HMS *Endurance*, as well as in the training role at RNAS Portland.

Surplus Wasps have found a new lease of life with several navies. This ex-Netherlands Navy example is seen under flight test following refurbishing for the Indonesian Navy in 1981.

Overseas interest in the Wasp first crystallised in 1962 when the South African Navy ordered ten Series 1 aircraft for operation from three 'President' class (Type 12) frigates. These entered service between 1964 and 1966 and were followed by a second order for seven aircraft in 1971. In the event only six of the latter were delivered, a newly imposed UK government embargo having prevented delivery of the final example in 1974. Eleven South African Wasps were still on strength in 1985.

In 1964 the Royal Netherlands Navy placed an order for 12 Wasp Series 2 for service on six 'Van Speijk' class ships. These entered service in 1967 and were later followed by a 13th aircraft in 1974. In 1981 the ten survivors were purchased by Indonesia for small ship operation by No 400 Sqdn of the Indonesian Navy.

A third major overseas Wasp customer was Brazil, which initially ordered three new Series 3 aircraft in 1964 and subsequently took delivery of a further seven ex-Royal Navy machines between 1977 and 1979. The acquisition of further Wasps has been frustrated by funding difficulties. In service the aircraft operate primarily from six 'Niteroi' class frigates as well as from Brazilian Navy cruisers and destroyers.

The final export customer was New Zealand, which took delivery of two Wasp Series 4 in 1966 for operation by the 'Leander' class frigates HMNZS *Waikato* and *Canterbury*. A third aircraft followed in 1971. Subsequently, ten ex-Royal Navy Wasps were purchased although some of these have been used for spares recovery.

Technical specifications

Helicopter Westland Wasp HAS Mk 1
Type Anti-submarine
Year 1962
Engine 968 shp Rolls-Royce Nimbus Mk 503
Rotor diameter 9.83 m (32 ft 3 in)
Fuselage length 9.24 m (30 ft 4 in)
Overall length 12.29 m (40 ft 4 in)
Height 3.56 m (11 ft 8 in)
Empty weight 1,566 kg (3,452 lb)
Gross weight 2,500 kg (5,511 lb)
Maximum speed 193 km/h (120 mph)
Hovering ceiling IGE 3,810 m (12,500 ft)
Service ceiling 3,750 m (12,300 ft)
Range 488 km (303 miles)
Capacity 2 crew + 3 passengers
Armament 2 × Mk 44 torpedoes or 250 kg (550 lb) weapon load

Westland Wessex HAS Mk 1,3,31

The last few single-engined Wessex in service operate with the Royal Australian Navy, relegated to a training and SAR role.

The Wessex helicopter was originally projected by Westland as an anglicised turbine-engined development of the Sikorsky S-58, to meet a mid-1950s Royal Navy specification for an anti-submarine helicopter.

This led to the signing of a licence with Sikorsky in 1956 and the importation of a standard S-58, powered by a 1,525 hp Wright R-1820-84 radial engine, for conversion as a Wessex prototype. The turbine powerplant selected for installation, an 1,100 shp Napier Gazelle NGa11, was mounted in a revised nose section with an air intake and side exhaust, and connected directly to the standard S-58 dynamics system.

In this form the aircraft, XL722, first flew on 17 May 1957, being subsequently followed by 12 prototype and pre-production machines assembled and flown by Westland in 1958-59 and used for various engine and equipment trials. As the HAS Mk 1, powered by the uprated 1,450 shp Gazelle NGa13 engine, production Wessex began entering service with the Royal Navy in the anti-submarine role in April 1960. Initial deliveries of the anti-submarine version were followed in 1962 by a number of aircraft fitted out for the commando assault role, in which task they operated until superseded by the later Mk 5 in 1965. Altogether 111 HAS Mk 1 were built by Westland. The last Mk 1s, serving in the SAR role, were retired in September 1979 but, in 1967, the development of the more sophisticated HAS Mk 3 with an uprated 1,600 shp Gazelle 165 engine, advanced AFCS and improved sonar equipment, led to the conversion of 43 Mk 1s to the new configuration. These continued in service until the last were finally replaced by the Navy Lynx (page 163) at the end of 1982.

The only overseas customer for the Gazelle-engined Wessex was the Royal Australian Navy, which took delivery of 27 Mk 31 in 1962-63. Basically similar to the HAS Mk 1, these aircraft served in the ASW and SAR role until 1968, when most were converted to HAS Mk 31B standard with improved avionics and the uprated Gazelle 165c powerplant. Replaced in the ASW role by the Sea King Mk 50 in 1975, the aircraft reverted to utility and SAR work but almost all were in storage by 1985, pending a decision on their future.

Technical specifications

Helicopter Westland Wessex HAS Mk 1
Type Anti-submarine/Utility
Year 1957
Engine 1,450 shp Napier Gazelle Mk
Rotor diameter 17.07 m (56 ft)
Fuselage length 14.74 m (48 ft 4.5 in)
Height 4.39 m (14 ft 5 in)
Empty weight 3,447 kg (7,600 lb)
Gross weight 5,715 kg (12,600 lb)
Maximum speed 212 km/h (132 mph)
Hovering ceiling IGE 1,800 m (5,900 ft)
Range 630 km (390 miles)
Capacity 2 pilots + 2 crew or 16 troops

Westland Wessex HC Mk 2, 5, 52-54

The Wessex HC Mk 2 is still in front line operation with the RAF as a tactical transport and is also used in the SAR role.

The arrival of smaller, improved turboshaft engines, such as the General Electric T-58 in the late 1950s, led to an early decision by Westland to investigate the use of twin turbine engines in their Wessex helicopter, then operational with the Royal Navy with a single 1,450 shp Napier Gazelle turboshaft.

Accordingly a prototype Wessex, XM299, was modified in 1961 with two 1,250 shp Rolls-Royce Gnome H1200 engines (licence-built T-58), installed side-by-side with a coupling gearbox in a redesigned nose section. Reflown on 18 January 1962, the aircraft thus served as a prototype for

The Royal Navy has replaced most of its Wessex HC Mk 5s, used in the commando assault role, with the Sea King HC Mk 4 but the type remains in service in second-line roles such as SAR.

the Wessex HC Mk 2, ordered by the Royal Air Force in August 1961 to fulfil a tactical transport role in support of army operations.

The power available from the twin-coupled Gnome powerplant vastly improved the qualities of the Wessex, offering almost twice the power of the original Sikorsky S-58 design with minimal changes in basic weight. It allowed the HC Mk 2 to carry up to 16 troops or an underslung load of 3,000 lbs (1,361 kg), with an engine-out safeguard, and provided good performance characteristics in extremes of hot/high operating conditions.

Following completion of a pre-production prototype in October 1962, deliveries of production

Wessex HC Mk 2s began in 1963, with the first squadron becoming operational in February 1964. A total of 72 aircraft were eventually delivered, to be based with units in the UK, Germany and the Middle and Far East. From 1981, with the arrival of the Boeing Vertol Chinook in RAF service, surplus Wessex HC Mk 2 were transferred to the training and SAR roles. In early 1986 Wessex were also still in service in the trooping role in the UK, Cyprus and Hong Kong.

Two special Wessex HC Mk 2, re-designated HCC Mk 4, also operate with the Queen's Flight. Delivered to the RAF in 1969, both aircraft are reserved exclusively for VIP duties and, like the standard Wessex HC Mk 2, are expected to remain in service until the end of the decade.

The arrival of the Gnome engine conversion was quickly noted by the Royal Navy, which had originated the Wessex programme with the single-engined HAS Mk 1. The advantages of twin engines for overwater operations were obvious, while the limited success of a squadron of Whirlwind HAS Mk 7s in the commando role in the early 1960s, made the Gnome-Wessex an obvious contender for a much-needed expansion of this requirement.

Accordingly, the Royal Navy issued a specification for a commando assault helicopter written around the Gnome-Wessex, and ordered a prototype. This aircraft, XS241, designated the Wessex HU Mk 5, first flew on 31 May 1963 and was followed by the first production machine on 19 November. An initial production batch of 40 Wessex HU Mk 5 was followed by a further 60 machines between 1965 and 1968, and the type equipped four front-line Fleet Air Arm commando units before being largely succeeded by the Sea King HC Mk 4 in the early 1980s. Following a battlefield swansong in the 1982 Falklands campaign, the Wessex HU Mk 5 was relegated to an SAR and training role and is expected to be withdrawn from use by 1990.

Export sales of the Gnome-Wessex were confined to three variants, the Mk 52 for Iraq, Mk 53 for Ghana and Mk 54 for Brunei. The two Mk 53 and two Mk 54 were later sold for civilian use but the 12 Mk 52, delivered in 1964 and early 1965, have remained in Iraqi ownership, although the current operational status of the known seven survivors is unknown.

Technical specifications

Helicopter Westland Wessex HC Mk 2
Type Tactical transport
Year 1962
Engine 2 × 1,250 shp Bristol Siddeley Gnome H.1200
Rotor diameter 17.07 m (56 ft)
Fuselage length 14.74 m (48 ft 4 in)
Height 4.93 m (16 ft 2 in)
Empty weight 3,842 kg (8,470 lb)
Gross weight 6,124 kg (13,670 lb)
Maximum speed 195 km/h (120 mph)
Hovering ceiling IGE 1,800 m (5,900 ft)
Range 770 km (478 miles)
Capacity Pilot + 16 passengers

Westland 30

The original Westland 30 features the Lynx rotor system and uprated Gem engines, and is being promoted as a utility tactical transport and VIP helicopter.

During the 1970s Westland Helicopters undertook a series of studies aimed at producing a medium-weight utility transport which took advantage of the proven Lynx dynamics system. These studies considered both military and civil applications, with a replacement requirement for the UK Wessex and Puma fleet providing much of the driving force on the military side.

Having rejected several ideas, including the WG-29 with rear ramp loading, the company settled on the WG-30, which retained the complete Lynx dynamics with a new box cabin fuselage, in a design that Westland felt would appeal to the growing commercial market as well as to military customers. Construction of a prototype was begun by the company in 1978 and this aircraft, G-BGHF, made its first flight on 10 April 1979.

As completed G-BGHF featured twin 1,120 shp Rolls-Royce Gem 4 engines, then powering the latest variant of the Lynx, driving main and tail rotors increased slightly in length over their Lynx counterparts. The main transmission sat atop a structural raft which was separated from the fuselage decking by elastomeric units to minimise vibration from the semi-rigid rotor. The large

cabin, accessed via a sliding door on either side, provided an area of 460 cu ft (13.02 m^3) which gave maximum seating for 14 combat-equipped troops or 17 passengers. The two-seat cockpit could be entered from the cabin or via individual pilot doors. Avionics and AFCS was initially based on the Lynx, as were other aircraft systems. Behind the cabin was a large luggage bay. A new retractable undercarriage featured short-legged main units mounted within sponson-type fairings, all fuel being contained within the fuselage.

Although a second prototype was used for structural tests, G-BGHF shouldered all the flight development programme alone for the next two years, during which period a number of changes were made. These included the decision to adopt a fixed undercarriage with smaller fairings, and the introduction of a reverse-rotation tail rotor to improve yaw control and reduce noise levels. In order to stimulate development and sales, the company now laid down an initial production batch of 13 aircraft, designated the Westland 30 Series 100 and aimed specifically at the civil market. Deliveries of these helicopters, including the second prototype, began in 1982.

The lack of power afforded by the Gem 41 powerplant, however, led to the Series 160, engined with the uprated 1,260 shp Gem 60, and the prototype Series 200 (G-ELEC) which first flew on 3 September 1983 with two 1,712 shp General Electric CT7 engines. This new power-plant installation required redesigned engine intakes and longer cowling area, with enlarged engine bays and associated modifications. Gross weight was increased from the 12,350 lb (5,602 kg) of the Series 100 to 12,800 lb (5,806 kg), with power to spare for good single engine hot/high operation.

Although the original first prototype was modified as a military TT30 demonstrator, interest in the Series 100 and 160 variants has so far failed to crystallise into any military orders. This is partly as a result of the lack of power and the payload of these versions, but also due to the financial problems experienced by Westland since 1984 and the British defence ministry decision to re-evaluate its Wessex/Puma replacement programme.

Nevertheless the company has continued W30 development and, on 5 February 1986, flew the more definitive Series TT300. This new variant represents a major step forward in the W30 programme, being based on the Series 200 but introducing a new five-bladed bolted titanium main rotor head, with aerodynamically improved BERP composite main rotor blades, and a five-bladed composite tail rotor. Other changes include a crashworthy undercarriage and fuel system, a third hydraulic system, a strengthened fuselage structure and tail boom, a new all-plastic tailplane with stabiliser fins, and a new three-point isolation raft structure for the CT7 engines. The TT300 also introduces on-condition health and usage monitoring equipment as part of an updated avionics package. As a result of these improvements, in particular the performance advances conferred by the new rotor system, gross weight of the W30-300 has climbed to 16,000 lb (7,262 kg), providing a major payload increase over the earlier versions.

While the TT300 represents the current stage of W30 development, and may attract renewed military interest, Westland is also proposing a Series 400 to meet the still pending UK defence

The Westland TT300 is the newest variant of the W30, introducing the BERP advanced main rotor on a new five-bladed head, crashworthy undercarriage and new powerplants.

requirement. This variant, specifically designated the W30-404, would introduce more powerful 2,100 shp Rolls-Royce/Turboméca RTM322 engines to the Series 300 airframe. The new variant would thus feature a further gross weight improvement to 17,950 lb (8,142 kg) maximum and a top cruising speed of 173 mph (278 km/h) at normal mission weight.

Technical specifications

Helicopter Westland TT 300
Type General purpose
Year 1986
Engine 2 × 1,712 shp General Electric CT7-2B turboshafts
Rotor diameter 13.31 m (43 ft 8 in)
Fuselage length 15.90 m (52 ft 2 in)
Height 4.72 m (15 ft 6 in)
Empty weight 3,411 kg (7,520 lb)
Gross weight 7,262 kg (16,000 lb)
Maximum speed 222 km/h (138 mph)
Hovering ceiling IGE 1,158 m (3,800 ft)
Range 352 km (219 miles)
Capacity 2 crew + 14 fully-equipped troops

APPENDIX

World Military Helicopter Fleets

While the majority of military air arms are naturally reticent at revealing details of their helicopter equipment, the following listing has been based on independently gathered data corrected to 30 April 1986. Bracketed figures indicate confirmed orders awaiting delivery.

AFGHANISTAN
Air Force: 12 × Mil Mi-4, 24 × Mi-8, approx 20 × Mi-24A, approx 25 × Mi-24B

ALBANIA
Air Force: 2 × Mil Mi-1, 2 × Mi-2, 20 × Mi-4

ALGERIA
Air Force: 6 × Aérospatiale SA 316B, 5 × SA 330C, 6 × Hughes 300A, 40 × Mil Mi-4, 4 × Mi-6, 12 × Mi-8, 28 × Mi-24

ANGOLA
Air Force: 20 × Aérospatiale SA 316B, (+ 6) × SA 342M, (+ 4) × SA 365M, 1 × SA 315B, 6 (+ 24) × IAR-316B, 4 × Mil Mi-4, 40 × Mi-8, 6 × Mi-17, 23 × Mi-24

ARGENTINA
Air Force: 8 × Aérospatiale SA 315B, 4 × Bell 47G/J, 6 × UH-1, 6 × 212, 1 × Boeing-Vertol CH-47C, 13 × McDD 500M, 2 × Sikorsky S-58T, 2 × S-61R
Army: 5 × Aérospatiale SA 315B, 4 × SA 330L/J, (+ 24) × AS 332B, 6 × Agusta A109, 15 × Bell UH-1H, 7 × 206A, 2 × 212, 4 × Fairchild-Hiller FH-1100
Navy: 1 × Aérospatiale SE 3160, 4 × SA 316B, 2 × SA 319B, 6 × Bell 47G, 5 × Sikorsky SH-3D, 6 × ASH-3H, 1 × Westland Lynx Mk 23
Coast Guard: 2 × Aérospatiale SA 330L, (+ 6) × AS 350F, 6 × McDD 500M

AUSTRALIA
Air Force: 18 × Aérospatiale AS 350, 30 × Bell UH-1H, 11 × Boeing Vertol CH-47C, (+ 14) × Sikorsky S-70A
Army: 46 × Bell 206B, 4 × Hiller UH-12ET
Navy: 6 × Aérospatiale AS 350B, 3 × Bell UH-1B, 4 × 206B, (+ 16) × Sikorsky S- 70B, 8 × Westland Sea King Mk 50/50A, 16 × Wessex 31B

AUSTRIA
Air Force: 11 × Aérospatiale SE 3160, 10 × SA 316B, 12 × Agusta-Bell 206A, 25 × 212, 12 × Bell OH-58

BAHRAIN
Defence Force: 2 × Bell 412, 3 × MBB Bo 105C, 2 × McDD 500D, 2 × Sikorsky S-76

BANGLADESH
Air Force: 4 × Aérospatiale SA 316B, 2 × Bell 206L, 24 × 212, 1 × Mil Mi-4, 12 × Mi-8

BELGIUM
Air Force: 1 × Sikorsky SH-34C, 4 × Westland Sea King Mk 48
Army: 35 × Aérospatiale SE 3130, 36 × SA 318C, 3 × SA 330H
Navy: 3 × Aérospatiale SA 316B

BENIN
Air Force: 2 × Aérospatiale AS 355M

BOLIVIA
Air Force: 2 × Bell 212, 3 × UH-1H, 8 (+ 3) × Helibras HB 315B, 12 × McDD 500M

BOTSWANA
Defence Force: 2 × Aérospatiale AS 350L, (+ 6) × Bell 206

BRAZIL
Air Force: 6 × Aérospatiale SA 330L, 8 × AS 332M, (+ 25-30) × AS 350, 3 × Bell 47D, 20 × 47G, 4 × 47J, 2 × OH-13H, 56 × UH-1D/H, 9 × 206B, 4 × Hughes OH-6A, 6 × McDD 500D
Navy: 4 (+ 4) × Agusta ASH-3H, (+ 6) × Aérospatiale AS 332F, (+ 11) × AS 355, 16 × Bell 206B, 15 (+ 11) × Helibras HB 350B, 3 × HB 315B, 4 × Hughes 269A, 4 × Sikorsky SH-3D, 8 × Westland Lynx Mk 21, 7 × Westland Wasp HAS Mk 1

BRUNEI
Air Force: 2 × Bell 206, 14 × 212, 1 × 214ST, 1 × 412, 6 × MBB Bo 105C, 1 × S-76

BULGARIA
Air Force: 20 × Mil Mi-2, 40 × Mi-4, 6 × Mi-8, 12 × Mi-24
Border Guard: 12 × Kamov Ka-26, 12 × Mil Mi-2
Navy: 6 × Mil Mi-2, 6 × Mi-4, 12 × Mi-14

BURKINA FASO
Air Force: 2 × Aérospatiale SA 316B, 2 × SA 365N

BURMA
Air Force: 10 × Aérospatiale SA 319B, 14 × Bell UH-1H, 7 × 206, 7 × Kaman HH-43B, 10 × Kawasaki-Bell 47G, 10 × Kawasaki-Vertol KV 107

BURUNDI
Army: 1 × Aérospatiale SE 3160, 3 × SA 316B, 6 × SA 342L

CAMEROUN
Air Force: 2 × Aérospatiale SE 3130, 1 × SA 315B, 2 × SA 318C, 1 × SA 319B, 4 × SA 342L
Government: 1 × Aérospatiale SE 3160, 1 × SA 330C, 1 × AS 332L, 1 × SA 365N

CANADA
Armed Forces: 63 × Bell OH-58 (CH-136), 42 × UH-1N (CH-135), 9 × UH-1H (CH-118), 14 × 206B (CH-139), 14 × Boeing Vertol 107 (CH-113), 7 × CH-47C (CH-147), 35 × Sikorsky SH-3 (CH-124)

CHAD
Air Force: 10 × Aérospatiale SE 3160, 4 × SA 330C, 1 × SA 341F

CHILE
Air Force: 6 × Aérospatiale SA 315B, 1 (+ 2) × AS 332B, 13 × Bell UH-1H, 2 × Hiller UH-12E, 4 × UH-12L-4, (+ 19)1 × MBB Bo 105LS, 6 × Sikorsky S-55T
Army: 13 × Aérospatiale SA 315B, 11 × SA 330H/L, 2 × Bell UH-1H, 2 × 206B
Navy: 8 × Aérospatiale SA 319, 3 × Bell 47, 3 × 206

CHINA (PEOPLE'S REPUBLIC)
Air Force: 9 × Aérospatiale SA 365N, 6 × AS 332B, 400 × Mil Mi-1, 500 × Mi-2, 300 × Mi-4, 30 × Mi-8, 24 × Sikorsky S-70C
Navy: 1 × Aérospatiale SA 365N, 10 × SA 321J, 30 × Harbin H-5 (Mi-4)

CISKEI
Defence Force: 2 × MBB Bo 105, 3 × MBB-Kawasaki BK 117

COLOMBIA
Air Force: 27 × Aérospatiale SA 315B, 12 × Bell 47G/J, 9 × UH-1B, 12 × UH-1H, 10 × 206, 1 × 212, 2 (+ 10) × 412, 4 × Hiller UH-12E, 7 × Hughes 300C, 6 × TH-55A, 12 × McDD 500C, 10 × 500M, 6 × 500MG, 2 × 500E
Naval Air Arm: 4 × Agusta-Bell AB 212AS, 2 × MBB Bo 105LS

CONGO
Air Force: 3 × Aérospatiale SA 318C

COSTA RICA
Air Force: 1 × Fairchild-Hiller FH-1100, 2 × Hughes 300, 2 × Sikorsky S-58T

CUBA
Air Force: 5 × Mil Mi-1, 2 × Mi-2, 12 × Mi-4, 20 × Mi-8C, 20 × Mi-8F, 14 × Mi-14, 16 × Mi-17H, 12 × Mi-24D

CZECHOSLOVAKIA
Air Force: 3 × Mil Mi-1, 2 × Mi-2, 60 × Mi-4, 30 × Mi-8, 30 + × Mi-17, 24 × Mi- 24D
Border Guard: 10 × Mi-2, 10 × Mi-8

DENMARK
Air Force: 7 × Sikorsky S-61A
Army: 14 × McDD 500M
Navy: 7 × Westland Lynx Mk 80

DJIBOUTI
Air Force: 1 × Aérospatiale SE 3130, 2 × AS 355F

DOMINICAN REPUBLIC
Air Force: 4 × Aérospatiale SE 3130, 1 × SE 3160, 1 × SA 316B, 1 × SA 365C, 2 × Bell 47G, 8 × Bell 205A, 2 × Hiller UH-12A, 7 × Hughes OH-6A, 2 × Sikorsky S-55C

ECUADOR
Air Force: 4 × Aérospatiale SA 315B, 4 × SA 316B, 1 × SA 330F, 4 × AS 332B, 2 × Bell 47G, 4 × UH-1H, 1 × 212, 2 × 214
Army: 2 × Aérospatiale SA 315B, 1 × SA 316B, 6 × SA 330, 5 × SA 342L
Navy: 2 × Aérospatiale SA 319B

EGYPT
Air Force: 6 × Aérospatiale SA 342K, 90 × SA 342L, 4 × Agusta-Sikorsky AS-61, (+ 24) × Bell AH-1S, 15 × Boeing Vertol CH-47C, 18 × Hiller UH-12E, 20 × Mil Mi-4, 6 × Mi-6, 50 × Mi-8, 5 × Westland Commando Mk 1, 16 × Commando Mk 2, 2 × Commando Mk 2B, 4 × Commando Mk 2E
Navy: 6 × Mil Mi-6, 10 × Mi-8, 6 × Westland Sea King Mk 47

EL SALVADOR
Air Force: 3 × Aérospatiale SA 315B, 2 × SA 316B, 60 × Bell UH-1H, 4 × UH-1M, 4 × McDD 500MD

EIRE
Air Corps: 8 × Aérospatiale SA 316, 5 × SA 365F, 2 × SA 342L

ETHIOPIA
Air Force: 5 × Aérospatiale SA 316B, 1 × SA 330C, 6 × Agusta-Bell AB 204B, 10 × HAL Chetak, 6 × IAR-316B, 2 × Mil Mi-2, 10 × Mi-6, 9 × Mi-8, 6 × Mi-24
Army: 6 × Bell UH-1H

FINLAND
Air Force: 6 × Agusta-Bell 412, 5 × Bell 206B, 2 × McDD 500D, 6 × Mil Mi-8

FRANCE
Air Force: 29 × Aérospatiale SE 3130, 42 × SA 316B, 8 × SE 3160, 12 × SA 318C, 30 × SA 330B/H, 3 × AS 332B, 2 × AS 350B, 6 (+ 46) × AS 355F, 1 × SA 365N
Army: 87 × Aérospatiale SE 3130, 48 × SE 3160, 50 × SA 318C, 22 × SA 319B, 134 × SA 330B/H, (+ 20) × AS 332, 108 × SA 341M, 86 (+ 60) × SA 342M
Navy: 13 × Aérospatiale SE 3130, 6 × SE 3160, 31 × SA 316B, 18 × SA 321, (+ 22) × AS 350, 38 × Westland Lynx HAS Mk 24

GABON
Air Force: 1 × Aérospatiale SA 316B, 3 × SA 319B, 5 × SA 330C/H, 5 × SA 342, 2 × AS 350L

GERMANY (DEMOCRATIC REPUBLIC)
Air Force: 19 × Mil Mi-1, 27 × Mi-2, 40 × Mi-4, 40 + × Mi-8, 20 × Mi-24
Navy: 8 × Mil Mi-4, 5 × Mi-8, 20 + × Mi-14

GERMANY (FEDERAL REPUBLIC)
Air Force: 80 × Bell UH-1D
Army: 107 × Aérospatiale SE 3130, 53 × SA 318C, 92 × Bell UH-1D, 99 × MBB Bo 105M, 207 × Bo 105P, 110 × Sikorsky CH-53G
Navy: 12 (+ 7) × Westland Lynx HAS Mk 88, 22 × Sea King HAS Mk 41

GREECE
Air Force: 11 × Agusta-Bell AB 205A, 2 × AB 206A, 2 × AB 212, 12 × Bell 47G-3B, 5 × 47G-5, 5 × Boeing Vertol CH-47C
Army: 3 × Agusta-Bell AB 204B, 43 × AB 205, 1 × AB 212, 5 × Bell 47G-5, 20 × UH- 1H, (+ 20) × AH-1, 8 (+ 2) × Boeing Vertol CH-47C, 2 (+ 18) × Nardi-Hughes NH300C
Navy: 4 × Aérospatiale SA 319B, 10 × Agusta-Bell AB 212 ASW

GUATEMALA
Air Force: 6 × Bell UH-1D, 6 × UH-1H, 1 × 206B, 3 × 212, 6 × 412, 1 × Hiller OH- 23G, 3 × Sikorsky H-19

GUINEA
Air Force: 1 × Bell 47, 1 × Hiller UH-12, 2 × Mil Mi-4

GUINEA BISSAU
Air Force: 2 × Aérospatiale SA 316B, 1 × SA 342L, 1 × SE 313B, 1 × Mil Mi-4, 1 × Mi-8

GUYANA
Defence Force: 2 × Aérospatiale SA 319B, 2 × Bell 206B, 3 × Bell 212

HAITI
2 × Hughes 269, 2 × McDD 500, 2 × Sikorsky S-58T

HONDURAS
Air Force: 10 × Bell UH-1B, 19 × UH-1H, 10 × 412SP, 8 × Hughes 269, 1 × McDD 500, 2 × Sikorsky H-19, 1 × Sikorsky S-76

HONG KONG
Air Force: 3 × Aérospatiale SA 365C

HUNGARY
Air Force: 15 × Kamov Ka-26, 30 × Mil Mi-2, 10 × Mi-4, 30 × Mi-8, 12 × Mi-24

ICELAND
Coast Guard: 1 × Aérospatiale SA 365N, 1 × McDD 500D

INDIA
Air Force: 30 × Aérospatiale SE 3160, 30 × SA 316B, 70 × HAL Cheetah, 120 × Chetak, 60 × Mil Mi-4, 70 × Mi-8, 10 (+ 30) × Mi-17, 12 × Mi-25, (+ 10) × Mi-26
Navy: 1 × Aérospatiale SE 3160, 16 × HAL Chetak, 4 × Hughes 269B, 5 × Kamov Ka-25, (+ 18) × Ka-27, 11 × Westland Sea King Mk 42/42A, (+ 20) × Sea King Mk 42B, (+ 3) × Sea King Mk 42C

INDONESIA
Air Force: 1 × Aérospatiale SE 313B, 2 × SA 318C, 18 × SA 330B/L, 8 × Bell 47G, 2 × 204B, 2 × 206, 9 × Hughes 300C, 12 × McDD 500D, 6 × Nurtanio-Aérospatiale NAS 332B, 1 × NAS 332L, 15 × Nurtanio-MBB NBo 105C, 12 (+ 4) × Sikorsky S-58T, 1 × S-61A, 4 × Soloy-Bell 47G
Army: 6 × Aérospatiale SE 3160, 16 × Bell 205A, 6 × 212, 15 × Nurtanio-MBB NBo 105
Navy: 3 × Aérospatiale SE 3160, 4 (+ 22) × AS 332F, 12 × Nurtanio-MBB NBo 105C, 9 × Westland Wasp HAS 1

IRAN
Air Force: 45 × Agusta-Bell AB 205, 68 × AB 206, 5 × AB 212, 2 × Agusta-Sikorsky AS-61/A-4, 39 × Bell 214C, 8 × Kaman HH-43B/F
Army: 185 × Bell AH-1J, 293 × 214A, 78 × Boeing Vertol CH-47C
Navy: 5 × Agusta-Bell AB 205, 10 × AB 206A, 8 × AB 212, 20 × Agusta-Sikorsky ASH-3D, 6 × Sikorsky RH-53D

IRAQ
Air Force: 44 × Aérospatiale SA 318C, 13 × SA 321, 15 × SA 330G, 9 × SA 341H, 60 × SA 342K/L, 6 × Agusta-Sikorsky AS-61A, 28 × Hughes 300C, 6 × MBB-Kawasaki BK 117, 30 × MBB Bo 105C, 32 × McDD 500D, 4 × Mil Mi-1, 30 × Mi-4, 15 × Mi-6, 60 × Mi-8, 20 × Mi-24, 2 × Sikorsky S-76A, 7 × Westland Wessex Mk 52

ISRAEL
Air Force: 11 × Aérospatiale SA 321, 2 × SA 342L, 2 × SA 366G, 34 × Agusta Bell AB 205A / Bell 205A, (+ 10) × Bell UH-1H, 19 × 206A/B, 10 × 212, 26 × AH-1G/S, 17 × AH-1Q, 30 (+ 6) × McDD 500MD, 30 × Sikorsky S-65C/CH-53D

ITALY
Air Force: 10 × Agusta-Bell AB 47J, 20 × AB 47G, 34 × AB 204B, 10 × AB 205A, 18 (+ 18) × AB 212, (+ 4) × AB 412, 2 × Agusta-Sikorsky AS-61A-4, 15 (+ 12) × AS-61R, (+ 50) × Nardi-Hughes NH500D
Army: 5 × Agusta A 109, (+ 24) × A 109EOA, (+ 66) × A 129, 12 × Agusta-Bell 47G, 10 × AB 47J, 18 × AB 204B, 92 × AB 205A, 136 × AB 206B, 14(+ 6) × AB 212, 6 × AB 412, 24 (+ 6) × Boeing Vertol CH-47C/D
Navy: 4 × Agusta-Bell 47G, 2 × AB 47J, 20 × AB 204AS 53 × AB 212AS, 34 × Agusta-Sikorsky SH-3D/H, (+ 36) × EHI EH 101

IVORY COAST
Air Force: 1 × Aérospatiale SE 3130, 2 × SE 3160, 1 × SE 316B, 4 × SA 330, 4 × SA 365C

JAMAICA
Defence Force Air Wing: 2 × Bell 206A, 2 × 206B, 3 × 212

JAPAN
Air Self-Defence Force: 39 (+ 4) × Kawasaki-Vertol KV 107, 2 (+ 12) × CH-47J
Ground Self-Defence Force: 3 × Aérospatiale AS 332L, 12 (+ 45) × Bell AH-1S, 82 × UH-1B, 92 (+ 40) × UH-1H, 65 (+ 64) × Hughes OH-6D, 115 × OH-6J, 38 × TH-55J, 57 × Kawasaki-Vertol KV 107, (+ 2) × CH-47C, 5 (+ 24) × CH-47J, (+ 10) × McDD 500D
Maritime Self-Defence Force: 2 × Hughes OH-6D, 2 × OH-6J, 6 × Kawasaki-Bell 47G, 9 × Kawasaki-Vertol KV 107, 10 × Sikorsky S-61A, 8 × S-62J, 48 × SH-3A, 54 (+ 30) × SH-3B, 2 (+ 36) × SH-60J, (+ 12) × MH-53E

JORDAN
Air Force: 12 × Aérospatiale SA 316B, (+ 4) × AS 332B, 24 × Bell AH-1S, 8 × McDD 500D, 16 × Sikorsky S-76

KENYA
Air Force: 4 × Aérospatiale SA 330L, 2 × SA 342K, 9 × IAR-330, 2 × McDD 500D, 20 × 500MD, 8 × 500E

KUWAIT
Air Force: 10 × Aérospatiale SA 330F, (+ 6) × AS 332F, 24 × SA 342K, 6 × SA 342L

KOREA (NORTH)
Army: 1 × Hughes 300C, 20 × McDD 500D, 66 × 500E, 20 × Mil Mi-4, 20 × Mi-8

KOREA (SOUTH)
Air Force: 5 × Bell UH-1D, 2 × UH-1N, 2 × 212, 2 × Boeing Vertol CH-47C, 56 × Hanjin-McDD 500MD, 48 × McDD 500MD, 6 × Sikorsky H-19
Army: 25 × Bell UH-1B, 47 × UH-1H, 6 × AH-1J, (+ 21) × AH-1S, 25 × McDD 500MD, 50 × Hanjin-McDD 500MD (TOW)
Navy: 23 × Hanjin-McDD 500MD

LAOS
Air Force: 2 × Aérospatiale SE 313B, approx 5 × Bell UH-1D/H, 10 × Mil Mi-8, 10 × Mi-24A, approx 6 × Sikorsky S-58

LEBANON
Air Force: 4 × Aérospatiale SA 316B, 6 × SA 330L, 4 × SA 342L, 9 × Agusta-Bell AB 212

LESOTHO
Police Mobile Unit (Air Wing): 2 × Bell 412, 1 × MBB-Kawasaki BK 117, 2 × MBB Bo 105C, 1 × Mil Mi-2, 1 × Soloy-Bell 47

LIBYA
Air Force: 4 × Aérospatiale SA 316B, 1 × Agusta-Sikorsky AS-61A, 10 × Mil Mi-8, 12 × Mi-14, 24 × Mi-24
Army: 10 × Aérospatiale SA 316B, 10 × SA 321G, 40 × SA 342K, 3 × Agusta-Bell AB 206A, 2 × AB 212, 8 × Bell 47G-4A, 20 × Boeing Vertol CH-47C

LIBERIA
Air Force: 3 × HAL Chetak

MADAGASCAR
Air Force: 2 × Mil Mi-8

MALAWI
Air Force: 1 × Aérospatiale SA 316B, 6 × SA 330, 1 × AS 350B

MALAYSIA
Air Force: 29 × Aérospatiale SE 3160/SA 316B, 4 × Bell 47GA-5, 5 × 206B, 6 × 212, 39 × Sikorsky S-61A

MALI
Air Force: 2 × Mil Mi-4, 1 × Mi-8

MALTA
Helicopter Flight: 2 × Agusta-Bell AB 204B, 3 × Bell 47

MAURITANIA
Air Force: 4 × McDD 500C

MEXICO
Air Force: 5 × Aérospatiale SE 3160, 5 × SA 330J, 2 × AS 332L, 1 × Agusta A 109, 5 × Bell 47G, 5 × 205, 5 × 206, 1 × 212
Navy: 4 × Aérospatiale SA 319B, 3 × Bell 47G, 1 × 47J, 6 × MBB Bo 105

MONACO
Government: 2 × Agusta-Bell AB 206A

MONGOLIA
Air Force: 9 × Mil Mi-4, 3 × Mi-8

MOROCCO
Air Force: 18 × Aérospatiale SA 342K, 6 × SA 342L, 47 × Agusta-Bell AB 205A, 5 × AB 206B, 5 × AB 212

MOZAMBIQUE
Air Force: 4 × Aérospatiale SA 316B, 4 × Bell 47G-5, 5 × 206B, 11 × Mil Mi-8, 13 × Mi-25

NEPAL
Air Force: 2 × Aérospatiale SA 330C, 1 × AS 332L, 4 × HAL Chetak

NETHERLANDS
Air Force: 4 × Aérospatiale SE 3160
Army: 63 × Aérospatiale SE 3160, 27 × MBB Bo 105C
Navy: 5 × Westland Lynx UH-14A, 9 × Lynx UH-14B, 8 × Lynx UH-14C

NEW ZEALAND
Air Force / Army / Navy: 6 × Bell 47G/OH-13, 5 × UH-1D, 9 × UH-1H, 11 × Westland Wasp

NICARAGUA
Air Force: 2 × Aérospatiale SA 319B, 1 × Hughes 269, 4 × OH-6A, 11 × Mil Mi-8, 16 × Mi-24, 1 × Sikorsky CH-34

NIGERIA
Air Force: 10 × Aérospatiale SA 316B, 15 × SA 330H, (+ 12) × AS 332, (+ 5) × Boeing Vertol CH-47, 15 × Hughes TH-55, 4 × MBB Bo 105C, 20 × Bo 105D,
Navy: 3 × Westland Lynx Mk 89

NORWAY
Air Force: 19 × Bell UH-1B, 3 × UH-1C, (+ 12) × 412SP, 6 × Westland Lynx Mk 86, 10 × Sea King Mk 43

OMAN
Air Force: 4 × Aérospatiale SA 330, 2 × AS 332C, 16 × Agusta-Bell AB 205A, 3 × AB 206A, 1 × AB 212, 2 × Bell 212, 5 × 214B, 6 × 214ST

PAKISTAN
Air Force: 7 × Aérospatiale SE 3160, 2 × SA 316B, 4 × SA 319B, 1 × SA 330J, 4 × Kaman HH-43B
Army: 1 × Aérospatiale SE 3160, 20 × SA 316B, 28 × SA 330F/J, 16 × Bell 47G/OH-13S, 6 × UH-1H, 22 × AH-1S, 2 × 206, 10 × Mil Mi-8
Navy: 4 × Aérospatiale SA 316B, 5 × Westland Sea King Mk 45

PANAMA
Air Force: 1 × Aérospatiale AS 332L, 8 × Bell UH-1B, 9 × UH-1H, 4 × UH-1N, 1 × 212

PARAGUAY
Air Force: 14 × Bell 47, 2 × Hiller UH-12E, 2 × UH-12SL-4
Navy: 2 × Aérospatiale AS 350B, 2 × Bell 47

PERU
Air Force: 7 × Aérospatiale SE 3160, 17 × Bell 47, 19 × 212, 9 × UH-1H, 6 (+ 6) × 214ST, 10 × MBB Bo 105C, 5 × Mil Mi-6, 6 × Mi-8, 12 × Mi-24
Army: 7 × Aérospatiale SA 318C, 8 × Bell 47G, 38 × Mil Mi-8
Navy: 2 × Aérospatiale SA 319B, 6 × Agusta-Bell AB 212AS, 12 × Agusta-Sikorsky AS-3H, 3 × Bell 47G, 2 × UH-1D, 4 × UH-1H, 9 × 206B

PHILIPPINES
Air Force: 110 × Bell UH-1H, 15 × 205, 10 × MBB Bo 105C, 10 × McDD 500, 2 × Mitsubishi-Sikorsky S-62A, 2 × Sikorsky S-70, 15 × S-76/H-76
Navy: 3 × MBB Bo 105C

POLAND
Air Force: 8 × Kamov Ka-26, 20 × Mil Mi-1, 140 × Mi-2, 10 × Mi-4, 28 × Mi-8, 30 × Mi-24
Navy: 10 × Mil Mi-2, 8 × Mi-4, 12 × Mi-8, 15 × Mi-14

PORTUGAL
Air Force: 14 × Aérospatiale SE 313, 36 × SA 316B

QATAR
Air Force: 12 × Aérospatiale SA 342L, 3 × Westland Lynx HC 28, 3 × Westland Commando Mk 2A, 1 × Commando Mk 2C, 8 × Commando Mk 3

ROMANIA
Air Force: 50 + × IAR-316B, 90 + × IAR-330, 10 × Mil Mi-2, 14 × Mi-4, 19 × Mi-8

RWANDA
Air Force: 6 × Aérospatiale SA 342L

SAUDI ARABIA
Air Force: 4 × Aérospatiale SE 3160, 1 × SA 316B, 1 × Agusta-Bell AB 204A, 14 × AB 205A, 26 × AB 206A, 29 × AB 212, 2 × Agusta-Sikorsky AS-61, 18 × Kawasaki Vertol KV 107
Navy: 4 (+ 16) × Aérospatiale SA 365F, 4 × SA 365N,, 3 × Agusta-Sikorsky ASH-3D, (+ 2) × Sikorsky VH-53E

SENEGAMBIA
Air Force: 2 × Aérospatiale SE 3130, 3 × SA 330H, 1 × SA 341F

SHARJAH
Amiri Guard Air Wing: 1 × Bell 206B

SIERRA LEONE
Defence Force: 1 × MBB Bo 105C

SINGAPORE
Air Force: 5 (+ 17) × Aérospatiale AS 332M, 6 × AS 350, 17 × Bell UH-1B, 30 × UH-1H, 3 × 212

SOMALIA
Air Force: 1 × Agusta-Bell AB 204B, 4 × AB 212, 4 × Mil Mi-4, 2 × Mi-8

SOUTH AFRICA
Air Force: 5 × Aérospatiale SE 3130, 57 × SE 3160, 46 × SA 316B, 14 × SA 321, 63 × SA 330F/J
Navy: 11 × Westland Wasp

SPAIN
Air Force: 3 × Aérospatiale SA 318C, 6 × SA 330, 11 × AS 332B, 20 × Agusta-Bell 47G, 2 × AB 47J, 11 × AB 205, 4 × AB 206A, 7 × Bell UH-1H, 17 × Hughes 300C
Army: 3 × Aérospatiale SA 319B, (+ 18) × AS 332B, 6 × Agusta-Bell 212, 59 × Bell UH-1H, 13 × OH-58, 11 (+ 6) × Boeing-Vertol CH-47C/414, 73 × MBB Bo 105
Navy: 9 × Agusta-Bell/Bell AB 47G/47G, 10 × AB 212AS, 4 × Bell AH-1G, 11 × McDD 500M, 13 × Sikorsky SH-3D/G, (+ 6) × SH-60B

SRI LANKA
Air Force: 2 × Aérospatiale SA 365C, 5 × Bell OH-13H, 20 × 206A/B, 16 × 212, 5 × 412, 2 × Kamov Ka-26

SUDAN
Air Force: 6 × Agusta-Bell AB 205, 5 × AB 212, 10 (+ 5) × IAR-330J, 20 × MBB Bo 105, 8 × Mil Mi-8

SWEDEN
Air Force: 8 × Aérospatiale SE 3160, 6 × Agusta-Bell AB 204B, 10 × Boeing-Vertol 107-11-4, 4 × MBB Bo 105CBS
Army: 12 × Agusta-Bell AB 204B, 39 × AB 206A, 16 (+ 10) × Hughes 300C, (+ 20) × MBB Bo 105
Navy: 5 × Aérospatiale SE 3130, 9 × Agusta-Bell AB 206B, 10 × Kawasaki-Vertol KV 107

SWITZERLAND
Air Force: 26 × Aérospatiale SE 3130, 76 × SE 3160

SYRIA
Air Force: 3 × Aérospatiale SA 342K, 41 × SA 342L, 12 × Kamov Ka-25, 18 × Mil Mi-4, 10 × Mi-6, 50 × Mi-8, 8 × Mi-14, 35 × Mi-24D

TAIWAN
Air Force: 10 × Bell 47G, 15 × UH-1H, 16 × McDD 500M, (+ 12) × Sikorsky S-70A
Army: 70 × Bell UH-1D/H, 3 × Boeing Vertol CH-47 Model 234, 2 × Kawasaki-Bell (KH-4), 10 × McDD 500M, 7 × Sikorsky CH-34
Navy: 12 × McDD 500MD-ASW
Marine Corps: 6 × McDD 500M

TANZANIA
Air Wing: 4 × Agusta-Bell AB 205A, 2 × AB 206B, 2 × Boeing Vertol CH-47C

THAILAND
Air Force: 27 × Bell UH-1H, 1 × UH-1N, 2 × 212, 2 × 214ST, 2 × 412, 18 × Sikorsky S-58T
Army: 12 × Bell 47G/OH-13, 99 × UH-1B/D/H, 1 × 206A, 10 × 206B, 8 × 212, 2 × 214B, 2 × Boeing Vertol CH-47A, 4 (+ 20) × Schweizer-Hughes TH-300C
Navy: 4 × Bell UH-1H, 8 × 212

TOGO
Air Force: 1 × Aérospatiale SA 315B, 2 × SA 318C, 1 × SA 330

TRINIDAD & TOBAGO
Defence Force: 1 × Aérospatiale SA 341H, 2 × Sikorsky S-76

TUNISIA
Air Force: 5 × Aérospatiale SE 3130, 3 × SE 3160, 4 × SA 316B, 18 × Agusta-Bell AB 205A, 6 × Bell UH-1H

TURKEY
Air Force: 20 × Bell UH-1D, 12 × UH-1H, 4 × UH-1HEW, 25 × UH-1HSAR, 1 × Sikorsky UH-19D
Army: 14 × Agusta-Bell AB 204, 15 × AB 205A, 8 × AB 206, (+ 3) × AB 412, 18 × Bell OH-13H, 25 × TH-13T, 25 (+ 25) × UH-1H, (+ 26) × AH-1S, 28 × Hughes 300C
Navy: 3 × Agusta-Bell AB 204AS, 3 × AB 205, 6 × AB 212AS

UNION OF SOVIET SOCIALIST REPUBLICS
Frontal Aviation: 225 × Mil Mi-1, 235 × Mi-2, 35 × Mi-4, 260 × Mi-6, 1,615 × Mi-8 C/E, 150 × Mi-17, 1,035 × Mi-24, 30 × Mi-26
Transport Aviation: 8 × HAL Chetak, 350 × Mil Mi-1, 250 × Mi-2, 100 × Mi-4, 350 × Mi-6, 900 × Mi-8, 60 × Mi-10
Naval Aviation: 125 × Kamov Ka-25, 100 + × Ka-27, 25 × Mil Mi-1, 35 × Mi-2, 100 × Mi-4, 100 × Mi-8, 120 × Mi-14

UGANDA
Air Force: 2 × Agusta-Bell AB 205, 3 × Bell 206, 4 × Bell 212

UNITED ARAB EMIRATES
Air Force: 3 × Aérospatiale SA 316B/319B, 8 × SA 330, 6 × AS 332B, (+ 8) × AS 332F, 2 × AS 332L, 11 × SA 342, 10 × Bell 205A, 6 × Agusta-Bell/Bell AB 206B/206B, 3 × MBB Bo 105S

UNITED KINGDOM
Air Force: 38 × Boeing Vertol Chinook HC 1, 43 × Aérospatiale SA 341, 43 × SA 330E, 19 × Westland Sea King HAR 3, 15 × Wessex HC 2, 2 × Wessex Mk 4, 8 × Wessex Mk 5
Army: 9 × Aérospatiale SE 313B, 4 × Agusta A 109, 182 × Aérospatiale SA 341, 104 × Westland Lynx AH 1, (+ 5) × Lynx Mk 7, 98 × Scout
Navy: 31 × Aérospatiale SA 341, 45 × Westland Lynx HAS 2, 33 (+ 7) × Lynx Mk 3, 77 (+ 5) × Sea King HAS 2/5, 10 × SeaKing AEW Mk 2, 24 (+ 10) × Sea King HC 4, 36 × Wasp, 18 × Wessex 5
Marines: 12 × Aérospatiale SA 341B, 6 × Westland Lynx AH 1

UNITED STATES OF AMERICA
Air Force: 25 × Bell TH-1F, 120 × UH-1F, 18 × UH-1N, 59 × HH-1N, 22 × HH-1H, 2 × AH-1G, (+ 80) × Bell-Boeing CV-22A, 6 × Boeing Vertol CH-46B, 6 × CH-47A, 12 × CH-47C, 35 × Sikorsky HH-3E, 29 × HH-53B/C, 10 × HH-3F, 18 × CH-3E, 9 × HH-53H, 10 × UH-60A, 1 × HH-60A
Army: 334 × Bell UH-1, 10 × EH-1H, 220 × UH-1V, 1828 × OH-58A/C, 16 (+ 100) × OH-58D, 86 × AH-1G, 193 × AH-1S, 10 × TH-1S, 126 (+ 23) × Modernised AH-1S, 407 × Mod AH-1S, 124 × Boeing Vertol CH-47, 106 × CH-47B, 265 × CH-47C, 113 (+ 215) × CH-47D, 348 × McDD (Hughes) OH-6A, 240 × TH-55A, 50 (+ 625) × AH-64A, 685 (+ 363) × Sikorsky UH-60A, 72 × CH-54, (+ 40) × EH-60A
Coast Guard: 22 (+ 74) × Aérospatiale SA 366G, 60 × Sikorsky HH-52A, 36 × HH-3F
Marine Corps: 200 × Bell UH-1E, 20 × TH-1E, 50 × TH-1L, 170 × UH-1N, 8 × VH-1N, 56 × AH-1J, 49 × AH-1T, 2 (+ 42) × AH-1W, (+ 552) × Bell-Boeing MV-22A, 18 × Boeing Vertol CH-46A, 43 × CH-46D, 267 × CH-46E/F, 99 × Sikorsky CH-53A/D, 18 × VH-53D, 82 (+ 15) × CH-53E, (+ 9) × VH-60E
Navy: 27 × Bell UH-1E, 27 × TH-1K, 32 × TH-57A, 49 × TH-57B, 89 × TH-57C, (+ 50) × Bell-Boeing HV-22A, 46 × Boeing Vertol HH-46A, 19 × UH-46A, 12 × UH-46D, 127 (+ 36) × Kaman SH-2F, 12 × Sikorsky VH-3E, 96 × SH-3G, 109 × SH-3H, 12 (+ 24) × CH-53E, (+ 32) × MH-53E, 15 × RH-53A, 23 × RH-53D, 52 (+ 156) × SH-60B, (+ 76) × SH-60F

URUGUAY
Air Force: 5 × Bell UH-1B, 4 × UH-1H, 2 × 222
Navy: 4 × Bell 47G-2, 1 × 222A, 2 × Sikorsky CH-34

VENDA
Air Force: 1 × Aérospatiale SA 316B, 1 × MBB-Kawasaki BK 117

VENEZUELA
Air Force: 4 × Aérospatiale SE 3160, 8 × Agusta A 109, 4 × Agusta-Sikorsky S-61R, 14 × Bell UH-1B/D/H, 2 × UH-1N, 7 × 206L-1, 2 × 212, 2 × 214ST, 2 × 412
Army: 12 × Aérospatiale SA 316B, (+ 6) × Agusta A 109, 2 × Agusta-Sikorsky AS- 61, 12 × Bell UH-1H, 2 × 205A, 3 × 206B
Navy: 12 × Agusta-Bell AB 212AS, 2 × Bell 47G

VIETNAM
Air Force: 4 × Bell UH-1D/H, 10 × Boeing Vertol CH-47A, 30 × Mil Mi-4, 10 × Mi-6, 60 × Mi-8, 30 × Mi-24D
Navy: 17 × Kamov Ka-25A, 10 × Mil Mi-4

YEMEN (NORTH)
Air Force: 2 × Aérospatiale SA 316B, 2 × Agusta-Bell AB 204, 6 × AB 206, 6 × AB 212, 2 × Mil Mi-4, 12 × Mi-8

YEMEN (SOUTH)
3 × Mil Mi-4, 8 × Mi-8, 12 × Mi-24

YUGOSLAVIA
Air Force: 15 × Aérospatiale SE 3160, 3 × SA 341G, 17 × SA 341H, 2 × Agusta A 109, 5 × Agusta-Bell AB 205, 2 × AB 212, 10 × Mil Mi-4, 29 × Mi-8, 110 (+ 22) × Soko-Aérospatiale SA 341H, 10 × Soko-Westland Whirlwind Srs 2

ZAIRE
Air Force: 4 × Aérospatiale SE 3160, 3 × SA 316B, 1 × SA 321J, 11 × SA 330, 1 × AS 332L, 7 × Bell 47G

ZAMBIA
Air Force: 5 × Aérospatiale SE 313B, 8 × SA 316B, 16 × Agusta-Bell AB 47G-4A, 20 × AB 205A, 3 × Bell 206, 2 × Bell 212, 11 × Mil Mi-8

ZIMBABWE
Air Force: 3 × Aérospatiale SE 3160, 10 × SA 316B (+ 30 stored), 8 × Agusta-Bell AB 205, 2 × AB 412, (+ 10) × AB 412 Griffon